George Burns

George Burns

An American Life

LAWRENCE J. EPSTEIN

McFarland & Company, Inc., Publishers

Jefferson, North Carolina, and London

Unless otherwise indicated, all photographs are from the author's collection.

LIBRARY OF CONGRESS CATALOGUING-IN-PUBLICATION DATA

Epstein, Lawrence J. (Lawrence Jeffrey)
    George Burns : an American life / Lawrence J. Epstein.
       p.   cm.
    Includes bibliographical references and index.

    ISBN 978-0-7864-5849-3
    softcover : 50# alkaline paper ∞

    1. Burns, George, 1896–1996.   2. Comedians — United
States — Biography.   3. Entertainers — United States —
Biography.   I. Title.
PN2287.B87E78   2011
792.702' 8092 — dc23
[B]
                                              2011029016

BRITISH LIBRARY CATALOGUING DATA ARE AVAILABLE

Front cover: Publicity photograph of George Burns for *Oh, God!
You Devil,* 1984 (Photofest)

Manufactured in the United States of America

*McFarland & Company, Inc., Publishers
  Box 611, Jefferson, North Carolina 28640
   www.mcfarlandpub.com*

For Sharon,
A Woman of Valor

Table of Contents

Acknowledgments

It is always a pleasure to thank the many kind, intelligent, and considerate people who helped me with my research for this book.

I spoke with Ronnie Burns about a year before his death, and he was generous with his time and memory.

A variety of wonderful writers and journalists provided help, materials, and insights. They include Joe Adamson (who also provided guidance to work with people at the Margaret Herrick Library of The Academy of Motion Pictures Arts and Sciences), Cynthia Clements, Wes Gehring, Donna Halper (the friend I always turn to for matters regarding radio history), Pat Mellencamp, Jim Neibaur, Abe Novick, Ben Schwartz, Anthony Slide, Rob Snyder, Tom Tugend, Larry Wilde, and Jordan Young.

As always, librarians were of enormous help. I owe a significant debt to Ned Comstock of the Cinematic Arts Library at USC. He provided invaluable suggestions and material. It's impossible to imagine film and television scholarship in this country without Ned's contributions to many writers. I also appreciate the suggestions and help of Janet Lorenz of the National Film Information Service at the Margaret Herrick Library. I'm pleased to thank the entire staff at the Billy Rose Theatre Division of the New York Public Library of the Performing Arts. They tracked down materials I needed and provided them to me. Finally, I appreciate the efforts of Charles Greene, AnnaLee Pauls, and Ben Primer of the Princeton University Library.

Professional help came from Bruce Abrams of the Division of Old Records, The County Clerk and Clerk of the Supreme Court in New York; Reg Bacon of Variety Arts Enterprises; Marshall Berle (Milton's nephew), who offered material I didn't know existed, Barry Dougherty, the Historian at the Friars Club; John Keene at the National Comedy Hall of Fame; Laura Leff, President of the International Jack Benny Fan Club; Larry Mintz, from the University of Maryland; Don L. F. Nilsen, Historian of the International

Society for Humor Studies; and Bob Thompson, Director of the Bleier Center for Television and Popular Culture at Syracuse University

Suggestions for the book came from Shaun Gerien, Larry Yudelson, as well as my good friend Stanley Barkan. Another good friend and former office mate, Tony DiFranco, heard tales of the book at many lunches. Assemblyman Mike Fitzpatrick is always there to offer help and advice.

Doug Rathgeb, my friend of almost 50 years, always offers great writing advice. He listens patiently and offers consistently insightful ideas.

My literary agent, Don Gastwirth, encouraged this book with his characteristically profound compassion and enthusiasm. His brother, Joseph Gastwirth, always offers words of support.

My cousins Toby Everett and Sheldon Scheinert keep listening to me talk about my writing. I'd like to thank them and my extended family.

My four children, Michael and his wife, Sophia Cacciola; Elana and her husband, Justin Reiser; Rachel and her husband, John Eddey; and Lisa are always enthusiastic about my writing and always willing to help.

Finally, this book is dedicated to my wife, Sharon. She's there every day to talk about our children, our lives, and our work. Her steadfast goodness and honesty supports my life and my work.

Preface

George Burns was always willing to sacrifice truth for a good line. He liked, for instance, to tell the story of the stage manager who heard him singing and fired him on the spot. But Burns could never tell it the way it really happened. He retold it with comic exaggeration to hide the pain. In real life, Burns was playing at the Folly Federal theater in Brooklyn. He was rehearsing his music at ten in the morning. The manager heard the rehearsal, didn't much like the voice, and canceled the young performer. It was common to be fired after the first show, but rare to be let go before the opening.

But Burns learned how to deal with such rejection and pain. He would re-tell tales from his life, keeping in the essence of the truth but filtering it through the strainer of humor. As Burns re-cast the sad moment, "I was in the middle of my act ... and just before my yodeling finish the manager walked out and canceled me.... To make matters worse, the audience applauded him. And as he dragged me off the stage, the musicians gave him a standing ovation."[1]

The life of George Burns was funnier when he told it than when he lived it. This cigar-puffing icon of American humor, this spectacular straight man in one of the most famous comedy teams of all time, this man who remained ageless even as he aged, always provided a twist to his tales. He was after laughter, not truth. So, despite his anecdote-laced memoirs, the real George Burns story remains to be told.

It was a remarkable life, one that virtually overlapped the twentieth century. He was there for every modern entertainment innovation, for all of the triumphs and tragedies of American life during the century, and for all the dizzying changes in American culture. His personal life is important, that is, because he became a symbol of American life. But it was also a life that defined the cruel emotional cost of success. George Burns had to suppress his feelings, his anger at his early failure as a comedian, his having to make the woman in his team the star, his hiding his Jewishness behind an Irish name, his inability to deal with tragedy because of the early death of his father, and much more. George Burns was a happy man. The man deep inside him, though, was another story.

All of this is the story told in *George Burns: An American Life.* The book begins with his poverty-stricken childhood on New York's Lower East Side, where Burns developed a deep emotional need for the acceptance that came from audiences and a fierce determination to succeed, a determination that saved him during his lengthy and numerous failures in vaudeville, his disabling dyslexia, and his early struggle against hunger. The book traces his meeting and marriage to Gracie Allen, their fabled romance that was marred by infidelity, and their groundbreaking career in every modern entertainment medium. His journey put Burns in contact with the most influential actors and comedians of the century such as his best friend, Jack Benny, and his comedic and personal rival Groucho Marx. Just when his career seemed to have ended after Gracie's death, Benny's death propelled Burns into a new movie career that won him an Academy Award, a new generation of fans, and new women who became his romantic partners. His graceful lessons to the world on the art of aging and accepting death and his being cast in the title role in the movie *Oh, God!* combined to make him a towering figure in popular culture. Additionally, this book includes the various entertainment innovations that Burns made, from transforming the role of women comedy team partners in vaudeville to speaking directly to the audience in television.

I was a child in that television audience when he spoke. I didn't then know much about vaudeville or radio, but the comedy on television fascinated me. Later, I wrote a book about Jewish comedians and another about comedy teams, and George Burns was a central character in both books. I began to read about him, and suddenly the simple television character had shades and angles. His life as a child on the Lower East Side so intrigued me that it led to a book about Jewish immigrants in that New York neighborhood.

Finally, I realized, I had wandered all around the life of George Burns. It was time to tell the story, to fill in the missing pieces, to translate his funny tales into hard facts but to try to do so without burying the great humor.

I gathered materials from archives and published materials. The particulars of my enormous debt to others are detailed in the book's acknowledgments section. As I read, I noted that specific details were sometimes difficult to determine. This led me to focus on an area others had avoided: public documents. I obtained many birth, marriage, and death certificates, census records, draft registration forms, information from cemeteries, and other information to fill in George Burns' colorful comic exaggerations with the grayer details of reality. Using this material I was able, for example, to determine new facts about the exact death date of Burns' father and the town he and his wife had lived in before coming to America. The book includes new information about Burns' first wife and the small-time vaudeville actor she married after she and Burns divorced.

I also wanted, in a way that I hadn't previously seen, to focus on Burns' Jewish connections and his complicated relationship to his religion and the Jewish community.

George Burns: An American Life tells a uniquely American story about a uniquely American institution. It is an incredible story of a life that lasted for one hundred years. It is a story filled with constant laughter, incredible tensions and struggles all along the way, a journey back and forth between obscurity and fame, great love, tragic loss, resilient triumph, and entry into the limited pantheon of the greatest American entertainers. It is the story of an American man who is widely beloved but not yet well understood.

CHAPTER ONE

Looking Back

George Burns drove his own car until he was 93. But after several accidents, he decided that Conrad, his chauffeur, ought to take him in the Cadillac limousine to Glendale for his visits to Forest Lawn Memorial Park. It's a majestic setting for a funeral home. Ronald Reagan and Jane Wyman were married there in 1940. Indeed, there have been over 60,000 weddings on the 300 acres meant primarily for the dead.

Gracie Allen was entombed there in 1964. From then on Burns — her husband, her partner, her booster and defender — visited her monthly. He went to the northeast corner of the Park, to the Court of Freedom. He stopped to look at the statue of George Washington opposite the entrance of the Freedom Mausoleum. Once inside the main entrance, he turned right. The Sanctuary of Heritage is on the left hand side. Gracie's vault is on the right.

Burns would sit down on the marble bench in front of Gracie and light his ever-present trademark cigar, as much a part of him as his hands. He would say a prayer, and talk to Gracie, tell her what happened, even ask for her help. When he was up for a part in the movie *The Sunshine Boys*, he said, "Gracie, maybe you can help, maybe you can put in a good word for me up there. But don't bother the head man, he's very busy. Talk to his son, and be sure to tell him I'm Jewish, too."[1]

That was Burns, funny and irreverent about death and God and all else except Gracie and show business. But under the patter lay a more disturbed George Burns, a man who had to suppress much of himself to achieve the success he so craved and loved, a man who had to push down his Jewishness and even his own name, who had to push down the anguishing reality that he had not succeeded as a comedian early in his career despite his desperate need for love and approval. It was a tension released through smoking cigars, sexual escapades, yelling at Gracie and his brother Willy among others, and telling the same show business stories over and over so that they provided him a comforting if inaccurate narrative of his life.

Burns told anyone who listened that he lied when he told his stories, but even that wasn't true. Burns used what was called a "vaudeville shine," an exaggeration of a story to highlight its comic potential and push aside its tensions and disturbing elements. Burns put a vaudeville shine on life. He didn't want to hear life's horrors; he had seen enough of those.

But there, sitting with Gracie in the silence of what he knew would be his own eternal home, he could talk plainly, or at least talk as much as he could allow himself, as much as he was able after all those decades of stopping himself. "I'd tell her some of the funny things that happened to me. If I went to a party, I'd tell about all the amusing things that went on, but I made sure I always told her the truth. I figured she'd know if I was lying again."[2]

But there came a realization that even here there wouldn't be the promised eternal paradise. "Sometimes I tell her a joke, but Gracie doesn't laugh. She's heard all my jokes."[3]

This recognition that there was not going to be everlasting peace came out in the regularity of his visits. For the first year after Gracie's death, Burns brought flowers and visited her weekly. During the second year he came every other week. After that, he had monthly visits. The first visits were marked by tears. It was after they stopped that he began to talk to her.

At the end, there was no sanctuary even in this spot; there was no place where the world ended and the soul's peace began. Perhaps that is why he agreed to a *60 Minutes* television interview with Ed Bradley that aired on November 6, 1988. He took the crew to Forest Lawn for part of that interview.

Burns held Ed Bradley's arm as they walked into the Sanctuary of Heritage. Burns stopped in front of the vault, put his finger to his lips and then touched his fingers below a floral ornament to the right of the vault and then below one on the left. This is a gesture, conscious or not, that resembles the Jewish religious gesture of holding a kissed prayer book up to the Torah, the parchment holding the first five books of the Hebrew Bible.

"Hi ya, Googie," Burns says, using his pet nickname for his wife. "We're working together again." He turns to Bradley. "I talk to her all the time. I hope she hears me. If she doesn't, it makes me feel good."[4]

Bradley seems confused by Gracie's epitaph, which read:

Grace Allen Burns
Beloved Wife and Mother
1902–1964

But Bradley isn't confused by the incorrect date given for Gracie's birth, rather by the placement of the plaque. He assumes Burns' name will be on top eventually.

"No, no, no," Burns tells him. "I'm going to change the billing. It's going to be Gracie Allen and George Burns. Yeah, she's going to get top billing."[5]

He then says goodbye to her, promises to return in a month, and then puts his hand to his lips and reverses the kissing routine, this time touching the floral ornament on the left first.

Burns has brought the world to this most private of places. He always gives the audience what it wants.

Still, it is easy to imagine George Burns puffing away on that marble bench all alone in the room, talking to Gracie and then sitting silently. She was gone, but she was right there, as though Death had to laugh at Gracie, just like all those audiences, and, therefore, could never control her.

For Burns, sitting there was time as detached from the world's clocks as he could find, as close to Gracie and to heaven as it was possible to feel on earth, as near a perfect place for quiet contemplation as a noisy life would ever allow.

It was at just such a time that it was possible for George Burns to think back to when it all began, to the television shows with Gracie, to the radio shows, and films. Pushing further into the past, he might have contemplated the moment he met Gracie in vaudeville. In a way, all his life before that had been a preparation.

But what a preparation. Surely, as Burns sat in this mournful place, he thought about his mother and his father, who had died so young. After all, his story began with them and their fateful decision to come to the United States without money, a job, or a grasp of the English language. All his father had was his faith and all his mother had was a determination and an unshakeable, abiding love of her children.

The George Burns story, then, begins with those parents in a faraway land with what they truly had in common: a dream that the fabled America was the Golden Land.

CHAPTER TWO

The Land of Hope
and Tears

The village of Kolbuszowa in southeastern Poland lies on a river with the same name as the town. Pine forests surround the town, including its large pond. The whole region is sandy and wooded, but the town's gardens and orchards and its sturdy wooden houses made it look like a lush and pleasant place amid all that sand.

During the last half of the 19th century, fully half of Kolbuszowa's population of 4,000 was Jewish. Despite any of the town's charms, the Jewish population lived in dire poverty. They studied their faith, married young, and produced what they most valued — children.

It was here in about June 1855 that Eliezer Shrager Birnbaum was born. He was the son of Naftaly Birnbaum and a woman whose Yiddish name is unknown but whose name in English was Theresa. Young Eliezer was called by his nickname, Lipa. The standard derivation of the surname "Birnbaum" is that it comes from a house in Frankfurt, Germany, with a sign that had a pear tree ("birnbaum"). It's probable, then, that Lipa Birnbaum's ancestors came from Germany prior to migrating to Poland.

Like other young Jewish boys, Lipa received an Orthodox Jewish education, studying religious texts at an early age. He learned the laws of keeping kosher, the chants to all the prayers, and all else that a learned Jew needed to know.

At an early age — probably at age 18 or even earlier — Lipa was introduced to the woman he would marry. Arranged marriages were common, though sometimes couples met at a market fair or a celebration such as a wedding. Travel was extremely limited; villagers relied on their horses and their carts, so almost always young men and women lived near each other.

At some young age, then, Lipa was introduced to Hadassah Bluth for their arranged marriage. Hadassah, nicknamed Dassah, was the daughter of Isidore and Gertrude Rosenblum Bluth, and was born around November 1857, probably in a village near Kolbuszowa.

Lipa and Dassah were married in about 1874. Two of their children, either in Europe or America, died. Morris, the oldest child who survived, was born sometime before 1880. Annie was born in about February 1880. Isidor, named after Dassah's deceased father, was born in about May 1881. Esther was born about March 1883. Sarah was born in June 1885.

It was around this time that Lipa and Dassah decided to move to America. Many people in Kolbuszowa decided to leave. They had heard the tales of America's gold-lined streets, of the opportunities for their children, away from the poverty, and away from the fear of attacks on Jews which had been accelerated in Russia in 1881 following the assassination of Czar Alexander II. Two-thirds of the Jewish population in Eastern Europe stayed, but for the young there was a dreamland across the ocean, a land rich in opportunity and hope, a better place for the children — always a determining factor in life's decisions for a Jewish family. A religious people could believe in dreams, and America was the land of dreams. Of course, the reality that would face them was jarring. As one immigrant wryly noted, "When I left for America, I was told the streets were paved with gold. When I got here, I found that not only were they not paved with gold, they weren't paved at all. And not only weren't they paved, but I was expected to pave them!"[1] Other immigrants were angrier or sadder. America was a land of hope, but for many it was also a land of tears.

The first group of Jews who left Kolbuszowa journeyed to Memphis, Tennessee, and many became peddlers. But Lipa was part of a later group that went to the Lower East Side of New York City. Some of the town's Jews planned to go to America, gather in the wealth that was available to any hardworking young man, and return. For those who wished to bring their families, the cost of steamship tickets, even for a place in steerage (the lowest-class because passengers stayed in the crowded, claustrophobic area below the ship's decks), was prohibitive. It was common, therefore, for the young men of Kolbuszowa to journey to America alone. Some would bring back the money, and others, like Lipa Birnbaum, would save up enough so that the family could join them in America.

Lipa made his journey probably around 1885, and Dassah came perhaps a year later with the children.

Lipa had a tough time in America. He tried various jobs, earned enough as a coat presser to send for his family, but never found an economic identity suitable for the sprawling, quarrelsome, competitive urban land to which he had immigrated. The family lived in squalid tenements, with no lights on the stairways leading to the tiny apartments, with privies in the back yard, with deafening noise, dead horses in the streets, streets so crowded that nimble nurses had to walk across rooftops to reach the sick.

More children came along for the Birnbaum family. Sadie was born in about December 1887, Mamie about April 1891, Goldie about May 1894.

And on January 20, 1896, Naftaly Birnbaum, named for his deceased paternal grandfather, was born in the family tenement apartment at 95 Pitt Street in New York. Lipa, sometimes called Louis in America, was already 40, and Dassah, now Dora, was 38. Lipa's occupation was listed as a tailor on his new son's birth certificate, and so he must have been continuing to work as a coat presser, an unwilling conscript in the army of Jewish immigrants who worked in sweatshops, the all-too-accurately named places where labor extended for hours in impossible heat. Pressers typically earned about $500 a year; they worked 60 hours a week.

Three more children would enter the Birnbaum family after Naftaly. Theresa was born in about April 1897, Samuel in about August 1899, and William on March 12, 1902.

Young Naftaly, soon called Nathan, was like other young boys. He didn't know a different world, so for him the noise and sights were exciting. The crowds were an early audience, even with his long curls, which he had until he was five.

Also at five, the family moved to 259 Rivington Street up on the third floor of a four-story tenement. The grocery store and the butcher shop were downstairs, and the Birnbaum apartment was one of four on the floor. The whole family lived in three cramped rooms, a front room with windows looking out on a crowded street below, a kitchen area, and a back bedroom that didn't have any windows. Communal bathrooms would be built in tenements eventually, but the Birnbaums had no such convenience. The children, understandably scared of the dark stairs, were forced to walk down if they needed to use the privy in the backyard at night. Their mother stood on the stairs, yelling down words of encouragement. When they reached the door, she rushed to the window to yell out more comforting words. Privacy was not an alternative on the Lower East Side. As Burns transformed this terror into humor, "So when my sisters went to the toilet they knew it in Altoona."[2]

With so many children, bathing wasn't easy, either: "We took baths in the kitchen tub. There was only enough hot water for one tubful, so the oldest got the first bath and the rest of us took turns, according to age, in the same water. You can imagine what it was like when it got to me. I was cleaner when I got in."[3]

There was also a lack of light. Here is the way Burns put it: "We had gaslight but very little of it, because about once a week when the gas ran out you had to put a quarter in the meter. My mother always kept the flame turned down very low to make the quarter last as long as possible ... I was eight years old before I knew what my sisters looked like. Then one night my mother turned up the light. I got a look at my sisters and blew it out."[4]

There is a magic trick going on here. Painful, embarrassing reality goes into the hat but out comes a funny, warm memory. That was how Burns dealt with pain all his life, by transforming it. Humor was not just a reflex or an income. It was necessary for survival. Burns became a master at blocking out the painful and seeing all of his life as funny.

Less funny was the reality of hunger. One of the grandmothers lived with them, and she was known to take food at weddings, hide it in her petticoat, and bring it home. Burns developed a lifelong habit of putting ketchup on all foods because it would mask any bad taste. Sometimes when young Nathan was hungry, he put ketchup in a cup of hot water as a makeshift version of tomato soup.

Dora was a master of figuring out how to stretch the food she had. She'd buy Vienna rolls, two for a penny, and a can of tomato herrings for about six cents. For 15 cents, she'd feed nine children.

But it was not enough for young Nathan (nicknamed Natty, sometimes spelled Nattie) Birnbaum to keep reality away. He had a deep need for approval, applause, and recognition; for him all code words for love. He certainly received such love from his mother, but his father was a different story.

Beyond his work as a presser, Lipa Birnbaum's long, gray beard and strict observance of Jewish law made him proud. There were dreams behind his brown eyes. He lived by carrying with him a vision of an afterlife. He was respected. He refused to have pictures taken of him because he thought such practices were egotistical. He loved discussing the sacred texts with others.

He eventually gave up being a presser and worked, when he could, for whatever money he could get, as a religious functionary. He inspected meat to ensure that it was kosher. Indeed, the Birnbaum family was strictly kosher; they had, for example, two sets of dishes, one for meat and one for dairy.

Natty was sent to cheder, or Hebrew school. Lipa would take Natty to the mikveh, a ritual bath, to bathe before each Sabbath. The mikveh had three cubicles, one with lukewarm water, one with hot water, and one with very hot water. Lipa consistently took his son to the very hot option.

Most of all, Lipa wanted to be a cantor, someone who sang the Hebrew prayers, but he had no training, so he settled on being a ba'al tefillah, someone untrained who led the congregation in prayer. Lipa loved to sing, and young Natty joined his father in these songs, humming along as his father sang and then also singing with him, no doubt finding his father's most intense approval during such shared raising of voices.

Lipa found work as a ba'al tefillah in small synagogues that couldn't afford the real cantors. Unfortunately, Lipa's voice was evidently less than angelic. As Burns put it: "After he sang in one little synagogue, the following synagogue, instead of hiring him, they kept it closed during Rosh Hashanah and Yom Kippur."[5] Most often, Lipa didn't get paid for his singing services, but he was proud to be there at all. He once was ecstatic when he was asked to return even though he earned no fee.

Like his father, young Natty wanted to be a performer. Lipa did it for God; Natty did it for people. Both father and son were desperate for the approval of their respective audience.

Besides singing, Natty liked to dance. His first chance to find an audience for his talents came when he was five. Organ grinders were popular on the Lower East Side. Most of the major ones played over on Second Avenue, but Luigi, a large and kind man, wandered over to Rivington Street with his pet monkey, Toto, who wore a red-velvet pillbox hat with a matching red velvet suit. The gold buttons and green sash completed the outfit. Luigi played his organ while people in the tenements looked out their windows and threw pennies at Toto, who made an effort to catch the flying coins in his hat. Young girls gathered around Luigi and danced to the music, even though the organ wasn't very good and the music came out flat.

Natty noticed how a performer could entrance an audience and attract young females. He no doubt also noticed the resulting money and applause. Luigi and Toto had what he wanted. And, so, young Natty joined the girls in the dancing, noting the steps, most of which were made up as they danced. The girls approved of his dancing, heartily applauding his efforts. Natty loved all of it.

That was the beginning, the burning desire to hear approval from a crowd, the fire in every vein.

In all this, George Burns wasn't very different from other young Jewish children of his generation who emerged as major comedians. When Samuel S. Janus conducted a study of Jewish comedians in 1975, he discovered that their early lives were frequently haunted by suffering and deprivation. Almost all had come from poor families. The comedians were closer to their mothers than their fathers, who were, like Lipa, often frustrated failures in America. Those comedians, Janus said, always "live for acceptance.... There is never enough respect."[6]

But getting the respect of a wider audience meant rejecting the very Jewish values their parents had taught them — study hard in school, be passive, be frugal, be cautious about taking chances in life. Still, Burns always admired his father for teaching him the difference between right and wrong, as well as a strong sense of personal responsibility. Indeed, George Burns, like so many other Jewish comedians, was proud of being Jewish, but he could not accept all of its emotional requirements, much less its ritualistic obligations.

The harsh living conditions, the need for approval, the applauding crowd, the loving mother — these were the ingredients that shaped young Natty Birnbaum. All of these might have taken some time to develop, but Natty Birnbaum didn't have the luxury of time.

Late in the afternoon on Saturday, August 22, 1903, Lipa Birnbaum was in his rocking chair and, appropriately enough for the Sabbath, he was reading from a religious book. Dora was at one of the front windows, watching the organ grinder in the street and the neighborhood children dancing. Natty was playing nearby on the floor. Suddenly, Natty heard his father call out, "Dassah," but the music made her unable to hear the plea for help. Natty yelled in a louder voice, "Mama ... papa's calling you."[7] Dora turned around. Lipa dropped his book. At age 47, he died of heart disease.

Keeping with the Jewish tradition of a quick burial, Lipa Birnbaum was buried the following day at Union Field Cemetery in Queens. Lipa had bought a plot from a society organized by people who came from Kobaschow, and he was buried in that area.

In the traditional Jewish mourning custom, ten men (called a minyan) were required to say the Kaddish prayer for the seven-day mourning period (called shiva) following burial. Dora Birnbaum did not have enough male relatives for a minyan, and so she had to pay some men to pray for her husband. Young Natty could never erase the memory of his mother desperately seeking the money to pay for the mourners. As Natty observed his mother's continuing anguish, his distaste for formal religion was formed.

His father's death was a pivotal moment in Natty Birnbaum's life. He watched as his mother frequently burst into tears and joined in with her. There would be no more singing with Lipa, no more chances for the seven-year-old Natty to earn his love.

As Burns later reconstructed his life, the age of seven became supremely important. It was, as Burns told and retold, at seven that he left school, and it was the age at which he entered show business, at least of sorts, by joining in a singing group with three other boys. It seems improbable that all this chronologically happened at the same time. But whatever the factual truth, the psychological truth is indisputable. For young Natty Birnbaum, life was entirely different after his father died. After that, he would never again have the benefit of his father's approval. This meant that there could never be enough approval, enough applause, enough audience love. There would always be some void that could not be filled.

Perhaps, if he had been a good student, he might have walked the more common path to communal and familial approval. But Natty was not a good student at all. He attended P.S. 22, then on Sheriff Street, and dropped out of school in the fourth or fifth grade, sometime around 1904. Natty wasn't dreaming about school, but about singing. And he couldn't grasp mathematics. Worst of all, he could barely read or write. What he had was later termed dyslexia, but no one could diagnose that during his school years. He knew he was smart, but sitting there trying to decode the printed words was a painful experience. Beyond the frustration of not pleasing his teachers or his mother, the inability to read well made Natty feel apart from the rules of society and of his family. Other young Jewish children were discovering schooling as the golden gateway to success in America. But Natty found the classroom useless and difficult.

The poverty and the culture of the Lower East Side made it inevitable that young children who felt like social outsiders acted outside the legal rules. Like many others, Natty began stealing. He told of going to the Automat with his sister's hairpin and standing by the glass window with the beef stew. When someone bought the stew, Natty would slip in the hairpin before the window closed. Then he would steal the next stew, either eating it or selling it to another customer.

Another illicit practice required Natty to cut the bottoms from his coat pockets. He would then go to one of the area's numerous fruit peddlers and, with one hand, point to the top of the pile and ask the cost of the item. As the peddler looked to where the finger pointed, Natty would reach through the hole with his other hand and grab any fruit he could reach. He had other "businesses" involving various small thefts as well.

Perhaps if his father had lived, Natty Birnbaum would have had a more powerful restraining force. But as it was, Natty was poor and powerless. He didn't have school as a way into society. His parents' influence did make crime an unsuitable possibility. His mother, in particular, made known her disapproval of any illegal activity. Natty might have gone into the tailor trade, but he found that prospect to be unappealing.

Instead, young Natty tried to make money in any way he could. He sold papers. He shined shoes. But it was his job at Rosenzweig's candy store on Columbia and Stanton that changed his life. He worked there after school from three in the afternoon until five for five cents a day making syrup for the ice cream sodas the store sold. Natty worked with three other boys stirring the syrup in the four large copper vats. The boys grew bored, and, as was common on the Lower East Side, they began singing. Here, he realized, was a way out: a place where schooling wasn't required, where people would approve him, where he'd be successful. Starry-eyed Natty Birnbaum discovered early that he wanted to go into show business.

One day, Lou Feingold, a letter carrier who so frequently thought of himself as a budding impresario that he even adopted the professional name of Lou Farley, went down to the basement to deliver a letter and overheard the boys. He was impressed and began to teach the boys how to sing harmony. Natty was the tenor in the group.

One day as the boys sang, people threw pennies down. The boys counted, and they discovered they had made more money from such tips than from stirring syrup. Natty Birnbaum's career had begun.

With Farley's help, the four boys — Natty, Mortzy Weinberger, his bother Heshy, and Moishe Friedman, nicknamed Toda — formed the Peewee Quartet. (The original spelling was "Quartette," but that is most often simplified in writing about the group.)

The boys sang on street corners, in backyards, any place they could. They began singing on the Staten Island Ferry. Burns thought it was a perfect arrangement: "Every trip we had a captive audience. The only way they could get away from us was to jump overboard."[8] The boys soon learned that young men romancing women would pay them to go away and leave the couple alone.

The Quartet continued playing for several years. Then their voices changed. In Natty's case, not only did his voice change naturally when he was thirteen, but he also contracted diphtheria, the result of which was a gravelly voice. For whatever reason, it was also about this time that he began to develop a slight stammer.

From this point on, the boys went their separate paths. Mortzy and Heshy went into the taxicab business. Toda became an insurance broker. But Natty Birnbaum was stuck. He never left show business. It was a life he loved. It added a twinkle to his eye. And if his father blocked out reality as he viewed Heaven, young Natty could block out reality to view the heaven of a show business life. Despite his bar mitzvah, Natty Birnbaum had no interest in following his father's religious inclinations.

Natty Birnbaum wanted to enter show business. For him that meant entering vaudeville. The word "vaudeville" evidently derives from the Vau de Vive, a river valley in Normandy that inspired French drinking songs. The word eventually got transposed to *voix de ville*, or street voices.

Vaudeville began with a man named Tony Pastor who decided that the raucous entertainment then available was inappropriate for families. It was, after all, meant to get men to order more drinks in saloons. Entertainment in theaters included rough language and women in revealing outfits. Pastor thought an alternative was needed, and so, in 1881, he opened the 14th Street Theater in New York. It was a new theater with new rules. No liquor was allowed. The words liar, devil, damn, slob, son of a gun, or sucker would not be tolerated; any performer using such language was fired immediately. Pastor knew he could also attract families by giving door prizes; potatoes and silk dresses were among the most popular.

The singers and comics in Pastor's theater, the wholesome atmosphere, the chance for new immigrants to find some escape from the drudgeries of life, all led to enormous success. That very success led to competition, most especially from Benjamin Keith and Edward F. Albee who built a chain of theaters in the Northeast also providing clean entertainment. Keith and Albee knew people so enjoyed the shows that they would return, which began the idea of continuous shows. Keith and Albee were the first who used the term "vaudeville" for this new kind of entertainment.

Many of the theaters were beautiful, considered palaces to the mostly poor audiences. For performers, however, the theaters meant being backstage in cramped rooms. The performers weren't paid well. They were fired if the theater manager didn't like them. The firing took place when the manager returned the performer's photographs. Theater managers also compiled reports on individual acts and sent to the home office of the chain. These "review books" could determine a performer's future.

A vaudeville show reflected the variety of entertainment available and the different needs of the audience. A typical show usually began with a "dumb act," that is one that didn't require speaking. Such an act was for those in the audience with a tenuous grasp of the English language. It was also a courtesy to the audience members already in their seats; they could enjoy the performance — the acrobat, or cyclist, or dog or seal performing tricks — without having to worry about hearing lines above the sounds of incoming people. The second act, or "deuce spot," was for people who had yet to achieve status in vaudeville. It was often performed in front of a closed curtain, or "in one," so that scenery could be set up out of view. Audiences didn't always pay attention to the act, typically a singing or dancing pair of performers. Among some performers, the deuce spot was also called the burying ground because performers "died" there. The third, or "flash," act had sets and many performers. Here was an act — perhaps a magician or a comedy sketch or a playlet — meant to excite audiences, to get them to feel they were getting a good value for their admission price. The fourth spot kept the momentum going. A singer, a comedy team, or a dance act were typical. The fifth act was the headliner, the big star, the person meant to cause chatter during intermission and keep people in the theater. The headliner in this spot was not the top headliner in the show — who would appear in the next-to-closing spot — but a rising star or someone who had been at the top and was no longer there. The nature of the act depended on what had preceded it in order to provide balance. So if the fourth act had been a comic, then the headliner might be a singer.

Intermission for vaudeville theaters was crucial. They sold goods at the concession stands for large profits. Because of this, managers were strict about how long an act ran. If it went over, crucial intermission minutes were lost. This vital economic reality made performers precise in their timing. They developed the necessary skills to leave time for laughs, to space their silences, to pace their speaking.

The sixth spot, right after the intermission, was a challenge for the performer who had to get the audience calmed down after the intermission. A high-quality "dumb act" usually worked the best, maybe a juggler. A musical act also often succeeded. A large musical number or dramatic sketch typically filled the seventh spot — novelty orchestras, dramatic sketches, and the like. The eighth spot, the one next to closing, was for the headliner. The spot might feature a comedy team, a comedian or a singer, but whatever the nature of the performance, the spot was filled with the most famous performer the theater could afford. The ninth spot was the chaser, or "haircut act" (so called because the performer usually played to the backs of departing audience members' heads). This spot was not for competent performers. Boring, strange, or worthy of derision: these were the descriptions that comedy managers wanted for this act. Loud was also good so the act could be heard above the sound of exiting audience members. Managers wanted to get the people out and get a new audience in for the next show — which would be simply a repetition of the show that had just been completed. Performers were in four to six programs a day in what was appropriately nicknamed "the grind." For those in small-time theaters, nicknamed "the death trail," life was never easy. In later years, movies served as the chaser, mostly because they were obviously not live and included shots that were typically static and hazy. Audiences who wanted live performers simply left and those who liked the movie knew its completion was a prompt for them to leave the theater.

At its height in the 1920s, there were 4,000 vaudeville theaters. Two million people a day paid the average admission price of 25 cents to see the show. There were 25,000 performers of widely varying talent. That is, it was a huge business with lots of opportunities. For those with little schooling and no money it was a genuine path to success.

And young people like Natty Birnbaum wanted to make money, be famous, attract good-looking partners, and lead an adventurous life. The entertainer's life stressed enjoyment of the present, not the delayed gratification inherent, say, in religious teaching. For Natty and thousands like him, the identity he sought as a vaudeville entertainer carried with it a belief system and lifestyle diametrically opposed to the Jewish values he had learned at home. But all audiences, including American Jews, were absorbing these lessons from the entertainers, so in that Natty Birnbaum's ambitions were hardly his own.

To keep his dream alive, Natty started a dance act with Abie Kaplan, a neighborhood friend. Seeking a stage name, the two boys settled on The Burns Brothers. Burns always claimed that they took the name from the Burns Brothers coal yard. According to his version, Burns and his brother would steal coal, prompting the neighbors to call them the "Burns brothers." It's unclear whether or not that is true. Natty may have chosen "Burns" as a shortened form of Birnbaum. Most families, including his own, didn't think highly of show business. Additionally, "Burns" sounded Irish, not Jewish, and so it would be easier to "pass" in the wider world. Abie became Al Burns.

Natty couldn't call himself Nat Burns because there was already an entertainer with that name. He settled on "George" because his older brother Izzy had begun using the name George, and young Natty liked it. "George Burns" began his career. George and Abie first worked at Seiden's Theater on Columbia Street — pulling the curtain up and down.

During one week, the Seiden had a Yiddish sketch titled "Religion Versus Love," about a young Gentile woman who wanted her Jewish partner to renounce his religion and marry her. At the end, the boy called out, "No! A Jew I was born, and a Jew I shall die!"[9] Natty Birnbaum used this line whenever someone asked him if he had legally changed his name to George Burns.

Abie, who was not meant for show business, soon left. One evening Natty was singing and a man named Mac Fry came over to offer a job in the act "Mac Fry and Company." Burns did some singing, dancing, and acting. They played a burlesque house and then the Windsor Theater in the Bowery. That was it. Fry and Company was no more.

Sam Brown was Natty's next partner. Brown had been in an act called "Brown and Williams" in which the partners sang, danced, and roller skated. After Williams left, Natty adopted a new stage name; he was the new Williams. The act began with a soft-shoe dance. Then Natty let loose with the no doubt entrancing song, "Don't Take Me Home." Brown, meanwhile, donned his roller skates and circled around while "Williams" put his skates on to join his partner in a dance on the skates. Vaudeville stages often slanted toward the audience, so poor Natty kept sliding toward the footlights, relying on Brown to pull him back.

The real Williams who had left started his own act eventually returned, and the young Natty Birnbaum was once again without a partner. Indeed, it was time to earn some legitimate money.

Natty went to work for Borgenicht and Kornreich printing the size tickets for children's dresses. He worked from eight until six in the evening, five days a week, and until one in the afternoon on Sundays. His pay was $5 a week. He was eventually promoted to be an assistant cutter for $12 a week. Of course, the irrepressible Natty began singing harmony with some of his co-workers. He'd even get up on a table and dance. He'd charm the young women who worked in the loft above them. Natty was fired but found that his work as an assistant cutter was much in demand, so he went to work for Mursky and Company, a company that manufactured kimonos. Unhappy with the job, Natty left to work as a cutter at the Gaiety Waist Company, where his sisters Mamie and Goldie worked. But Natty's mind was not on his work; he thought only about show business. It didn't take long for him to get fired.

Natty was unemployed for six months and finally determined to take a job he had avoided: cutting fur. He found a job, but it lasted only four days.

Natty Birnbaum, age 16, was getting a quarter a day from his mother. Other young men his age were working hard in business, but Natty, still undiscouraged, was out of work for another half-year.

Natty met Hymie Goldberg and Nat Fields, two young men who also wanted to enter show business. The three began an act. Natty's new stage name was Glide, and Hymie became Goldie, so Goldie, Fields, and Glide were ready to conquer show business. (Years later, George Burns, Jack Benny and Bing Crosby did a singing and dancing act on Benny's show that they called Goldie, Fields, and Glide. They were a considerable improvement over the original act.) The young men weren't exactly a success. They did, however, make good money selling umbrellas in front of the theaters on Broadway. The act finally found a booking at Miner's Bowery Theater. Natty appeared in blackface doing the best Jolson impression he could, which was not especially reminiscent of the real singer. Nat Fields put tissue paper on a comb and tried to make music. He had a beard to make the audiences realize he was supposed to be Jewish, not exactly a stretch for him. Ethnic acts were then very popular. Even so, the manager let them go.

Natty took to sitting in a booking agency in the Putnam Building. One day a man came in asking if the booker could find George Burns. Natty jumped up announcing that he was George Burns, though, of course, the man wanted someone else with that name. Borrowing some money for a new suit and stealing an older performer's act, Natty went onstage and started his number. The manager interrupted him and fired him on the spot.

More months followed with no work. It's probable that most people would begin to get the message that they weren't going to succeed in show business. But Natty Birnbaum didn't believe that. He loved the life, and if he would remain small-time his whole life, so be it. He didn't want to leave the world he loved for the dreary world of reality.

But he needed money. And so he became a ballroom dancer. He entered every contest he could find and won a few of them. He looked at women's feet, not their faces, and searched out the best partners. He finally settled on one young woman in particular. Nettie Curlin was not only a great dancer, she had the added advantage of having a father who owned a pickle stand. The pair got paid $5 a night to exhibit their dancing skills and continued until Nettie found a better dancing partner.

Natty, now 17, joined "The Fourth of July Kids," five males and four females, all between 14 and 18 years of age. For his $15 a week, Natty sang; his stammering prevented him from the acting parts in the act. The group was promised that if the group was successful during its three-day run in Gloversville, New York, they would be booked in Wilkes-Barre and Scranton, Pennsylvania. They were so spectacularly unsuccessful that the manager tried to skip town. He was caught and jailed, and Natty Birnbaum was on the street again.

With his dancing skills intact, Natty got a job at Bennie Bernstein's Dancing School on Avenue B. The customers, mostly immigrants, were attracted to the place because Bernstein spoke seven languages. Men paid a dime, women a nickel. Bernstein spoke and Natty taught. Natty was doing well; he earned $25 a week and was so popular that Bernstein asked him to become a partner. The two opened B.B.'s College of Dancing. One night, however, a man came in, checked his package, and left. The police soon arrived. The man had walloped a woman over the head at a hotel on Broadway. He had stolen her money and jewels and hidden them in the package he had checked. The criminal, Bernstein, and Natty wound up at a police station. It wasn't long before the police closed the school.

There was one blonde side benefit to working at the school. Her name was Jean DeFore, a 23-year-old who wore make-up so heavily she looked 30. Natty took her home to meet his mother, who was less than impressed. Dora Birnbaum smiled, stared at Jean, and asked Natty in Yiddish if this woman planned to adopt him. She then went over to Jean and said she had just told her son how charming she was.

Natty Birnbaum, alias George Burns, tried out many other aliases during the next couple of years. He failed so often that a manager would refuse to book him, so he had to come up with a new stage name. He lived next door to despair and failure but he refused to move there. It seems reasonable that he might have considered changing his act, but that he was unwilling to do. He loved performing. It's not, though, that he had so many bookings. He worked with a seal for three days. It wasn't even his act, but Captain Betts, the man who worked with Flipper, as he was called, became ill and asked Natty to take his place. And so, armed with a ball and fish in his pocket, young Natty went to work. He threw the ball to the seal, who'd bounce and twirl it on his nose and then flip it back to Natty, who then rewarded the star by throwing him a piece of fish. When the seal finished, he applauded with his flippers. Natty bowed, the curtain descended, and the act was over. Only in retrospect was this a good story. "Flipper and Friend" (as the act was billed) was not a high point of Natty's career. After all, the seal got top billing.

But Natty never quit. He saw his life as funny. He simply blocked out what was bad. He saw the world through a vaudeville lens. He transformed life's burdens into comedy bits, seeing them as raw material, not suffering.

At one point he had an act with Harriet Gibson and lived with her for a time. He tried a double act with a woman named Janie Malone. Natty decided to call himself Jed Jackson, and so Jackson and Malone sought work.

After that, Natty joined with someone else for a two-man dancing act called "Burns and Links," only in this act, Natty was Links. The two were sitting in an office when someone walked in saying he wanted to hire a dog act in Ronkonkoma, on Long Island. Natty declared himself to be in a dog act. Burns and Links went to 44th Street, found two dogs and did their regular act with the exception that this time they held the dogs under their arms.

Unable to find further work, Natty went back to ballroom dancing, then especially popular because of the success of the husband-and-wife dance team of Vernon and Irene Castle. Natty entered every dance contest he could find, perfecting his tango.

Natty duly filled out his draft registration card on June 5, 1917. He listed himself as a performer on various circuits and indicated that he had blue eyes and brown hair (and not yet bald). He was 5 feet 8½ inches tall. He sought exemption from the draft as he was the sole support of his mother and his sister. He was clearly not above a little vaudeville shine even on official documents.

After performing an exhibition dance at P.S. 188, Natty watched as everyone else danced. He was particularly taken by one young woman, Hannah Siegel. Natty arranged an introduction. They got along immediately, and Natty asked her to be his partner in a dance act. Deciding on a Spanish name for her to match their tango, Natty selected Hermosa Jose. "Hermosa" means a beautiful woman in Spanish, but George Burns always insisted that he selected the name because he smoked Jose Hermosa cigars.

Natty had started smoking cigars as a teenager. He thought they made him look grown-up and important. They were also useful onstage. He could puff while planning the next line or waiting for the applause to stop. It became part of the act, and so, part of the person. Hermosa Joses were long, cheap cigars. He wanted cheap ones because they stayed lit. He needed a dependable prop.

Hannah Siegel was born in New York on April 20, 1899, to Simon and

Lena Morris Siegel. Simon Siegel was a shoemaker who eventually owned a shoe store. And Natty's eye had been good. She was a terrific dancer. They won enough contests to feel confident about trying a vaudeville act, billed as Jose and Smith.

For the rest of his life, George Burns told the story of what happened after a few one-week runs. They were, he would repeat in print and in person, offered a 36-week (or some variation in his different stories) engagement. Her parents, the tale continued, wouldn't allow that unless she was married, and so young Natty married her, went on the road, and they divorced immediately afterward.

What really happened is not clear, but a lengthy engagement like that was for headliners not unknowns, so even on the face of it the story is suspicious. This much is known. On September 5, 1917, 21-year-old Nathan Birnbaum, giving his address as 272 East 7th Street, and 18-year-old Hannah Siegel were married in Hannah's apartment at 247 Broome Street in New York by a man, presumably a rabbi, named Oscar Geller. What happened during the marriage and when they decided to separate is unclear. What is known is that they were officially divorced in 1921 (file #16490/1921). The Burns story is inaccurate, but it does reveal one of George Burns' characteristic psychological strategies. He compressed time in order to avoid subjects he didn't like. If the actual marriage lasted four years, and he didn't like that, he simply said it lasted for an unconsummated 36 weeks. It was hardly the last time he took such an approach in retelling his life. (Statutory law restricts access to divorce records to the parties and their attorneys for one hundred years, so that the file will not be available to the public until 2021.)

But despite the date of the divorce, there is probably some version of the truth in George Burns' account. As Hermosa Jose, Hannah Siegel Birnbaum appeared in *The Schubert Gaieties of 1919*, which ran from July 17, 1919 to October 18, 1919; *Cinderella on Broadway*, which ran from June 24, 1920 to September 25, 1920; and *The Whirl of New York*, from June 13, 1921 to September 17, 1921. In all of these (and perhaps other plays as well) she seems to have had very small roles as a dancer. It is unclear whether she and Natty had, by then, split up their act, or that they had so few engagements Hannah felt ready to take what she hoped would be long engagements in shows. Either way, they clearly did not have a successful vaudeville act.

Hannah Siegel, now divorced, married again on June 22, 1922, to another vaudevillian named Al Klein (Alexander Kleinman). Klein, born on August 16, 1885, was almost 14 years older than his new wife. He later appeared in at least 14 films, but was uncredited in ten of them. Klein died on September 5, 1951.

His wife was known for the rest of her life as Hermosa Klein.

Burns didn't forget her, either. And neither did Gracie Allen. For Christmas 1926, George and Gracie used a photo of Hermosa and George, had it enlarged, tinted, and mounted on cardboard. The picture was offered as a jigsaw puzzles with the pictures broken into pieces. Many years later, on a May 29, 1979 television program, Burns told Barbara Walters that he had seen Hermosa a few years before her death, and that they had great fun going around with her introducing him to her friends as her first husband. (Hermosa Klein, who had been living at the St. Moritz Hotel, moved to New Jersey to be with her sister and died on February 28, 1981. Her body was cremated. She left no children.)

After the separation, Natty kept failing in vaudeville. His anguished brother Izzy had by then moved to Akron, Ohio, where he had opened a women's clothing store. Izzy suggested that Natty come out to Ohio and work in the store. Natty, on Izzy's advice, did enroll in the Manhattan Preparatory School, but the tortures of his public schooling returned, and he left after four days.

Natty Birnbaum was 24. His peers had married and stayed married, settled down into jobs, and began to have children. Natty, on the other hand, was on the verge of divorce and had almost no job prospects. He had clean spats, some cigars, and a failing act with the Rosebud Sisters. But the life of a vaudeville entertainer was exciting. There were chances for a new romance in every town. If no romance was possible, there were houses of prostitution in every town. There were the young women in the various acts to joke with. There were stories to collect, people to meet, and always, always the thrilling sound of applause and laughter. The lure of tomorrow's applause made it easier to get through some long nights. And it was easy to stay in vaudeville. All you needed were black and white publicity pictures a theater could put in the lobby, some business cards, some music, and your act.

Natty wasn't about to leave the business. In 1920 he teamed up with Sid Gary, born Sidney Garfunkel in Boston in 1901. Natty suggested they call themselves "Two Boys from Rhode Island in an Act of Providence." Gary, wisely, refrained from considering the name. The silly pun, though, is important: Natty's offbeat humor eventually became needed. But that was in the future. The act with Gary included singing and talking. Gary had an incredible soprano voice which the audience first heard offstage. He'd walk on singing and the audience was always surprised the voice belonged to a man.

Burns and Gary stayed together for about a year before breaking up. One evening Natty heard Billy Lorraine singing, was impressed, and asked Lorraine to team up with him for an act. The two couldn't have a comedy act because Billy Lorraine stuttered except when he sang, so they became "Burns and Lorraine — Two Broadway Thieves." Lorraine imitated popular singers of the day such as Al Jolson and Eddie Cantor, and Natty imitated popular dancers. They criss-crossed the country, not very successfully.

But, as always, the vaudeville life had its own crazy tales. Dolly Kraeger was a woman on their bill. She and Natty began seeing each other. Unfortunately for Natty, she neglected to mention that she was the girlfriend of a Detroit gangster. Hearing of the romance, the gangster wrote her a letter threatening Natty's life. He wrote that he would prove how serious he was by shooting himself in the leg. And he did. While he hobbled around for several months, Natty and Dolly continued to see each other, but when the tour neared Detroit, she left to marry the gangster.

On October 2, 1922, Burns and Lorraine reached the Broadway Theater at Broadway and 41st Street. The performance was a big chance for the team because bookers were going to see their supposedly improved act and promised to raise their pay on the East Coast to $175 a week if they were good enough. The excited Burns got up early. The theater gave out rehearsal checks to the entertainers, and the lowest number went first. This was crucial because no songs could be duplicated; thus if an act rehearsed first and offered a number then no later act could repeat it. Sybil Vane, a pretty, bobbed-hair soprano, was the headliner. Both she and the Burns and Lorraine team wanted to sing "Yankee Doodle Blues." Natty beat her, and they sang it.

But his efforts did not impress the reporter for *Variety* whose review appeared in the October 6, 1922 edition. Here, in full, is what the reviewer wrote: "Burns and Lorraine held the second spot. The dancing brought them through, but the impressions of Jolson and Cantor by the vocalist [Lorraine] marks the turn as a small time buy. The double dance routine brought some scattered applause."[10] Ouch. This after Natty had spent years in show business. He knew it was time for a new act. He saw attractive women who could dance and considered joining with one of them.

But he had also been collecting jokes, reading the humor magazines *Whiz Bang* and *College Humor*, finding jokes he liked and then switching them around a bit. He decided he wanted to do a talking act, some humor with a partner. Of course, he would be the comedian. He just needed a woman as a partner. He sought a partner in the common way, by putting up notices at the National Variety Artists Club and at the office of The White Rats, the vaudeville union.

And so, soon after the Broadway Theater fiasco, Burns and Lorraine played their last date, at the Union Hill Theater in Union Hill, New Jersey. Rena Arnold was the headliner on the bill. After the first matinee, Natty spoke to Rena and told her that the act was splitting up and that he planned to do a talking act. He then told her a risqué joke, one she did not find amusing. The next day, one of Rena's roommates at the Coolidge Hotel, a block from the Palace Theater, went backstage to see her. (Mary Kelly was the other roommate; she was the sweetheart of a rising young comedian named Jack Benny.) The young woman, who had been out of work for a year and miserable in secretarial school, wanted to get back into show business. Rena mentioned that Burns and Lorraine were splitting up. Recalling the offensive joke, Rena suggested that Lorraine might make a good partner.

The young woman sat in the audience and watched the show. The way George Burns sometimes told the story, Rena took the young woman backstage where she introduced herself to the stuttering Lorraine, who said his name was Burns. That seems less likely than the probability that the woman shrewdly sized up the two and determined that, even if he told some mildly dirty jokes, the Burns part of the team was the one with talent. The woman knew a lot about dancing, and she could tell.

When Natty first saw her he thought she looked stringy and tired and that she "acted uppity and tossed her long black hair from her shoulders."[11] For her part, Grace Allen was equally unimpressed. "George acted outrageously conceited over a split-week engagement [appearing in multiple venues during a week rather than being good enough to be hired in one place for the whole week] in a five-a-day grind house and wore a loud checked suit and used out of date slang."[12]

In one way or another, Grace Allen and the man who should now be called George Burns met that night and made a date to meet at Wiennig and Sberber's restaurant, near the Palace Theater in New York, the next day. They had breakfast together and agreed to form an act. Her only demand was that he remove his gold tooth.

Two days later Burns and Allen began to rehearse.

CHAPTER THREE

The Not-So-Dumb Dora

If George Burns re-created a life history as he fashioned his biography, so did Gracie Allen. Both of them were evasive about Gracie's year of birth. While census records are notoriously unreliable, it does seem clear that Gracie was born before George, on July 26, 1895, rather than sometime during the 1902–1906 era they both offered as her birthdate. (The San Francisco earthquake and fire on April 18, 1906, destroyed the official records.) If she had been born in 1906, George's relationship to her would have been entirely different, more of a mentor, much older sibling, or even a bit of a parental role. In 1923 when they met, she would have been 17, still a young woman. Instead, she was 28, with a lot of experience and failure behind her, experience that made her shrewder than a youth would have been. At 28 she would have felt that she had less time in which to succeed.

Gracie was born in San Francisco. Her father, George Allen, was Scottish. He was born in San Francisco in February 1862. Gracie's mother, Margaret Darragh, was born to Patrick, an Irish immigrant, and Clara Darragh, around July 1867.

George Allen was a dancer and entertainer; the Darraghs hired him to teach Margaret ballroom dancing. They married in 1883. Bessie Allen, the oldest child, was born in April 1884; Pearl was born on February 28, 1886; George was born on March 29, 1888; and Hazel was born on September 18, 1889 (or 1891).

When she was 18 months old, Gracie had the first of two childhood accidents. In the first, she pulled a pot of boiling water off the stove. The burning water poured down on her shoulder and right arm. The doctors managed to save her arm, but for the rest of her life she felt a need to hide the scars by wearing long sleeves. (So, Gracie Allen was hiding more than her birth date.) Soon after the first incident, Gracie pulled over a lamp. Pieces of glass went into her eye. Again, she was saved, but she became especially sensitive to bright light.

These childhood injuries did not dim her lively spirit. Her father had various jobs including performing in vaudeville. When she was three, therefore, her father evidently encouraged her singing by having her perform an Irish song to benefit a local church. She had a top hat and suit coat, but as she would not wear the red beard she was supposed to, she simply carried it onstage.

At some point in her early life, George Allen abandoned his wife and family. During the family tumult that followed, Gracie spent several years away from her mother, living instead with her mother's sister Clara.

The struggling Margaret Allen eventually met Edward Pidgeon, who drove a patrol car for the police. They married in 1905. In the 1910 census, Gracie is listed as Pidgeon's stepdaughter. Pidgeon died on December 6, 1923, not living long enough to see Gracie's success.

The young Allen sisters, like their father, loved to dance. Pearl Allen opened a dance studio, and all the sisters helped in the teaching. Bessie decided to try show business, performing in vaudeville. At age six, Gracie went to see her older sister. Her sister got her on stage, but Gracie began to cry. Undeterred, Bessie insisted and Gracie, bawling all the while, danced an Irish jig. The audience loved it. It didn't take long, however, for Gracie to get over her shyness. She, like her future husband, was in love with show business. Also, like him, school held no interest, no promise to be a gateway to a prosperous future. Gracie enjoyed going to theater lobbies and looking at the pictures of the entertainers. It was her art gallery. Gracie began performing as a singer and dancer when she was a teenager. Various members of the family would join her on stage, and she, in turn, joined their acts. Gracie received a business diploma in 1914, and from then on her focus was entirely on vaudeville. But vaudeville didn't entirely focus on her.

She had to spend about a year teaching at the family dancing school. Then she toured with Larry Reilly in an Irish act. Although the act allowed for comedy, Gracie was assigned just the dramatic roles. Joined by her sisters Bessie and Hazel, Gracie went on tour with the act "Larry Reilly and Company." The sisters grew tired of the act and went back home. Gracie was now "and Company." It was while she was working with Larry Reilly that she went out with a comedian who would one day become famous, but it was not George Burns. Gracie met Groucho Marx when the Marx Brothers were on a vaudeville bill with Larry Reilly and Company. Groucho invited Gracie to dinner at Luchow's, a famous German restaurant in Manhattan, and she accepted. It is not known whether there were other dates, but it is interesting that Gracie found the quick, Jewish comedic temperament attractive. Groucho and George eventually became comedic rivals, and Gracie's early date with Groucho no doubt contributed to that friendly feud.

Unhappy with the non-billing in Larry Reilly and Company, Gracie left. Searching for a future, she turned to various friends, including Benny Ryan, who toured as a dancer with his wife. Ryan wrote an act for her, and she went on tour looking for new partners. No one worked out, but Benny Ryan had inadvertently given Gracie Allen an incredible gift.

The act he wrote for her was a "Dumb Dora" act. In a typical Dumb Dora act, the male was a straight man and the woman was the comic. She could be vulgar, suggestive, brassy, and might say suggestive lines indicating her availability blended with some stupidity.

But Benny Ryan and Harriette Lee had changed that pattern. It was still a flirtation act, but in theirs Lee was not a wisecracking, attractive woman. She was simply dumb, dressed in ordinary clothes, not the outlandish costumes of the earlier Dumb Doras. She had a mind that could not be penetrated. What also made Ryan and Lee different was that they both did comedy, though comedy that by today's standards was simply not funny enough. The lines fall flat.

Ryan began writing for other acts, seeking to imitate his own.

The beloved character Gracie Allen eventually embodied had its start in Dumb Dora acts, and Benny Ryan was the first to see her comic potential. By some accounts, Ryan wrote the very first Dumb Dora acts that Gracie eventually did with George Burns. Benny Ryan, it seemed, liked more than just Gracie's acting talents. After splitting with Harriette Lee in 1918, Ryan and Gracie became romantically involved. Gracie may even have worked with Ryan while Harriette Lee was ill.

But George Burns was not ready to accept the gift that Benny Ryan had given to Gracie. George's usual explanation (and it's a reasonable one) is that the required "drop" (or set) for the act would have cost several hundred dollars that the couple didn't have. It's not clear whether they could have borrowed the money, but they should have. Benny Ryan's original Dumb Dora with Burns' insightful modifications would have accelerated their success enormously. Instead, because of cost, jealousy, or one other reason, he rejected the act outright.

The other reason is that George Burns wanted to be the comic in the act. He didn't, at the beginning, want a Dumb Dora. He wanted to wear flashy clothes and get the laughs. Indeed, he wore a large red bow tie, a hat with its brim turned up, and baggy pants. And so, armed with such an outfit and jokes re-written from the various humor magazines he found, George put together his own act, one filled with wisecracks, one that didn't find Gracie Allen's character.

The two rehearsed for about three weeks after their first meeting. And then they were ready for their first performance. George N. Burns and Grace Allen were about to storm vaudeville.

B.F. Keith and Edward Albee's circuit of vaudeville theaters was the largest during the decade, but they had rivals, most especially from the Orpheum, Pantages, and Loew's circuits. (In 1927, Keith-Albee merged with the Orpheum circuit.) Additionally, there were individual talent promoters, people like Fally Marcus, Gus Sun, or B.S. Moss. They booked mostly in small theaters, often in small towns, and often for only one performance a day.

Fally Marcus was the first promoter of Burns and Allen. He got them their initial performance, for three days at five dollars a day, at the Hill Theater in Newark, New Jersey. Gracie's dressing room at the Hill Theater had a mirror on the dressing table. Gracie sat down at the table, which shook. The mirror fell on the floor and cracked. Gracie, superstitious about the broken mirror, was in tears, fearing their new act was doomed. George told her about a Jewish superstition, one he invented as he calmed her down, that breaking a mirror was good luck, just like the Jewish custom of breaking a glass at the end of a wedding. Gracie did calm down and they went out to face the 15 people in the audience. They then worked for a week at a theater in Boonton, New Jersey, for ten dollars a day.

They didn't work again until March 15, 1923, when they performed for four days at the Myrtle Theater in Brooklyn. On April 9, they played the Fifth Avenue Theater. *Variety* noted about this performance that it was a "talking skit" with "his efforts at lovemaking consisting of 'wisecracks' ... it will hold a spot on any of the intermediate bills."[1] *Variety* liked their personalities but not the material.

For the rest of his life, George Burns gave a vaudeville shine to this seminal performance. He claimed, over and over, that, during the performance, the audience laughed at Gracie's straight lines and kept silent at his punch lines. Realizing this, the story continued, he immediately grasped the fact that Gracie was the comic in the act, and he needed to be the straight man. As in his retelling of how long he had been married to Hannah Siegel, George compressed reality in his reconstruction of reality. It took about a year for George to accept the fact that he could not succeed as a comic and to make the necessary switch.

The reluctance and the delay can be tracked through reviews in *Variety*. In June, for example, George remained the wisecracking hick. A perceptive reviewer noted that a "brighter and smarter vehicle will have to be secured eventually if they expect to advance."[2] On November 1, *Variety* reviewed an October 29 performance at the Riverside Theater in New York, noting that "George Burns and Grace Allen followed, dealing out some wisecracking chatter that didn't take them far."[3]

The Dumb Dora act slowly made its entrance. Gracie's sweet innocence, her freshness and her petite figure all helped. And, of course, they had some material provided to Gracie by Benny Ryan. George searched for Dumb Dora jokes, but the type had been played many times before in vaudeville, and they knew what was expected of them. It is unclear whether Ryan's actual material was used, but Gracie was familiar and comfortable with the type. It seems plausible as well that George, deeply upset at having to change the act, found it more palatable for Gracie to be a Dumb Dora than a smart and sassy comic. If he couldn't be the funny one, at least he could be the smart one. As if to illustrate this, George named the act "Sixty-Forty," an inside joke about how they split the money; Burns got 60 percent and Allen 40 percent, because, he claimed, he wrote the act, and he deserved the money.

They were doing the act by December 1923, but it still lacked punch. Gracie, bathed in the spotlight, walked onto the stage searching for George. He showed up by lighting a cigar in the dark. She started to berate him, saying he was constantly late and enumerating his other faults. She concluded with, "Here I've talked to you for three minutes and you don't even answer me. Aren't you going to say something?" George's response was, "Hello, Babe." Then he puffed his cigar again.[4] This line was supposed to get a laugh.

They had 21 bookings in 1924, mostly as a "disappointment act" in the smaller theaters on the Keith circuit. That is, they waited until a performer was too ill or drunk to perform, didn't like the billing, or had some other reason not to appear. The calls would come to their hotel rooms (always separate) on a Monday or a Thursday evening. Then Burns and Allen found some means of transportation, a subway for local venues or a train to go to places like Minneapolis or Portland or Los Angeles or one of the other cities they played that year. During all of 1924 they signed contracts for a week at a time, playing three or four shows each day. They probably earned $350 a week for the year — during the 21 weeks they played.

Just as Natty Birnbaum required tenacity, so, too, did George N. Burns and Gracie (still called Grace) Allen. Their life as vaudevillians had no guarantees. It was difficult, always. It's a fair question to ask why they stayed at it for the several years it took them to succeed. The obvious answer is that they both were smitten with show business. They also were inherently driven people: they refused to quit. And, it should be noted, they were making slow and then accelerating professional progress, in making Gracie the comic, in finding Gracie's character, in getting audiences to like them, and, excruciatingly slowly, in finding the lines to magnify their genuine skills. It's crucial to note that George's character also had to evolve. George stuttered. He suffered from stage fright. As Gracie watched the audience warm up to her and not him, it's easy to imagine she might have dropped him for another partner, especially because they were not romantically involved. But she liked the way he treated her. She believed in him, perhaps, despite his bluster, even more than he believed in himself. George's character needed to have perfect timing, to be suave and sophisticated. None of this was immediately obvious from George's early performances. Gracie was not just a passive partner. It was not merely her character or her acting and comedic skills that merited applause. Her loyalty to George under difficult circumstances for an extended period of time is remarkable.

For his part, George immersed himself in improving the act. He paid careful attention to the audience, always listening to its reactions for cues, always saying lines differently to see which version got the most laughs. He knew he needed to modify the Gracie character. By coincidence, his mother's American name was "Dora," and she had her own logic, and was funny without being aware of it. Consciously or not, Dora Birnbaum played an important role in the creation of Gracie's character. George loved his mother. She was his ideal of what a Jewish mother should be, and if she had an unusual way of seeing the world it wasn't because she was dumb.

George took the Dumb Dora character as modified by Benny Ryan and modified it yet again by applying an idealized Yiddish mama. This not-so-dumb Dora was dignified. In a way, she was the one who made sense, and it was the rest of the world that was out of step. As a woman worthy of respect, she couldn't be mocked or spoken to harshly. George couldn't blow cigar smoke in her face, and was careful not to do so onstage. This Dora had to dress well. From his mother's hard-earned, shrewd observations about people and society, George could smuggle truths through Gracie's innocent character. The Jewish nature of such social satire was not evident in Gracie's character, but its sharpness added to her appeal.

All of this was helped by Gracie's appearance, delivery (especially her laugh and a thin, high-pitched voice that was unlike her real voice) and her delicacy. All of this was added to her bubbly charm.

George evolved the Gracie character all through 1924 and 1925. He now had an appealing character and Gracie was an extraordinarily appealing woman to play that character. But he didn't have what could be judged good lines.

Consider, for example, the sharpness of one of the best of the original Dumb Dora skits titled, "Dialogue Between Master of Ceremonies and a Dumb Dora." It was supposedly written by a man named James Madison, though the accuracy of the name is improbable. Still, the lines are good. The flirtation act is much crisper than any lines Burns and Allen were using. One section of the routine went like this:

> MASTER OF CEREMONIES: If you do well this week, I may hold you over.
> DUMB DORA: Hold me over what?
> MASTER OF CEREMONIES: I mean I'll renew your engagement.
> DUMB DORA: Has it been broken?
> MASTER OF CEREMONIES: Has *what* been broken?
> DUMB DORA: Our engagement.
> MASTER OF CEREMONIES: *We're* not engaged. Getting married is foreign to my thoughts.
> DUMB DORA: That's all right. I'm a foreigner.
> MASTER OF CEREMONIES: You intrigue me.
> DUMB DORA: What's that?
> MASTER OF CEREMONIES: I said, "You intrigue me."
> DUMB DORA: Not while all these people are watching.[5]

Burns and Allen couldn't have used those lines, but they needed patter of that caliber. George couldn't get adequate material from the joke books. His own lines were good, but not great. But the changing character helped. It crystallized in a few lines during their next act, "Dizzy," which they started doing sometime around the end of 1925. Here are the crucial new lines:

> GEORGE: You're dizzy.
> GRACIE: I'm glad I'm dizzy. Boys like dizzy girls and I like boys.
> GEORGE: I'm glad you're glad you're dizzy.
> GRACIE: I'm glad you're glad I'm glad I'm dizzy.[6]

These lines, still not very good, finally were on the right track to Gracie's ultimate character.

Life, though, was not without its reality checks. Once they were on the bill right after the famous actress Ethel Barrymore. The audience adored her. As soon as she completed the performance, they left. George and Gracie walked out to an almost empty theater.

Additionally, sometimes the social status of being a vaudevillian made an unpleasant entry into George's life. One day, for instance, George received a call from the Cosmos Theater in Washington, D.C. They wanted Gracie and him for $450 a week. It was more than he had ever earned in his life, and he was excited. But when he informed Gracie of this great opportunity, she said she was not going to go, and he needed to call back and cancel. George was deeply upset, not just because of the money, but also because he had verbally agreed to the performance, and he considered it as crucial that he keep his word. But Gracie was adamant. Only later did he learn that she didn't want to go to Washington because her brother-in-law was just starting out as a diplomat, and she was concerned that his career could be adversely affected if his superiors learned that his wife's sister was in vaudeville.

Even with all that, the lines did get better. Armed with a more precise character, one in which Gracie was completely clear in her own mind that she was correct and that it was the world that didn't grasp the truths she did, George wrote or acquired better lines:

> GEORGE: I'm a pauper.
> GRACIE: Congratulations. Boy or girl?[7]
> [Building on this, the response was later modified:]
> GRACIE: My sister had a baby.
> GEORGE: Boy or girl?
> GRACIE: I don't know, and I can't wait to find out if I'm an aunt or an uncle.[8]

George Burns, already a proven master at suppressing the difficult, had other feelings to suppress as well. He was concerned that if he told Gracie he loved her, she would be forced to quit. She was by then engaged to Benny Ryan who, understandably, wanted Gracie to leave the act with George. Ryan was getting impatient; he wanted to get married. It couldn't have been lost on him that in marriage he would also acquire an incredible talent.

If Gracie didn't — or didn't want to — see George's interest in her, at least it was clear to her friends. As Mary Kelly noted, "It was obvious from the very first that he was head over heels in love with Gracie. He waited on her hand and foot. Half the time she didn't know at what theater they were playing. George did everything but carry her there. After he had arranged a booking for them, he would phone Gracie, tell her when to start for the theater, what subway to take, where to get off, where the stage entrance was and the number of her dressing room. [In most theaters, women dressed together, so even after she married George, Gracie dressed with the other women in the show.] Once a week they'd go dancing at a night club. As they grew to know each other better, they would have dinner together every night — but Gracie was very strict about paying her check, unless George had invited her out."[9]

Mary Kelly's boyfriend, Jack Benny, joined Gracie and George on double dates. The two Jewish men were both in show business and were both dating Irish Catholic women. That in itself was enough to provide enormous material for conversation. But Jack Benny turned into George Burns' lifelong best friend, and for a reason. They could talk for hours about comedy, about vaudeville (and later radio and television), about using assumed names (Jack Benny's real name was Benny Kubelsky), about submerging their Jewishness for the larger audience, and much else. And Jack Benny was the audience every performer loved. For George, he was a gift from Heaven. He laughed at all of George's jokes, and when Jack Benny really laughed he was on the ground, slapping his hand against the floor. Benny's singing voice was even worse than George's, but Benny loved to hear George sing. The two men played tricks on each other, told stories of women, tried out new lines. They understood each other as only struggling or successful performers can. In a way, they needed each other. Failure may bring bitterness, but success carries its own demons. Every successful performer needs a friend who can appreciate the success and not change. Success changes both the person experiencing it and the people he knows. Since both Jack and George were successful, they could form their own fraternity. There may not have been secret handshakes, but there might as well have been because they lived in a very closed, very small society, and they needed someone who could understand what it was like to live there. Actors were often seen as wild and morally loose characters, people whom refined citizens didn't want to have around. Some rooming houses had signs alerting would-be renters that actors were not welcome. People changed their names because their families disapproved of their show business life.

Jack Benny had been brought up in a middle-class family; he didn't experience the grinding poverty or the urban clutter of George's life. Additionally, Jack was more tortured about his relationship with a Gentile woman. For her part, Mary Kelly felt she should marry a Catholic man. Their relationship constantly wavered between devotion and termination. Indeed, ultimately Benny ended up marrying a Jewish woman (Sadie Marks, later known as Mary Livingston). As he had done in the case of poverty and rejection, George was able to suppress any guilt about dating Gracie. His Jewishness was private. He didn't feel a need to prove it by marriage or ritual or in any other way. His skin formed the borders of his private self. Only what went on internally mattered. Externally, he was George Burns, great performer, not great Jewish performer. Jack Benny couldn't create such a wall between himself and the world.

George's relationship with Gracie was muddled, but in a different way from Jack Benny's and Mary Kelly's. He loved her, and she admired him. She loved him in a certain way, but she was engaged to Benny Ryan. There was a crucial moment in 1924 when she was prepared to leave the act and marry Ryan.

Just then fate intervened. Burns and Allen were offered a tour on the Orpheum circuit that would include a stop in Gracie's home town of San Francisco. She very much wanted to perform there, to be seen as a success in her home town, but she felt pulled in another way as well. The tour would take months, and Benny Ryan didn't want to delay the wedding any longer. Unsure of what to do, she told George that the $350 a week they had been offered was not enough, but that if they got $400 she would go. George was heartbroken, but he had an ally. Mary Kelly was then dating Ray Myers, who booked acts for the Orpheum circuit. Mary offered an ultimatum to Myers: she'd stop dating him if Burns and Allen didn't get $400 a week. Evidently, Mary Kelly's charms were sufficient, because Burns and Allen got offered the additional money. Gracie now had no choice. Marriage to Benny Ryan was delayed.

Unfortunately, right after the May 19, 1924 performance at the Orpheum in Oakland, Gracie became ill with appendicitis and many of the shows did have to be cancelled — including the one at the Orpheum Theater in San Francisco — but because Gracie was now near her family, she was able to return to her mother's house after leaving the hospital. George brought flowers to the hospital and visited her each day. At some point during Gracie's illness, George was given the task of sending a telegram to Benny Ryan informing him of what had happened to Gracie. But Ryan never sent any flowers, never acknowledged the illness. Gracie became upset with him, believing he was angry that she had gone on the tour. A desperate George conveniently "forgot" to send the telegram — though he lied to her when she asked if he had sent it — and he undoubtedly pointed out Benny Ryan's indifference to poor Gracie's suffering, which stood in clear contrast to his devotedly staying by her and filling her room with beautiful flowers. He'd ask her several times each day if she had heard from Benny yet.

Now it was a contest for her affections. George knew how great she was on stage, how much he loved her — even needed her — offstage as well.

He searched for the final piece of the Burns and Allen puzzle — good material. In October 1925, he decided it was time to get a new act. A then-common source of humor was the notion of a woman dating a man and spending his money on food in a fine restaurant. That seemed like a perfect idea for Gracie. And George had another perfect idea. He had already given up being the comic because he recognized that Gracie had more talent. He swal-

George Burns and Gracie Allen starred in their first film, *Lambchops*, for Warner Bros. in 1929. The film was an eight-minute recreation of their first successful vaudeville act. The act was about eating, a popular comedy subject of the era.

lowed some more pride and accepted that comedy writers had more talent than he did. George was particularly impressed by a young man named Al Boasberg, who was hired to write the new act about eating, an act called "Lamb Chops."

Boasberg was a character. He saw the whole world as a joke. No words came out as straight lines. With a mind situated somewhere between character disorder and comedy genius, Al Boasberg was not just reflexively funny. He was like George in another way; he was a student of comedy. Boasberg watched acts, studied them, considered their characters and the jokes. It was Boasberg who told George to make Gracie smarter than he was, to make the world bend to her mind.

Boasberg had begun his career in Buffalo, New York, selling jewelry and then jokes in vaudeville houses to the comics who passed through the city. Boasberg wrote while sitting in a bathtub filled with hot water up to his neck. He talked into a Dictaphone that stood a few feet away. He had built a bookshelf into the shower stall in case he needed to refer to some books.

The key lines in "Lamb Chops" went like this:

GEORGE: Do you like to love?
GRACIE: No.
GEORGE: Do you like to kiss?
GRACIE: No.
GEORGE: What do you like?
GRACIE: Lamb chops.
GEORGE: A little girl like you? Could you eat two big lamb chops alone?
GRACIE: No, but with potatoes I could.[10]

The lines are not great yet, but they demonstrate a gradual sharpening of the Gracie character. She wasn't dumb, and she wasn't a "dizzy," a confused or bewildered character. She was illogically perfectly logical, as George used to say when attempting to explain the character. And she was sincere. "Gracie" the character didn't think she was telling a joke. She'd never wink knowingly at an audience. Her character wasn't trying to be funny, but simply making observations by using the tools of her unique perceptions. George had already learned that he couldn't touch Gracie on stage. That was crucial because the distance marked her off as being in a special world, and as not being loose like all the other Dumb Doras.

At some point "Grace Allen" became "Gracie Allen." The name change was vital, for the "Gracie" made her less formal, having more of a childlike innocence. That was an underappreciated part of Gracie's appeal. When audiences watched Gracie, they were pulled from their worlds of adult responsibilities back to their childhoods, when the whole world made sense on their terms. Gracie was funny, but she was also an escape into an audience member's own innocence, a cherished, vanished time of life that can't reappear except during those moments when one was listening to Gracie Allen. In heightened moments of social tension, this form of escape was especially valued.

The audience felt protective of Gracie. She was a hothouse flower, and they wanted to make sure her partner on stage didn't destroy her beauty or ruin her rareness. She was pretty and, therefore, attractive to men in the audience. Men could also see in her an adherence to the stereotype of women as illogical. But if that was a source of attraction, those men missed the incredible subtlety of her character's logic.

If men liked the Gracie character, so did women. It may seem odd that an illogical woman would not cause resentment. But Gracie was dignified. Most crucially, to the discerning members of the audience, Gracie wasn't conforming to a male stereotype of how women should think. Instead, she was slyly parodying such a stereotype and proving herself more logical — and far funnier — than the male straight man.

Gracie's character was perfect for the times. In the 1920s, women were caught between identities, between being prim and restrained or modern, American, and released from the constraints of Victorian morality. Internal struggles between the two identities were not always conscious and not always easy. Many women in vaudeville illustrated the flapper, that wild, sexually unrestrained woman of the twenties. Surely, the release from the psychological bonds of Victorian propriety were attractive to women, but many must have felt guilty at the prospect of violating the rules of their upbringing. They wanted to be free, but they wanted to be respected. They wanted men to love them, but they didn't want to lose their parents' approval. Gracie's character was attractive, confused, free not to act out sexually like other women in vaudeville but to act out linguistically, to control the world on that stage, to get the better of a man, to emerge triumphant. She challenged roles, but she didn't lose her self-respect. She was the perfect release for the era's women.

Even at this point, though, playing "Gracie Allen" must have been difficult for the real Gracie. The person and the character had the same name. They occupied the same body. It is understandable that audiences confused the two. Letting down her guard would have caused consternation, so Gracie had to stay in character during interviews and when meeting fans. That caused psychological tension that would ultimately take the form of migraine headaches.

Once Gracie's character was solidified, it was equally important that George as straight man had to react. He did this in various ways. His cigar was always there for timing. But even more crucial was his transformation from just a flirting line-feeder to someone who is anguished and long-suffering. This character would change significantly in the years to come — especially during their television years — but also in vaudeville, the movies, and radio, "George Burns" suffered, trying in an exasperated fashion to deal with "Gracie."

George became a master of comic timing. As a straight man, he had a difficult task. He had to wait for the audience to stop laughing, but not so long that there was an awkward silence between the end of the applause and his next line. He couldn't let the audience get bored or confused. The pause between lines is called a "beat." The "pace" is the speed of the delivery. An act was allotted a certain amount of time. They couldn't run under or over or the manager would be upset. If there was less laughter than expected they had to slow the pace, but quicken it for more than expected laughter. They had to find a rhythm, almost a musical rhythm, to their delivery. It was not so easy, but George and Gracie each had a keen ear. Their staccato rhythm had to remain steady through the delivery, the silences, and the laughs. Maintaining that rhythm required immense concentration. But they knew not just to focus on their own minds but also on how to listen to an audience to vary their delivery according to its needs. They were comfortable with each other.

George and Gracie practiced over and over. They pronounced and emphasized words in different ways, testing them out both onstage and offstage. They learned to control their voices, the sacred instruments of their act. They considered what to do between lines, after laughter had ended. Gracie started to giggle. The sound itself was funny and infectious and prompted audiences that had just finished laughing at a line to laugh again. As a straight man, George had to control Gracie's pace and the audience's reaction to it. His role was vital for the audience to grasp the premise of the joke. He needed to repeat her lines to make sure they got it, to set up the laugh line.

George had, in many senses, an easier time on stage. He had the cigar as a prop to fill in the silences, an easier device than Gracie having to giggle in a funny way. He could react. He could be amused. He could, that is, break character in a way Gracie could not. His tension could be released; hers couldn't. Her mask had to be worn tightly in place. But Gracie's job was more gratifying than George's. She was beloved. He was accepted. She got the laughs. He couldn't be a comedian because he had to feed the straight lines

Gracie and George found characters that fit their era perfectly. Gracie used "illogical logic," in which the world made sense to her even if her explanations exasperated George.

and could not break the carefully structured patter. Additionally, he had to react to Gracie's seeming craziness as a stand-in for the audience. For someone who had wanted to be a comic, that must have been frustrating. Luckily for him, George Burns was the master suppressor, a man who had built his life on his abilities not to think about troubles but to bury them. Slowly, he came to appreciate his role, to accept it, and to understand that fate would grant him fame in a way he had not planned.

In the fall of 1925, he also had a confrontation with his Jewish identity. George Jessel, George's friend and fellow vaudevillian, starred in the new play *The Jazz Singer,* which opened at the Fulton Theatre in New York on September 14, 1925. George went to see the play, the plot of which involves a cantor's son who breaks with family tradition to become an entertainer. George immediately saw the play as representing his own life, and he began to cry as he saw played out what might have been his own story had his father not died so early. Seeing the confrontation between father and son on the stage let George imagine the sorts of fights he would have had, and the emotion overwhelmed him. But George Burns, the master of suppression, pushed back any emotions and simply continued his life.

Burns and Allen prepared to start their new act at the beginning of 1926. But before they could, their relationship problems boiled over during Christmas week of 1925. They had been professional partners for three years with excruciatingly slow but clear progress. George was convinced that the new act would be the turning point. They were poised for success. George was sure that he'd won his love and would soon win show business glory.

And then, during that Christmas week, as George and Gracie sat in a cab on the way to shop for Christmas, he turned to her and said, "What if we go out and do a little celebrating tonight?"

"I'd love to, but I'm afraid I can't," Gracie responded. "I have a date." George immediately realized Benny Ryan was in New York and ready once again to marry Gracie.

George screamed, "Driver, pull over to the curb. I guess this is where I get out." Gracie remained silent, not even saying goodbye to George.[11]

A Christmas party was scheduled for the next evening in the apartment Gracie shared with Mary Kelly and Rena Arnold. George had agreed to dress as Santa Claus and give presents to everyone. He had already bought the costume along with a blue beard for laughs. Even Jack Benny couldn't get jokes out of George that night. Jack tried to tell some one-liners, but they didn't improve George's mood. George's eyes were focused on Gracie. He had bought her a bracelet with a single diamond on it, intending to add a diamond for each year they were together.

Gracie opened the present and walked over to thank George. Then George took another present out of the bag. It was Gracie's present to him. He read the card aloud to everyone there: "To Nat — all my love."[12]

George snarled at her. He told her that she didn't know what love really meant. Gracie began to cry and ran into the bathroom. Her roommates complained about her lack of Christmas spirit, but George yelled at them, defending Gracie. He walked over, knocked on the bathroom door, and said, "Listen, Gracie, we've got five weeks on the Gus Sun [circuit], time to break in our new act. After the second week, we have a three day layoff. In that three-days we either get married or it's good-bye."[13]

He took off his beard, hung it on the bathroom door, and stormed out of the room. Gracie came out after he left and sat down to talk with Mary Kelly, who always took George's side. Gracie was supposed to call Benny Ryan at midnight to wish him a merry Christmas, but she didn't make the call. He called her instead, but to complain that she hadn't called. He confronted her in the call:

> "Don't you love me anymore?"
> "No, I don't."
> "Then please hang up the phone."[14]

George lay in bed that night. His entire world was cracking in front of him. He had regularly proposed to Gracie, sometimes as often as once a week. She thought he was kidding. But there was no kidding in what he had to say that night. The jokes had stopped.

George had, in truth, been unfair to Gracie. He didn't consider how deeply she had been hurt by her father's abandoning the family, how profoundly she needed a sense of security, one hard to find for a vaudeville performer. She was struggling. Benny Ryan was like her father, a handsome dancer and an Irish charmer. But perhaps, she feared, he was too much like her father. By contrast, George was Jewish, not so successful, but someone who clearly loved her, someone who made her feel. The Jewish element was a genuine dilemma. Gracie attended Mass every Sunday when she could do so.

There was a knock on George's door in the rooming house at three in the morning. The man at the door announced to George that there was a phone call for him, and added that he shouldn't be getting phone calls at that hour. George raced downstairs and picked up the phone. Gracie was on the line:

> "You can buy the wedding ring if you want to," she said.
> George answered, "You'll never be sorry."[15]

The next day she told him she had chosen him because he had made her cry and that meant she really loved him. On Christmas, they made love for the first time.

George was elated, but before he could marry Gracie he needed his mother's blessing. In fact, because George and Gracie had been together for so long, both mothers had a chance to consider the relationship. They assumed the Burns and Allen relationship had not been entirely platonic for the three years the two had been partners. Such was the reputation show folks had. And Dora Birnbaum knew George had married a nice Jewish girl and it hadn't worked out. Now he was almost 30. All Dora wanted was a nice girl. Similarly, Gracie's mother had an experience with a wandering Irish husband. She just wanted someone to be nice to her daughter.

Naturally, though, George could make fun of himself about the wedding. Years later on a radio broadcast, Gracie told the audience, "It seems like only yesterday that my mother tripped him as we walked down the aisle."

George said, "I guess your family didn't approve."

"Oh, sure they did," Gracie responded. "In fact they applauded her when she did it."

Later in the same radio program, Gracie seemed to turn serious about the marriage. "I'm a very lucky woman. I was courted by the youngest, handsomest, most charming, most sought-after star in show business."

"Thank you," said George, clearly flattered.

"But I still married George because I loved him."[16]

In fact, George, using his real name of Nathan Birnbaum, married Grace C. Allen on January 7, 1926. Perhaps George wanted to get married before his 30th birthday. Perhaps he feared that if he delayed Gracie would change her mind again. It is odd that they didn't wait to get married either in New York or San Francisco and that they didn't get married in a church. Justice of the Peace J. E. Chizek performed the ceremony in Cleveland, Ohio. But Cleveland had its advantages. There was no one to double-check when George said he had not been previously married. There were no questions when Gracie said she was 26.

The marriage, perhaps, was only a ceremony, but it was the turning point in their lives in more ways than one. Their relationship was clarified. Their characters were defined. Their experience was invaluable. Their material was good and on its way to being great.

They were ready for such greatness, and they found it.

On January 18, eleven days after their wedding, they began a week-long engagement, performing "Lamb Chops" at the Keith Theater in Syracuse, New York. The two were so well received that the theater manager immediately called Keith's booking office and George and Gracie were offered four days at the Jefferson Theatre in New York City. The place had a brutal reputation as the toughest theater to play because the audience was always loaded with talent scouts. Failure at the Jefferson sealed a very unhappy vaudeville fate.

Success, on the other hand, was the gateway to greater opportunities. Burns and Allen played there starting on February 24, and at some time during that run the Keith organization sent a talent scout. The scout did what he was paid to do: he recognized upcoming talent and signed Burns and Allen to a five-year contract that ranged from $450 to $600 a week. It was big money, and they no longer would have to do three or four shows a day. Now they would be a two-a-day act, appearing in a matinee and an evening performance only. This was the Big Time.

After that, their rise was meteoric. It was almost as though getting married was literally the turning point of their lives. Of all

Although they always appeared happy to the public, it wasn't easy for George to convince Gracie to marry him. She was originally expecting to marry someone else. It was only after an ultimatum from George that she made her decision.

the theaters in vaudeville, the one most prized, the one every vaudeville performer dreamed of playing, was the Palace Theatre, known to vaudevillians simply as the Palace, on Broadway and 47th Street in New York. It was a narrow, tall building with gold and crimson decorations. The Palace's sidewalk was nicknamed "The Beach" because it was a favorite gathering spot "where vaudevillians, would-be vaudevillians, and dazzled members of the public met and mingled, discussing jokes and acts, wages and sins, and the hazards and joys of the profession."[17]

Burns and Allen were signed to play The Palace's bill for a week beginning

August 23, 1926. The opening performance for the week was always held on a Monday at 8:15 P.M. The critics all came to that performance.

George bought a new suit and new spats with pearl buttons. His walking stick now had a silver tip.

On the morning of the 23rd they had come to rehearsal and checked the chalkboard to see their spot on the bill. They would play in the third spot. They returned that evening to dress. The dressing room on the first floor were reserved for the stars, so George and Gracie climbed into the rickety elevator and rode up, got out, and found a small dressing room. Gracie put on her lipstick three times before she was satisfied. Her long sleeves covered her scarred arm. They didn't speak to each other, avoiding even their nicknames. Gracie called him by his real nickname "Natty," and he called her "Googie." That nickname originated one night when Gracie couldn't sleep. She asked her husband to say something funny. Even George Burns couldn't be very funny at two in the morning, so he said the first words to come to his mind: "Googie, googie, googie." Gracie laughed, and her nickname was born.

Oddly enough, for those performers making their debuts at The Palace, the venue was relatively easy. The headliners had to succeed without help, but the audience was filled with other actors who always laughed and applauded at newcomers. Burns and Allen had brought along many friends that evening to cheer them on to vaudeville victory. Mary Kelly wanted to send flowers up to Gracie and asked George for advice about when to time the delivery. He was confident; he told her to send them up after the second encore.

The heart of the Burns and Allen appeal that would last for the following three decades until Gracie's retirement can be seen in that Palace performance.

George and Gracie walked onstage holding hands. Gracie stopped, gazed toward the wings, and waved a hand. She then let go of George's hand and walked toward the opposite side of the stage still waving her hand. As she got close, she stopped. A man came onstage, put his arms around Gracie, and she kissed him. They waved goodbye to each other as he walked offstage. Gracie then walked back to George at center stage.

GRACIE: Who was that?
GEORGE: You don't know?
GRACIE: No, my mother told me never to talk to strangers.
GEORGE: That makes sense.
GRACIE: This always happens to me. On my way in a man stopped me at the stage door and said, "Hi ya, cutie. How about a bite tonight after the show?"
GEORGE: And you said?

GRACIE: I said, "I'll be busy after the show but I'm not doing anything now," so I bit him.

GEORGE: Gracie, let me ask you something. Did the nurse ever happen to drop you on your head when you were a baby?

GRACIE: Oh, no we couldn't afford a nurse. My mother had to do it.

GEORGE: You had a smart mother.

GRACIE: Smartness runs in my family. When I went to school I was so smart my teacher was in my class for five years.

GEORGE: Gracie, what school did you go to?

GRACIE: I'm not allowed to tell.

GEORGE: Why not?

GRACIE: The school pays me $25 a month not to tell.

GEORGE: Is there anybody in the family as smart as you?

GRACIE: My cousin Hazel is even smarter. If it wasn't for her, that canary would never have hatched that ostrich egg.

GEORGE: A canary hatched an ostrich egg?

GRACIE: Yeah, but the canary was too small to cover that big egg.

GEORGE: So?

GRACIE: So Hazel sat on the egg and held the canary in her lap.

GEORGE: Hazel must be the smartest in your family.

GRACIE: Oh, no. My brother Willy was no dummy either. [In real life, of course, Willy was George's brother.]

GEORGE: What's Willy doing now?

GRACIE: He just lost his job.

GEORGE: Lost his job?

GRACIE: Yeah, he's a window washer.

GEORGE: And?

GRACIE: And he was outside on the twentieth story washing a window. When he got through he stepped back to admire his work.

GEORGE: And he lost his job....

GRACIE: When Willy was a little baby my father took him riding in his carriage, and two hours later my father came back with a different baby and a different carriage.

GEORGE: Well, what did your mother say?

GRACIE: My mother didn't say anything because it was a better carriage.

GEORGE: A better carriage?

GRACIE: Yeah, and the little baby my father brought home was a little French baby so my mother took up French.

GEORGE: Why?

GRACIE: So she would be able to understand the baby —

GEORGE: When the baby started to talk?

GRACIE: Yeah.

GEORGE: Gracie, this family of yours, do you all live together?

GRACIE: Oh, sure. My father, my brother, my uncle, my cousin, and my nephew all sleep in one bed and —

GEORGE: In one bed? I'm surprised your grandfather doesn't sleep with them.

GRACIE: Oh, he did. But he died, so they made him get up.[18]

After the banter was finished, Gracie stood in the spotlight and she sang a song, then did an Irish jig. When the audience finished applauding, the two did ten more minutes of comedy. Then they sang and danced together. Four times during the dance, George stopped the music and they would tell a joke before continuing. Two of those interludes went like this:

GEORGE: Gracie, how's your Uncle Harvey?
GRACIE: Oh last night he fell down the stairs with a bottle of scotch and never spilled a drop.
GEORGE: Really?
GRACIE: Yeah, he kept his mouth closed.

And, drawing on a previously used line:

GRACIE: My sister Bessie had a brand-new baby.
GEORGE: Boy or girl?
GRACIE: I don't know, and I can't wait to get home to find out if I'm an aunt or an uncle.[19]

Burns and Allen were a triumph at The Palace. Here, for example, is the review from *Variety* (by Abel Green, then a journalist and later the paper's editor for 40 years):

George N. Burns and Gracie Allen have a new skit in "Lamb Chops," by Al Boasberg; funny stuff, almost actor-proof, but further enhanced by the team's individual contributions.
Miss Allen is an adorable "dizzy" with an ingratiating prattle. Burns foils and wise-cracks in turn and the laugh returns are that and many. They dance off before the routine encore, which brings him back for a bit wherein he reclines on a prop mat on the stage, "feeding" his partner.
A tip-top comedy interlude for the best vaudeville.[20]

After The Palace, it was not only the best of the vaudeville theaters that wanted them, but all the others as well. They began to take seriously the vaudeville practice of going to a smaller theater to test out lines before trying them in major houses. Scranton, Pennsylvania was a favorite place to test out the new jokes, to make sure audiences thought the lines were as funny as George did.

The success affected them in different ways. George was ecstatic; all his dreams were realized. His life had been justified. All the time he spent dragging his trunk to catch a train or illegally cooking over a hot plate in a cheap hotel room, all the indifference he had withstood from managers and audiences, all the doubts and worries he had heard for so long from some members of his family, all that vanished in 18 minutes. George Burns was a success.

George's mother, Dora Birnbaum, had been the one who believed in him. It pained George that she had been too ill to see him play The Palace. So when he and Gracie came back for a return engagement on March 28, 1927, George hired a limousine. Sammy and Willie, two of his brothers, went to 1710 Carroll Street in Brooklyn to get her at the tenement where she lived. The two men lifted Dora from the limousine and carried her to her seat in the front row. There she was, at the most important venue in vaudeville, ready to watch her newly successful son, the one she thought was going to have a tough life because he couldn't get show business out of his mind. It was almost as though seeing Nathan Birnbaum's great success, letting the roars of laughter and the thunderous applause wave over her, gave her permission to die in peace. Dora Birnbaum passed away five months later, on August 25, 1927, from a coronary thrombosis. She was buried alongside her husband.

While George and his family struggled with his career, Gracie Allen never had comparable doubts. She loved to perform, but show business wasn't her life. When she was on stage she was "Gracie" and she was perfect. Even there, though, she used the footlights to pretend the audience wasn't there. Such was her shyness. And as soon as she left the theater, her mind was out of the business and on to her private life.

Given their talents and success, George Burns and Gracie Allen could have continued for decades as successes in vaudeville. But, ironically, they reached their success just as vaudeville was dying. Other performers might have been angered. Many vaudeville performers, after all, saw their careers end in the decade after George and Gracie's first Palace performance.

It is easy to blame motion pictures for vaudeville's decline, but the cause was really a combination of sound film, made popular in 1927, and radio. Silent films had lived comfortably alongside vaudeville for decades, precisely because vaudeville could offer the voices that film couldn't. But sound film and radio proved to be too much. Burns and Allen continued while they could in vaudeville, but other forms of media began to beckon — especially radio, which would bring them the sort of dazzling economic success and dizzying fame of which they had not dared to dream.

CHAPTER FOUR

The Theater of the Mind and the Silver Screen

George Burns and Gracie Allen had found the formula for success. And if George Burns the man was jealous of his wife, angry with fate for giving her the laughs instead of him, or infuriated with managers and audiences for not recognizing his talent, George Burns the comedian was immensely pleased with the money and the fame. He continued to supply lines to Gracie about his inadequacies. She'd tell audiences, "I don't want a husband with money and good looks and personality. I'd rather have George. And I'm not the only one who feels that way about him. Plenty of women have told me how relieved they are that he's with me.

"I know there were a couple of people who thought he wouldn't be a good husband: Mama, Papa, Grandma ... Grandpa ... sister Bessie ... Uncle Dan ... Aunt Clara ... the ice man ... Schwab the druggist ... the U.S. Senate ... California."[1]

George and Gracie were a talking act. Had they been spectacular acrobats or dancers, or if George had continued with his seal act, they would have been finished by radio. Radio was built for talking acts. The comedians went directly from vaudeville to radio because they could take their lines about marriage, or flirting, or their families and speak them into the radio microphones. Many other vaudevillians were stuck.

And if radio was made for verbal comedians, so were talking movies. Burns and Allen didn't have a physically wild act. They weren't slapstick comedians, and they would not have even been asked to make a silent film. Both were good dancers, but neither had the precise movements of a Chaplin or the physical exaggeration of a Fatty Arbuckle.

Burns and Allen, the quiet talking act, had timed their rise perfectly.

As vaudeville was winding down in 1929, Burns and Allen received an offer to perform at the Palladium Theatre in London as part of a 26-week tour of England. The first show was scheduled for February 25. George and Gracie set sail to conquer foreign shores. It wouldn't be so easy. When they arrived, they discovered that their 18-minute act had been allotted only 11

In 1929, Burns and Allen received an offer to perform at the Palladium Theatre in London. They sailed to England for a 26-week engagement. As vaudevillians, they had learned to love to travel.

minutes. For a precisely structured act that had been rehearsed over and over, such demands were incredibly difficult. If that weren't enough, not every line in "Lamb Chops" got the laughs that American audiences gave. It took George a couple of performances to realize that British audiences didn't know what lamb chops were; they were called lamb cutlets in England. But George Burns, literally and figuratively, was quick on his feet. He made the adjustments. British audiences loved them, though British critics seemed more taken with Gracie's lavish dresses than any merits to their act.

Because British audiences had been so appreciative, Burns and Allen were asked to appear on radio. Although they had never been on American radio, the team agreed to appear on *Vaudeville*, a BBC radio show. And so, on June 10, 1929, Burns and Allen first appeared on radio, doing a version of "Lamb Chops." The show was so successful that they were asked back. And then each week for fifteen weeks they returned to the studio to perform for different British regions.

Vaudeville eventually was just vaudeville, but the radio broadcasts were a revelation for George. He was watching a new entertainment venue being born right in front of him.

But before he could explore radio, there was another entertainment world to start conquering. They arrived back in the United States and that very night they were at a party for Jack Benny. Benny's agent, Arthur Lyons, had arranged the party, during which Lyons asked Benny if he wanted to make a nine-minute film and earn $1700. Warner Bros. had set up Vitaphone Studios in Brooklyn to shoot short films. They had contracted for a movie with another comedian named Fred Allen (who would later become an extremely popular radio personality), but Allen was ill and couldn't make the film. Benny said he couldn't do it either, but George Burns, despite being a grade school dropout, figured out very quickly that there was money to be made in this new industry. Burns offered to make the film. Gracie was reluctant; she suggested that George do it alone, but he knew there was no act without Gracie. As so, as part of a lifelong behavior pattern, a reluctant Gracie went along with her ambitious husband's plans.

Lambchops, released in October 1929, opens with George and Gracie entering a fancy room. They look around under tables and chairs, searching, it turns out, for the audience. George suddenly spots the audience and tells Gracie. They begin their act with lines like:

GEORGE: What man in the army has the biggest hat?
GRACIE: The one with the biggest head.

GEORGE: What sings with four legs?
GRACIE: Two canaries.

Determined to get into the act, George asks a riddle and then answers it. "What gives more milk than a cow? Two cows!" They end by dancing and by singing "Do You Believe Me?"

The jokes seem extraordinarily dated now. They had not mastered the camera. George's fedora is slanted in a way that sometimes hides his face. But it is interesting, especially in light of their later television program, that even in their first screen appearance, George ignores the conventions of pretending there is no audience watching them, just as he would speak directly to the audience on his show. For her part, Gracie was shocked at her appearance; she didn't like the way she looked at all.

Burns and Allen may have pocketed Warner Bros. money, but the studio brass wasn't so happy with the result. No contract was forthcoming. As he had with his radio experience, George saw a replacement for vaudeville, indeed a replacement with the promise of great reward for minimal effort. Ignoring the Warners' dismissal of their talents, George sought more films. He began writing a screenplay, eventually called "Fit to Be Tied," and sold it to Paramount, which had a studio in Astoria, Queens. Paramount offered the team a three-year contract to make four films a year. The films they made were essentially skits drawing on their vaudeville material. That is, they hadn't understood the true nature of film, pictures that moved. Their films were really recorded bits of stage material. To ever-more sophisticated audiences, the results seemed static. They found Gracie endearing and laughed at her, but Burns and Allen did not fully grasp the new art form; only a way to adapt their old art form.

Burns and Allen continued in vaudeville, having to live in two worlds: the one that they had contracts for but which was dying, and one in which they had to find a home after vaudeville's inevitable death. And George didn't just count on films. He approached advertisers about a radio show, but they were reluctant. Some thought all they had was one act and after their 18 minutes were up, they would have no more material for radio. They did get an audition in 1930, but the advertiser who heard it thought Gracie's high-pitched voice unsuitable for the medium and one, they feared, audiences would not find attractive. Gracie might have switched to her real voice, an octave lower than her character's, but then the full force of the character would have been lost.

And so they continued on stage and began making films for Paramount. *Fit to Be Tied* was released on August 2, 1930. The ten-minute film has George walking in to a store to buy a tie, but he can't get any attention. He goes to Gracie, who's making up a crossword puzzle. The film is laced with bad puns, such as confusing a lizard with a snow storm, or after being asked to use poppies in a sentence, Gracie says, "A cat has kittens and a dog has poppies." As in their vaudeville act, she says goodbye to the audience at the end. It should be noted that it is commonly thought that Gracie simply repeats what George says when he announced "Say Goodnight, Gracie." In fact, starting with this movie in what would become perhaps their most famous tag line, Gracie offers a dainty and simple "Good night."

The film is symptomatic of what went wrong in their film career. The setting is unnatural for them, the lines seem plucked rather than hierarchically arranged to produce an overall result as in their vaudeville act, and the lines now seem hopelessly dated, though in keeping with the restrictions imposed on them at the time both in radio and film.

Between January and August 1931 they made four more films: *Pulling a Bone* (released January 10); *The Antique Shop* (released, March 7); *Once Over Light* (released, May 23) and *100% Service* (released August 1). All these movies have similar premises, with none of them standing out. Burns and Allen recycle familiar vaudeville patter. In *100% Service*, for example, George says, "I'm a pauper" and Gracie responds, "Oh, congratulations. A boy or a girl?" At one point Gracie says, "When I was born I was so surprised I couldn't talk for a year and a half."

On October 31, 1931, Burns and Allen were back at The Palace, but this performance turned out to be a turning point, both for them and for vaudeville. Eddie Cantor and George Jessel were also on the bill. The Palace survived for two weeks after the end of the run. According to many vaudeville historians, this show was the final triumph, the capstone on a dying entertainment form.

Although the precise routine Burns and Allen used is not clear, it is likely similar to one they had recorded in 1930 that included lines like:

> GRACIE: Well, I guess I'll be going home now.
> GEORGE: Going home? I'll take you home in my car.
> GRACIE: Oh, no thank you. I'm too tired. I'd rather walk.
> GEORGE: Yes, I'll walk you home. I'll walk home with you if you give me a kiss. I'll take you home.
> GRACIE: Well, if you take me home I'll give you a kiss.
> GEORGE: But just a minute, before I take you home I would like to find out whether or not your mother is home.
> GRACIE: She is, but my father wouldn't let you kiss my mother....
> GEORGE: Let's do something.

GRACIE: Let's do crossword puzzles.

GEORGE: That would be fun.

GRACIE: I'm very good at them now. You know, I make them up.

GEORGE: Well, make one up.

GRACIE: All right. What is it that starts with "c" and, uh, well, I don't know how many letters. What is it?

GEORGE: Hmm. That's very good. You made that up.

GRACIE: That came right out of my own head ... I have brains you know.

GEORGE: Have you?

GRACIE: Oh, I have brains I haven't even used yet.

GEORGE: I see ... It starts with a "c" and you don't know how many letters ... Does it jump?

GRACIE: No.

GEORGE: Does it swim?

GRACIE: No....

GEORGE: I give it up.

GRACIE: Well, look. Men shave with it.

GEORGE: Well the only thing I can think of that men shave with is soap.

GRACIE: Soap! That's it.[2]

Gracie and George had different appearances during their careers, searching for exactly the right look for their characters. Gracie raised her voice and changed her hair, while George, who had lost his hair early on, used hairpieces.

The show was important for another reason. Eddie Cantor asked Burns and Allen to join him in his stage show. During that run of Cantor shows, Eddie approached George. He wanted Gracie to appear on his radio show — but he didn't want George. It was, no doubt, one more crushing blow. George Burns was in an odd situation. He was a major entertainment star, and yet, legitimately, he could feel as though he wasn't appreciated. Disheartened but realistic about the need for vaudeville performers to get on radio, George agreed provided Cantor would let him write Gracie's lines. George didn't want any damage done to her carefully constructed character. Gracie made her appearance on Cantor's show, *The Chase and Sanborn Hour*, on November 15, 1931. Gracie herself was uncertain about the appearance. She had been on radio for the BBC but the microphone had bothered her, and there was no audience in the studio to laugh at the jokes. Fortunately, Cantor performed in front of a live audience, and that made her more at ease. In her skit, Gracie was a reporter who had come to interview Cantor about his earlier announcement he was running for president:

GRACIE: Mr. Cantor, what do you intend to do when you are elected sheriff?
CANTOR: What sheriff? President of the United States!
GRACIE: You can't be president of the United States. My father told me this morning that *he* is going to be president of the United States.
CANTOR: Your father?
GRACIE: Yes. My father said, "Gracie, if you can get on *The Chase and Sanborn Hour*, then I'll be president of the United States."
CANTOR: Well, that's fine.
GRACIE: And he will make a good president. He will be as good as Calvin Coolidge, the Rough Rider.
CANTOR: Calvin Coolidge, the Rough Rider. You remember George Washington, the fellow who freed the slaves?
GRACIE: Anybody knows that, and my father said that if Washington was elected, he would have made a great president.
CANTOR: How do you like Abraham Lincoln?
GRACIE: I read *The Life of Lincoln* four times.
CANTOR: And had trouble each time. Do you remember the Gettysburg Address?
GRACIE: I think they live in Buffalo now.
CANTOR: In Buffalo?
GRACIE: Maybe they moved.[3]

Cantor's ear for audience taste proved to be accurate. The ratings for Gracie's appearance were excellent. George now knew it was time to conquer radio, and so for a time their career had to weave together three threads: vaudeville, films, and radio.

The couple began a frantic pace. On January 4, 1932 they opened for four days at the Paramount in New York before heading to Cleveland on January 11. Meanwhile, their new film, *Oh, My Operation,* was released on January 16. In this one-reeler, Burns is mistaken for an accident victim and ends up in a hospital with Gracie as a nurse. Again, Gracie's lines are far weaker than her perfect delivery of them.

On January 28, Burns and Allen appeared on Rudy Vallee's radio show *The Fleischmann's Yeast Hour,* doing some of their "Dizzy" routine and singing "I Love Her, I Do." Once again ratings were good. Sponsors took note.

On February 15, Burns and Allen opened for seven

George was taller than the diminutive Gracie, but as the act continued that difference became symbolic of George's control over his partner. George was a brilliant comedic talent who loved show business and couldn't understand why Gracie did not.

days in Brooklyn. On the same date they appeared on Guy Lombardo's radio show. The bandleader's program was the highest-rated then on radio. They were on in two segments, each lasting a minute, but even that brief appearance was effective enough to warrent them being invited back the following week — just when they also opened at the Capitol Theatre in New York.

But their appearance was not without its difficulties. Their dialogue had taken place over the band's music, and several college students had written to J. Walter Thompson, the sponsor's advertising agency, to complain that those two people had spoken over the music — the very reason they listened to the show. Burns and Allen were reassured by the agency, but even more by the follow-up letters from the students several weeks later. The students wrote that they had gotten used to the speaking, that they had even grown to like it. This ability to turn even critics into fans was powerful support for Burns and Allen. They were made a regular part of the program and stayed on it until Guy Lombardo left.

Burns and Allen also served another purpose beyond just entertainment. Each radio show had a single sponsor, and the sponsors tried to integrate their product into each show. That was close to impossible with a band playing, but not at all difficult for a talking act. And so Burns and Allen did two four-minute spots for the sponsor, General Cigar.

Radio listeners who had never seen Burns and Allen got a taste of Gracie's logic and loved the high-pitched voice that an early executive had judged unsuitable for the medium:

> GEORGE: Gracie, how many days are there in a year?
> GRACIE: Seven.
> GEORGE: Seven?
> GRACIE: Seven. Monday, Tuesday, Wednesday, Thursday, Friday, Saturday, Sunday. If you know any more, George, just name them.[4]

Vaudeville was dying. Their film career would only last until the end of the decade. But radio was the haven for Burns and Allen, the venue that would propel them to national fame. With radio, Burns and Allen had perfect timing. In the 1920s people who wished to purchase a radio had to spend $120, an enormous sum at the time, and then still had to assemble the set. The batteries that powered radios in rural areas were unreliable and expensive.

Radio comedy came of age on March 19, 1928, when *Amos 'n' Andy* began broadcasting. Indeed, the program proved that radio itself was economically viable. President Coolidge told people that when the show was on, he did not allow anyone to interrupt him. Theater managers stopped shows and movies at 7 P.M., dragged radios out on stage, and played the entire 15-minute show. They feared that if they didn't audiences would stay home. Indeed it was witnessing one of those interruptions that helped convince George Burns that vaudeville was dying.

Radio had a profound effect on American life. People, of course, went out for entertainment, to a theater for a show or a movie or a museum, for instance. But there was no entertainment at home other than that which the family could provide for themselves. Families became proficient at reading books to one another, or staging plays, or standing around a piano while one family member played and everyone joined in singing. But with radio, as with the phonograph, entertainment came from the outside world into the home. With so many people hearing the same programs, mass audiences

Burns and Allen began their radio career early in 1932. At first, they had been turned down for a program because a sponsor decided that audiences wouldn't like Gracie's voice. As always, George and Gracie proved their critics wrong.

developed the same taste. Products advertised were bought whether they were needed or not, or whether they could be afforded or not. And radio was cheap entertainment. There was music and laughter — all right there in the home. Radio was a transformative invention.

But radio did more than entertain. It made Americans into good listeners. The audience rediscovered the beauty of sound. The shows affected how they thought about life, how they spoke with one another.

In the beginning, radio shows were controlled by the sponsors (that is, those whose products were advertised on the show) not the networks. In practical terms, that meant the advertising agencies who represented the products ran the programs.

Naturally, advertisers wished to reach as wide an audience as possible. Most of the radio audience had never attended college or even high school. Their vocabularies were simple. And writers had to be careful not only to write simply but not to offend anyone. No controversial material was allowed. That meant there could be no discussion about God, no mention of illness, no ethnic jokes, no obscenity, no discussion of body parts, and certainly no explicitly sexual material. That is, sponsors wanted bland, inoffensive, and wholesome material that was also entertaining. For musicians, such restrictions were virtually irrelevant. But for comedians, the restrictions were a straitjacket. The restrictions about allowable materials made finding jokes very difficult.

Punning was the standard way out of the dilemma. Making jokes about language itself allowed comedians to avoid the restrictions and try to be funny. Given the comedic environment of radio, Gracie Allen's character was about as perfect as possible. In a less restrictive radio world, Gracie might have been less attractive than a more sexually charged character or one who cracked ethnic jokes. But Gracie's competitors had to make puns, and she had a character ready-made to succeed in such a world.

And while the puns were frequently obvious and strained, punning itself was also subversive. Puns undermined language's authority by ignoring its rules. Because radio comedy came of age during the Great Depression, the puns became a way for audiences to survive psychologically. They didn't want to lash out at the government or legal authorities, but they were able to do so as they laughed at comedians who lashed out at the authority of language.

George had a perfect voice for radio. The sponsors didn't want accents. They wanted pleasant, American voices delivering lines at a pace listeners could comprehend. Burns and Allen had been doing that onstage for years, perfecting their vocal rhythms to meet an audience's needs. George's voice didn't have an urban ethnic rhythm like George Jessel's, and he didn't speak too quickly, like Milton Berle. Voices and pacing were crucial. Both Burns and Allen had pleasant, highly recognizable voices, and their pacing was not too slow to be boring or too quick to be incomprehensible. Burns and Allen not only were fit for the medium, but fit for the medium in that historical moment.

In the years between 1929 and 1932, the years just before Burns and Allen came on radio, American families lost 40 percent of their incomes. Americans needed explanations, relief, and solace. They were desperate. Given that, it is no surprise that radio's popularity only emerged after the 1929 stock market crash.

Americans felt they were living in a desperate present; they peered into an unknown and therefore threatening future. All they thought they understood was wrong; the government they trusted had betrayed them. They needed people to make them laugh, to find some way to tolerate lives in which they couldn't feed their families, buy presents for their children, or in many cases, keep their homes. What they could do is huddle around a radio at home and listen to the soothing music or the wholesome comedy that, for the moment at least, relieved their pain.

Despite all that, radio was a very competitive business. It was crucial for advertisers to determine just how many people were listening to the shows. Imprecise methods were originally used. For example, a show might offer a free item and determine the audience size from the number of requests they received for the item. After that, the Cooperative Analysis of Broadcasting (C.A.B.), which was popularly known as the Crossley ratings, began in 1929. The Crossley ratings were determined by calling random members of the public to ask them what shows they had listened to the previous evening, or even earlier. Unhappy about relying on people's memories, the Hooper ratings were developed to call people while the shows were still on the air. The Hooper people called listeners in 32 cities, but oddly enough, not in any rural communities. (Many years later, in 1949, the A.C. Nielsen Company bought out Hooper and the modern era of audience measurement began. Nielsen ratings were determined by installing electronic audiometers on radio sets chosen by statistical means.)

Burns and Allen survived and thrived because they spoke to those audiences and would continue to do so. Audiences loved Gracie; they could laugh at the mangled language and the hidden logic behind it. But Gracie wasn't just a comedian. What separated her from all her competitors was that she didn't just deliver a funny line. She created an alternate world. That was key. Radio has frequently been referred to as the "theater of the mind" because listeners were their own producers, visualizing the shows in their imaginations as they listened to the voices coming from the box. During the Great Depression everyone needed a good laugh, but it was even better if a performer could transport the listener out of their everyday world into another one, a fantastic one. Gracie's fantasy world was safe, protected, warm, funny, and inviting. It was a world that beckoned them, that released them. It was an Oz with no wicked witches, but rather a wonderful, high-pitched voice guiding them in their make-believe journey. Gracie's genius was not in creating a fantasy world that had no logic; it had, as George often explained, an illogical logic perhaps, but a genuine logic. Gracie's world modified the listeners' world; it was recognizable. A listener needed imagination but not so much imagination as to be a strain.

Escape into any fantasy world had its virtues for listeners during the Great Depression, but such escape was not without its dangers. Listeners could get addicted to escape, constantly searching for and living in such a way that imperils their real lives. To avoid this, they needed an escape hatch from the fantasy world. In some fantasy worlds, such as motion pictures, this escape was abrupt: the end of the film. But for listeners of Burns and Allen, the escape hatch was there every few seconds. George Burns, the straight man, would not let listeners live in the illogical world for too long. He was the tether to reality. George was the adult, Gracie the carefree child without obligations. George was the reminder that listeners could escape, but that they ultimately had to go back. Interpreted this way, the dialogue Burns and Allen read on radio was a battle between two worlds, a battle mimicking the struggles of audience members between their fierce desire to escape, and their realization that they were responsible for themselves and their families. It is no wonder that Burns and Allen were so successful; they met the needs of their audiences perfectly.

And audiences thought they knew the couple. Gracie's self-confessed great passion was not show business, but shopping. As George told the story, "One day the cook asked her to buy a rolling pin when she was out shopping. She came home looking a little shattered. 'I had a strange experience in Bloomingdale's,' she said. 'I picked up a rolling pin off the counter and the salesgirl said, "I suppose that's to hit George with?" Then she broke herself up over her own joke and pretty soon there was a big crowd around me and asking this kind of question. I got so embarrassed I dropped the rolling pin and bought two end tables instead.'"[5]

Gracie's incomparable success was more daunting than she let on. She was not only a great comic; she was a brave person. Gracie's mike fright was powerful. For their first year on radio Burns and Allen had no audience. Gracie didn't want them seeing her reading, didn't want any further intrusion on her private self. It was enough that they could hear her over the air. At the beginning, the show's producers had to tape paper over the studio's glass doors. Gracie didn't even want wandering visitors looking in at her. They even tried broadcasting from the Willard Hotel with 1,000 seats out front. But Gracie didn't want to see them. A giant mike was placed in front of them to block her from seeing the audience. George claimed that he asked the audience neither to laugh nor applaud, though it is difficult to see how he could have prevented such a reaction.

Gracie's struggles with audiences and microphones, combined with her ongoing illnesses and migraine headaches, illustrate how ambivalent she was about fame. The private Gracie was so different from the public one that the contradiction bothered her. But it did so without a fuss, and never through the press. Gracie struggled (and partially succeeded) because she separated herself from her character and believed it was the character "Gracie Allen" who was beloved and famous and wanted, and that the real Gracie Allen could keep a distance and remain a separate person. Still, Gracie, even in the 1930s, dreamed of leaving show business, of walking away from it all. Probably if George hadn't depended on her she would have. But George believed, armed with ratings proof, that Gracie was the fuel that propelled the Burns and Allen rocket. Without Gracie, there was no Burns and Allen. He couldn't substitute another woman in the act and keep going. Gracie, dutiful wife and dedicated trouper, kept going.

If there was one crucial emotional lesson she had learned from George Burns, it was how to suppress feelings. She did this for decades, loving the shopping, appreciating the joy she was bringing to so many people, no doubt proud of her accomplishments, but still, inside, the pain of being "Gracie Allen" never left.

If the astounding recognition they received indicated that George and Gracie's radio career was taking off, the same cannot be said of their film career. In the summer of 1932, they got away from the short, one-reelers and began work in their first feature film, *The Big Broadcast*, which was released on October 14. Bing Crosby was the main attraction of the film. Burns and Allen were relegated to supporting roles. George plays a studio manager and Gracie is his secretary. But they are still Burns and Allen, the vaudevillians.

They don't have new characters. They certainly didn't want new characters that would interfere with audience recognition of their well-known personalities, but that meant they also couldn't grow. There was no new Burns and Allen for audiences. The audiences didn't need to see them in films if they had heard them on the radio. In *The Big Broadcast*, for instance, they have several good scenes, but their limitations as believable characters make it clear that it would be difficult to have them carrying an entire feature film.

But if their film career was stalling, their radio career was about to hit great new heights. The show was going to move from 9 to 9:30 P.M. Stanley Holt of the J. Walter Thompson advertising agency went to network executive Paul White and said he wanted a cheap way to announce the change. Bob Taplinger, publicity head for CBS, approached George with the problem, as well as Holt and White's publicity stunt of Gracie looking for her lost brother. The bit would begin on their show, but — in a move never previously done — she would also appear on other shows and, while discussing her brother, mention the time change.

Burns and Allen had been using her brother (and she did have a brother, named George) as a source of their material for many years in vaudeville. They told vaudeville audiences her brother had developed a way to manufacture pennies for only three cents apiece. He created an umbrella with holes, Gracie said, so people could tell when the rain stopped.

The gag began on January 4, 1933. Eddie Cantor was in the middle of a story when Gracie showed up, in tears, and said she was looking for her brother who had gone missing. A half hour later, she was on Jack Benny's program:

GRACIE: I'm looking for my missing brother. Have you seen him?
JACK: Well, what does he do?
GRACIE: He was going to go into the restaurant business, but he didn't have enough money. So he went into the banking business.
JACK: Your brother didn't have enough money so he went into the banking business?
GRACIE: Yes. He broke into the banking business at two o'clock in the morning and was kidnapped by two men dressed as policemen.[6]

Two days later Burns and Allen were scheduled to be on Rudy Vallee's show. It was on the NBC network, a CBS competitor. NBC, fearing that it was giving publicity to a rival network, demanded that Vallee not mention Gracie's missing brother. Vallee would have none of it. He later claimed that, by mistake, he picked up the wrong script and did ask Gracie about her brother. George recognized a friend when he saw one. An engineer cut the sound and, for four seconds, there was dead air.

The publicity that resulted from this act of censorship resulted in a flood of demands for Gracie to appear on the Vallee show and discuss her missing brother.

Everyone recognized a great publicity opportunity. Gracie would walk in on various shows and offer a variant of the line: "Has anybody seen my brother George?" One of the people on the program would then respond that George hadn't been spotted. Gracie would then thank them and say goodbye. On one show, there was a dramatic moment involving a submarine. Suddenly, the phone on the submarine rang and a voice asked the captain if Gracie's brother was down

George and Gracie had a great career on CBS radio, including the publicity stunt of Gracie searching everywhere for her supposedly lost brother. She'd walk in on other radio shows and ask about him. Meanwhile, her real brother was not happy with the stunt.

in the sub. Everyone wanted to get in on the gag. No matter on whose show she appeared, Gracie always remained Gracie. For example, she was on a popular show called *Singin' Sam*, and Sam asked her what Gracie's brother called himself.

> GRACIE: Oh, you're silly. He doesn't have to call himself. He knows who he is.
> SAM: What I mean is, if your brother was here, what would you call him?
> GRACIE: If my brother was here, I wouldn't have to call him.
> SAM: No, listen to me. If I found your brother, and I wanted to call him by name, what would it be?
> GRACIE: It would be wonderful.[7]

Store advertisements around the country suggested that shoppers might find Gracie's brother if they just step inside their shop. The phrase, "You look like Gracie Allen's brother," became a national craze. Several men, upon being placed under arrest, claimed to be George Allen.

George (Burns, that is) was up to the task of keeping the joke going. He hired the Burns Detective Agency in a mock search. He sent Gracie to the Empire State Building, Coney Island, and the Statue of Liberty, where she was dutifully photographed supposedly looking for her missing sibling.

The running gag was perfect for Gracie, because it gave her a way to get into almost any event and meet almost any person. If there were radio listeners unfamiliar with Gracie before the missing brother stunt, there were very few afterwards. The couple received 350,000 letters in one two-week period. Some of the letters demanded ransom with the writers claiming they had her brother. Most added, tongue very much in cheek, that if George and Gracie didn't pay them, the brother would be returned immediately.

The publicity was enjoyed by everyone — except Gracie's real brother, George. He was a San Francisco accountant happily going on with his life until reporters discovered him and began tracking all his moves. George Allen had become a celebrity without doing anything. Advertisers sought his endorsement. He suffered the attention he didn't want for several weeks and then, in a case of life imitating comedy, decided to disappear. He sent an angry telegram to George and Gracie: "Can't you make a living any other way? The newspaper people won't leave me alone. As it is now, I'm ashamed to go out into the street. I don't like being laughed at."[8]

Of course, now the news media had the story of Gracie's brother really disappearing. Ironically, new life was breathed into the gag.

On May 24, 1933, Burns and Allen changed sponsors, and their show was called *The White Owl Program*. That lasted until June 13, 1934. Just three days after they began the new program, on May 27, their movie *International House* was released. In this all-star film, George plays a doctor and Gracie is his scatterbrained nurse. Again, they drew on their classic vaudeville routines. For example, Gracie kisses the hotel manager (played by Franklin Pangborn), turns to George, and says, "Who's that?" The film is riddled with their old routines. Mostly the film is remembered today not as a Burns and Allen vehicle, but for W.C. Fields, who is very good in his role of the hard-drinking Prof. Quail.

On July 5, George and Gracie's next film, *College Humor,* was released. It was one of many 1930s musicals set on college campuses. This was Bing Crosby's second feature — and the second film he made with Burns and Allen, but the comedy team was in the film briefly.

On October 9, 1933, Burns and Allen began their last week in vaudeville.

They were no doubt relieved, in large part because by then vaudeville was virtually dead. And if their film career was not soaring, their radio program kept them active enough so that vaudeville would have been an interference had it continued. In a literal sense, Burns and Allen's stage career was over, but only in a literal sense. Their career and their characters had been born on the stage. They would be vaudevillians for the rest of their lives, regardless of which venues were popular. They were vaudevillians on film, radio, and television.

But, most importantly, they were vaudevillians in life. "George and Gracie" were an act. For the rest of their lives they didn't break character in public. George loved it; Gracie didn't. But George gradually let the vaudeville stories congeal into a narrative of their lives that he told over and over, though with slight variations. The Burns and Allen narrative didn't always cohere with reality, but that, in George's mind, was reality's failure. He had a story to tell. He wanted to control the tale of his life, and, having constructed the story, he systematically presented it (with stunning repetition) until reporters could repeat his stories back to him. But in that very repetition they believed him. George Burns had done the impossible. He had suppressed reality first, and then he beat it.

Having concluded their vaudeville careers, Burns and Allen might have sought release from their motion picture commitments. But George saw it as easy money, and so they continued. During the first half of 1934, they appeared in three additional films: *Six of a Kind* (released February 7), *We're Not Dressing* (released April 27) and *Many Happy Returns* (released June 8).

On September 19, after Guy Lombardo had left the radio show, it was given a new name. Burns and Allen, that is, began the first of many shows. This one was called *The Adventures of Gracie* (although, technically, shows were known by the sponsors, so this one was also known as *The Vintage White Owl Program*). It ran until September 25, 1935, on CBS, for a half hour on Wednesdays starting at 9:30 P.M. There would be many other titles, but it makes more sense to think of them all as one, extended *George Burns and Gracie Allen Show*. The various series (after this one) were:

Campbell's Tomato Juice Program (October 2, 1935 to March 24, 1937). This was a half-hour program on CBS Wednesdays, starting at 9:30 P.M.

The Grape-Nuts Program (April 12, 1937 to August 1, 1938). This was a half-hour program on NBC Mondays, starting at 8 P.M.

The Chesterfield Program (September 30, 1938 to June 23, 1939). This was a half-hour program on CBS Mondays, starting at 8:30 P.M.

The Hinds Honey and Almond Cream Program (October 4, 1939 to April 24,

1940). This was a half-hour program on CBS Wednesdays, starting at 7:30 P.M. From May 1, 1940 to June 26, 1940, the program began on Wednesdays at 6:30 P.M.

The Hormel Program (July 1, 1940 to March 24, 1941). This was a half-hour program on NBC, Mondays, starting at 7:30 P.M.

The Swan Soap Program (October 7, 1941 to June 30, 1942). This was a half-hour program on NBC Tuesdays, starting at 7:30 P.M. From October 6, 1942 to December 26, 1944, the program switched to CBS, Tuesdays, starting at 9 P.M. From January 1, 1945 until June 25, 1945, the program switched to Mondays, starting at 8:30 P.M.

Maxwell House Coffee Time (September 20, 1945 to May 30, 1946). This was a half-hour program on NBC Thursdays, starting at 8 P.M. From September 5, 1946 until June 23, 1949, it shifted to Thursdays at 8:30 P.M.

The Amm-i-dent Toothpaste Show (September 21, 1949 until May 17, 1950). This was a half-hour program on CBS Wednesdays, starting at 10 P.M.

As this list makes clear, Burns and Allen were masters of the radio medium for almost two decades. Radio was simple for them. Vaudeville required constant travel, radio let them come to a studio. Although the lines were very familiar, in vaudeville they had to repeat lines from memory. In radio, they read from the scripts and no memory work was required. In vaudeville, they used the same routine week after week, and, early on, year after year. In radio, there was a new script each week, so that staleness or boredom with the material was not a problem. Radio, that is, was a dream job if the performers had the right material and right voices. Lacking either element meant disaster, even for successful vaudeville performers.

But Burns and Allen were the right people for radio. Their lives seemed perfect. They moved from the Edison Hotel to the more plush Essex House. But Gracie felt that something was lacking. The two were looking out their window toward Central Park one evening. George put his arm around his wife and said, "You know, Googie, if we never have more than this, we have more than anybody."

Gracie responded, "Yes, we've got everything except the most important thing."

"What's that."

"Children."[9]

George was surprised. At the outset of their marriage they had talked of having children, and Gracie had been the one who said they shouldn't because of their financial state and the vaudevillian's nomadic lifestyle. Gracie thought such a life unfit for a child. She had said, "I don't want a child I have to tie to a chair while we're on entertaining. I've seen too many of them, poor babies. I want a child when we can afford to give it a proper home."[10] George had not told her, but he was glad about her decision. He thought she was so small that giving birth might be very difficult.

Gracie's size always had affected her. When she was young she thought people took advantage of her because she was so small. George thought the diminutive size gave her a powerful determination to prove herself, to show that she was as capable as a taller person. George thought her size — and the fact that she was pretty — was an advantage for her because people wanted to take care of her. They were protective. Or usually so. Once Gracie was in an elevator and a stranger tried to get fresh with her. She hit the man over the head with her handbag.

But her size was not an advantage when it came to children. They later wanted children, and tried to have them, but Gracie was unable to conceive. (It's not clear who was responsible for their inability to have a child; in the era it was considered to be the woman's fault, but it is just as likely that George was the cause.)

Because he understood that a determined Gracie now wanted to have children, but that they could not, he asked her what she wished to do. Gracie clearly had thought out the plan and told him that she wished to adopt a baby. Many show business people in the 1930s adopted babies, though none of their friends had yet done so.

Gracie didn't waste any time. She was turning 39 that year (1934). She surely must have considered that waiting much longer would have made it ever more difficult to play with and care for a child, even if there were going to be nurses to help.

One day the couple had lunch with the actor Wallace Beery and his adopted daughter. The child smiled at Gracie, and that was heartwarming for her. The next day Gracie called Florence Walwrath, the founder of a home called The Cradle, a Catholic foundling home in Evanston, Illinois. Gracie was clear. She wanted a girl. She wanted to call the girl by the nickname Sandy. And she wanted to raise the child Catholic. George was all right with the decision. He never went to synagogue. He thought of himself as Jewish inside, but didn't much care for religious rituals. He spent his time thinking about show business, not God. He wanted to please Gracie, and she wanted to raise her child Catholic.

Gracie knew George would go along. He always did when he understood she really meant it, even if mostly she went along with his wishes. Gracie took a train to Chicago and went to the home. But there the problem was not George; it was simple bureaucracy. Gracie had to return to New York without a baby.

She spent the next four months like an expectant mother. She bought clothes, toys, and furniture, all in preparation of her child's arrival. She hired a nurse. Now, they had everything they needed except for a baby. And then the call came. Gracie was to go to Chicago to pick up a baby girl. Along with her old friend Mary Kelly, Gracie flew to Chicago. When they arrived, Mrs. Walwrath brought out the baby. Gracie held the infant in her arms and looked at it. Gracie was shaken; the baby simply didn't look like she expected. Mrs. Walwrath knew immediately what was wrong. The baby was too large and Gracie was so tiny. Mrs. Walwrath said the home wanted children to look as much as possible like the adoptive parents. She said she had picked the wrong baby, that there was a five-week-old girl who was one of the tiniest babies in the home. The other baby was brought out. Gracie took a look and knew she had found her Sandy. Sandra Jean Burns was about to enter one of the most famous show business families in America. (George later amended this version to say that Gracie was given three babies to choose from and that Gracie picked Sandy. The truth is not certain, but this version sounds like a characteristic softening of reality to make it sweeter.)

But Gracie was nervous. She and Mary Kelly tried not to sleep on the trip back. They wanted to make sure that Sandy would be all right. But, finally, Gracie fell asleep — and her fur coat fell over the baby. Gracie awoke, saw the coat, and removed it fearing the worst, that she had smothered the new baby. But the infant was fine.

Gracie came home to a party filled with show people, none of whom had a child. Gracie was delighted. George showed the baby off to everyone. It was their crowd: Jack Benny and his wife, Mary; Jack Pearl, a radio comedian, and his wife; Jack and Flo Haley; Benny Fields and Blossom Seeley; Fred Allen and Portland Hoffa; Eddie and Ida Cantor; Goodman and Jane Ace; Harpo and Susan Marx; and Jesse Block and Eve Sully. George called his group of friends "The Home Folks" because they spent time in one another's homes mostly talking, playing cards or even performing. The group knew when Burns and Allen were performing because Gracie would stop calling her husband Natty and start calling him George.

Now George and Gracie truly did seem to have it all. But Gracie still saw a missing piece. One night the following year she told George the final part of their lives, the part that would complete it, was adopting a baby boy. George saw that look, and Gracie made another call to Chicago. The couple and Sandy moved into a triplex in the Lombardy and waited. Gracie decided that, because Ronnie was her favorite nickname for a boy, they would name their new son Ronald.

Ronnie Burns was born prematurely, but Gracie took a look at his eyes and knew he was the right baby for her. George was more concerned that the baby was sickly, but Gracie saw those big, sad eyes and knew she could make him well. And so, in September 1935, Ronald Jon Burns joined the family.

George and Gracie were done with The Cradle, but the home wasn't done with them. Mrs. Walwrath called again a year later telling them she had a four-week-old girl up for adoption. The call came during dinner. Harpo and Susan Marx (George and Gracie's best friends after Jack and Mary Benny) were over for dinner. Gracie told Mrs. Walwrath that they didn't think it would be fair to the child, that their family was complete. Harpo was listening. He had already adopted three children. He rushed to the phone, and asked Gracie to hand him the receiver. He told Mrs. Walwrath that he'd adopt the girl. He was on the train the following day. After all the arrangements had been made, George asked Harpo just how many children he planned to adopt. Harpo replied, "We want to have one kid for every window we have in the house so that when we leave, we can look back and see one of our kids in every window waving to us."[11]

Burns and Allen had a hectic life. They had two young children along with a nurse, cook, and chauffeur to help them. They also had radio shows to do and movies in which to perform.

Their new movie, *Here Comes Cookie*, was released on September 10, 1935. At the time, "Cookie" was a common romantic nickname. In the film, Gracie's father provides his fortune to her for two months so that her sister won't run off with a fortune hunter. Eventually, Gracie turns the family home into a vaudeville theater. This is one of their few films in which they were the stars, and so it is a crucial film to evaluate. The movie is revealing. Critics loved it. It's certainly zany enough. And Gracie Allen is characteristically ebullient and charming.

But there is a subtle problem with the film: it distorts the Gracie character that had been so carefully crafted over the years in vaudeville and radio. In the film, Gracie is minus her usual illogical logic; she is merely illogical or scatterbrained. For example, she's found under a bed reading and says that someone told her to read *Dr. Jekyll* and hide. George says to her, "I've never seen that expression on your face before." Gracie answers, "I'm thinking." It's not that the line itself is bad, it's that the response alters the brilliance of Gracie's character. She's not empty-headed. She doesn't think of herself as dumb. She thinks the rest of the world is dumb and can't understand the clear reality of what she says. Similarly, George's character in the film is too manic. He doesn't have the controlled bemusement that makes his character strong. It's all right for his character to state, "The more I see of Gracie, the more I'm determined to stay a bachelor," but in the best of their repartee, especially as it evolved, George grew to be amused by Gracie. That's what works best. That is, the film is an excellent example of how even good material can be bad for Burns and Allen.

Beyond that, it's difficult to pinpoint why Burns and Allen were so great in vaudeville and radio and only lasted a decade in film, with many of the films being shorts or their being only supporting players. It may be a matter of how much of Gracie's character an audience could take. Vaudeville audiences saw her for just 18 minutes, and radio audiences heard her for thirty minutes. In films like this she was center stage for an hour or more. Focusing on short films might have been a better career choice, but those were often of dubious quality and had to be turned out quickly for little profit. Surely, the intense work wouldn't have appealed to Gracie, and the very low pay wouldn't have appealed to George. They might have continued having small parts in other films, but new acts came along, and audiences got their Burns and Allen quota from the radio. Additionally, the film lines were often simply "borrowed" from their acts, and audiences too rarely saw enough new material in the films.

Writing for Gracie seemed deceptively easy but was actually quite difficult. Live audiences — in theaters or at home — could respond to her. Movies were emotionally further away; there was an aesthetic distance between the character and the audiences in theaters. It's not clear why, because she would later succeed on television. Perhaps it was as simple as Burns and Allen not being able to fill a large screen. On stage, radio, and TV, their characters were the right size for the media. A Clark Gable, for instance, would have been oversized for television.

Most of the team's screen work was simply adapted from the stage, as though there were no differences between the media. This difficulty is illustrated by the failed efforts of one of America's greatest writers. F. Scott Fitzgerald met George and Gracie in 1934 while they were on a tour. He asked permission to write for them, and they agreed. The acclaimed author of *The Great Gatsby* and other works ended up writing an eight-thousand-word film treatment entitled "Gracie at Sea." But the treatment was never used to make a film; Fitzgerald simply couldn't capture the Gracie character.

Still, in some ways, their limited screen career is an oddity. It's clear from their later huge success in television that audiences enjoyed seeing Burns and Allen. Disembodied voices coming through the radio were no longer sufficient. Of course, their television show followed their radio show, so the venues weren't competing. Maybe audiences wanted a clearly delineated Burns and Allen. Vaudeville had died on its own, so they didn't have much of an overlap as they found success on radio. Burns and Allen, that is, were a single threat — either in vaudeville, radio, or television — but not simultaneously. Interestingly, the same observation can be made of Jack Benny.

Perhaps in considering their film failure it would make sense to compare Burns and Allen to another screen comedy team, Laurel and Hardy. Like Gracie, Laurel's character was apparently dimwitted. Like her, he had an appealing voice. Like Burns and Allen, Laurel and Hardy brought the audience into their world rather than simply letting the audience observe from the outside. But Stan Laurel and Oliver Hardy had two screen advantages over Burns and Allen. First of all, Oliver Hardy was part straight man and part dimwit. Ollie was halfway between Stan's world and the real one. He wasn't quite a parental figure, but more like an older brother. Burns tried to interpret Gracie for the world, never once entering into that illogical universe. Ollie was an intimate part of Stanley's clueless world. As Laurel once noted, they were "two minds without a single thought."[12]

That silliness worked well on the screen. It was comparable to that of the Marx Brothers. Zeppo tried to play a brother outside the brothers' world and in the normal one. It didn't work, and he eventually left the act. On screen, it worked better if there were two or even more people in the wacky world. The Three Stooges worked like that, for example. The team of Burns and Allen had to rely just on Gracie, and she was an under-populated alternate universe.

The second reason Laurel and Hardy worked better on screen than Burns and Allen is that "The Boys" were physical comedians. Burns and Allen could dance. Gracie had a funny voice. They both had pitch-perfect deliveries. But they didn't do any physical comedy. Physical comedy isn't needed on radio, which is one reason the Marx Brothers didn't succeed on radio (of course, there was the little added factor of Harpo's character not being able to talk at all). Film was founded as an almost exclusively visual medium. Sound helped — as an adjunct. Burns and Allen appear static next to Laurel and Hardy. Hardy had a perfect slow burn. He made precise small gestures, such as when he twiddled his tie. Laurel had been trained in pantomime. He had a perfect cry. His face developed a look of bewilderment, whereas Gracie's face was not expressive. Laurel had a grin and used make-up to make his eyes appear smaller. They knew how to use film. Burns and Allen simply applied their vaudeville act to film when they should have developed a new cinematic approach. Luckily for them, the vaudeville approach worked perfectly on radio.

Incidentally, the notion of a dumb character like Gracie, Stan or Ollie was part of the cultural milieu, not just in vaudeville, radio, and film. Take the character of Bertie Wooster in P.G. Wodehouse's stories and novels. Wooster, the empty-headed English gentleman, is served by Jeeves, his valet. Jeeves might be seen as playing a George Burns part. But Jeeves plays off the English interest in class, a subject of far less interest to American audiences. Jeeves is, by class distinction at least, inferior to Bertie, but in intelligence, cunning, and wit he is far, far superior. He can't say so because of his place in the class system and his employment status.

That is, Burns and Allen were working on a continuum of ways a dumb character could be used. They worked successfully in Britain as well, perhaps simply because the British enjoy eccentric characters. But Burns and Allen essentially failed in film.

Just a week after *Here Comes Cookie* was released, their film *The Big Broadcast of 1936* appeared. It's a classic example of a hodgepodge of a film. Burns and Allen are good in the film, but the overall effect is flat.

By the end of 1936, Burns and Allen decided to leave New York and live permanently in California. They could be there to make films. They could broadcast their radio show from anywhere. And for Gracie, there was the opportunity to be nearer to her beloved family. Gracie called her sister Bessie, who located a house for them. They moved that December. The house was huge, filled with servants, a swimming pool with a bridge over it, and a stable. The irony was not lost on George Burns. He had started out in a cramped three-room tenement, and now he had this.

They eventually moved out of the home into their more familiar house on Maple Drive in Beverly Hills.

It's not always clear from the character "Gracie Allen," but the real Gracie Allen was very religious. She regularly attended Mass. She wore a gold cross around her neck. George observed that sometimes, before the two went on stage to perform, she made the sign of the cross. In later life, she was thrilled to have an audience with the pope. In Gracie's home, the family ate fish every Friday, as was then a Catholic practice. (Not everyone in the family enjoyed fish. Sandy didn't like it. She used to tell people she was a Catholic for six days a week. For Friday's traditional fish meal, she took off.) The children, too, attended Mass every Sunday.

The children didn't always behave well. When they were older they skipped church. They engaged in normal childhood mischief. They had to endure the taunts that their mother was the dumbest woman in the world. They had another problem as well, one that revealed their innate sense of kindness.

Gracie continued to suffer incredible headaches. She developed a signal for her children; she drew the curtains in the bedroom. The children then knew to be quiet and not to disturb her. Gracie used to tie a bandana around her head to relieve the pain. Her dog, Suzy, would sit at the edge of the bed to protect her. Suzy only allowed Ronnie to enter the room, and he learned to adjust the bandage to make his mother feel better.

Meanwhile, Burns and Allen continued with their film efforts. *College Holiday* was released on December 19, 1936. The film, which also starred Jack Benny, was filled with gags and revue acts. Again, Gracie has reasonably good lines, but the film is overly long and not interesting. It's a surmise, but perhaps if George and Gracie had better scripts, their film career would have been stronger. But those script writers, as radio writers, faced enormous obstacles. To take one example, consider their next film, *A Damsel in Distress*, which was released on November 19, 1937.

The film was based on a novel by P.G. Wodehouse. It is set in an old English castle. An aunt imprisons a young woman because the woman wants to marry someone the aunt does not like. Fred Astaire starred in the movie, but it was his first musical without Ginger Rogers. It was also the last film George Gershwin ever scored. The Burns and Allen material is again familiar, and, although vintage Gracie, it does seem at odds with the usual Wodehouse sensibility and British humor. Gracie does some great dancing in the film, performing a delightful "whisk-broom" vaudeville routine with George and Fred. But again, Burns and Allen were trapped in a frothy romantic comedy that didn't really work. The film was not a box-office hit. This was despite a dedicated promotion effort. For example, George and Gracie appeared on the radio show *Hollywood Hotel* on November 5, 1937, along with the gossip columnist Louella Parsons, Fred Astaire, Joan Fontaine, Astaire's partner in the film, and George Stevens, director of the film. Gracie was Gracie. She bantered with Astaire about being in a dance scene and George spoke up:

GEORGE: Gracie, I was in those dance scenes too, you know! What did you
    think I was doing?

GRACIE: Oh, so you've begun to wonder, too?

GEORGE: Louella, I want to apologize for the way Gracie's breaking up your
    introductions. Just make out she hasn't said anything and go right
    ahead.

LOUELLA PARSONS: And now I'll tell you about a real sensation....

GRACIE: Oh, please, Louella, you embarrass me.[13]

But, despite all the talent assembled, the film — typical of Burns and
Allen's film career — didn't work. When audiences filled out cards after seeing
previews, Burns and Allen did far better than the general film. There were
comments like: "The whole picture was in distress except the comedy and
Burns and Allen." "I thought Burns and Allen came up a step from their last
picture." "Geo. Burns and Gracie Allen were exceptionally good, as always."[14]

While their radio career was spectacular, Burns and Allen had notably less success
in films. Here they are in *A Damsel in Distress* (RKO Radio Pictures, 1937) flanking
Fred Astaire. Audiences were surprised that the comedians could keep up with Astaire,
one of the screen's all-time best dancers.

Burns and Allen remained in this trap throughout the 1930s until their joint film career ended. They couldn't carry a whole picture and the films in which they were cast were weak and mostly unable to mesh their comedy seamlessly with the rest of the material. Audiences liked them enough, but producers didn't know what to do with them.

Part of the problem for producers lay outside the talent they could use. The industry Production Code was strict. In the case of *A Damsel in Distress*, for instance, Joseph I. Breen, the man who enforced the Code, sent letters to RKO (the film's studio) with comments on the script in several separate letters. His comments in a July 22, 1937 letter included such directives as:

> Page 9: This use of liquor seems unnecessary, and must be omitted, as well as all other showing of liquor which is not specifically required for proper character-ization.
> Page 11: We renew our request that you avoid playing these scenes in Maud's boudoir, substituting a private sitting room in her suite for her bedroom.
> Page 18: There must be nothing vulgar in this business of the armor "kicking Allen and Burns in the fanny."
> Page 25: We renew our warning that censor boards will cut the business of Fred locking the door after he is in Lady Maud's bedroom.[15]

Sponsors were strict in radio, but, by definition, there was no visual element to worry about. And Burns and Allen specialized in the verbal exchanges that defined radio comedy. In films, Burns and Allen could not offer a new product. Seeing them on the screen, especially seeing them dance, pleased audiences, but they weren't on screen very long in many of their films.

To their credit, they didn't quit. Their next movie, *College Swing*, was released on April 29, 1938. Burns and Allen were in the film with Bob Hope; it was only his second feature. The film takes advantage of Gracie's familiar character by having her attend college with the proviso that, if she graduates, the college will be hers. She rejuvenates the college with the introduction of swing music. Once again, the story was flat. Gracie delivers her lines well, but doing so only highlights the film's general weaknesses. It's once more a series of vaudeville skits. Clearly, the motion picture industry simply could not conceive of how to use Burns and Allen in an original way. Their film career was almost at an end.

But before they made their final film, George was involved in a scandal. One of the couple's strengths had been to avoid any scandals. Gracie's innocence in particular might have been affected by even a hint of inappropriate behavior. George was very discreet, and very busy. But this scandal did not involve romance, and that fact enabled them to survive it unscathed.

The case was odd. It involved a man named Albert Chaperau. Chaperau specialized in smuggling fine jewelry into the United States and was only caught because of a co-conspirator, Elma Lauer, who was the wife of Edgar J. Lauer, a justice on the New York State Supreme Court. The Lauers had a maid named Rosa Weber. Chaperau was among the guests at a Lauer dinner, and the talk turned to Hitler. Chaperau was outspoken in his denunciation of Nazism, and Rosa Weber was sympathetic to the Nazi movement. She supposedly announced to everyone there, "Ladies and gentlemen. I am a true German. I love Adolf Hitler. If you don't stop talking against him, I will stop serving the dinner right now."[16]

Justice Lauer fired Rosa Weber, and she, in retaliation, went to customs authorities to report that Chaperau had smuggled Parisian clothing for Mrs. Lauer. Chaperau's defense was that he enjoyed bringing gifts for his various friends. It turned out that many celebrities had accepted and paid for such gifts. Those celebrities included Jack Benny and George Burns.

The trouble for George started when Chaperau and his wife had dinner at New York's famous 21 with George and Gracie. George noticed that Chaperau's wife had a beautiful and wide diamond bracelet. Because Gracie always wore long sleeves, it was difficult to find such a bracelet for her. It was wide enough to cover her scar and thereby allow her to wear a dress with a shorter sleeve. Chaperau said he would sell the bracelet for $2,000, and George readily agreed, evidently without knowing that the bracelet had been illegally smuggled into the country.

Chaperau was indicted two more times. In the case of George Burns, the two were indicted in 1938 for smuggling $4,885 worth of diamond bracelets as well as a ring. It turned out that Mr. Chaperau had quite a history; he wasn't even an American citizen and he had served 18 months in Leavenworth Federal Penitentiary after a conviction for mail fraud in 1919. Rosa Weber received $8,000 for being a federal informant. George was facing 18 years in prison and a fine of $45,000. He immediately entered a plea of guilty to all nine counts of the indictment, thereby avoiding a trial. He claimed he didn't know the items were smuggled, although he did admit that he made the payments to Chaperau. George requested to be arraigned at once, and the judge agreed.

George was very nervous. He kept fingering his eyeglasses and chewing his nails. George was released on the recognizance of his lawyer.

On January 31, 1939, a trembling George Burns stood before the judge and was fined $8,000. This was in addition to the $9,770 he had already paid in duties and penalties. (George was then earning about $11,000 a week.) The judge seemed ready to send George to prison in order that a clear message be sent to other celebrities who were tempted to undertake similar actions. George was pale and his eyes kept blinking. His lawyer was ready. He argued that the judge shouldn't put a special burden on George Burns just because of his fame. And George had another advantage. He had fully cooperated with the government, and so the assistant U.S. attorney argued that the prison sentence be suspended.

George was sentenced to a year and a day in prison, but that sentence was suspended. If the charges against him had been felonies instead of misdemeanors, he would have lost the right to vote, but he retained those rights. As it was, he had to report to a probation officer each month for a year. Gracie was allowed to keep the jewelry, but she refused to wear it and eventually gave it away.

They tried a variety of parts in films, but they were always Burns and Allen. Audiences liked them enough, but they couldn't find the right film. In *Love in Bloom* (Paramount Pictures, 1935) Gracie is on the run from her carnival family.

George went immediately to Newark Airport, and, listed as "George Williams," he waited until the last possible minute before boarding a plane back to California.

His friend Jack Benny entered a plea of innocent, but he was found guilty at his trial, fined $10,000 and received the same suspended sentence of a year and a day.

Throughout the ordeal, George had worried that his sponsors would cancel the radio program, and, in fact, when the Burns and Allen contract expired the sponsor did not renew with them. The William Morris Agency found another sponsor for them — Swan Soap — but at a much reduced offer of $7,500 for what was then called "the package." That is, out of the money George had to pay for the musicians, writers, directors, and actors. Only after he paid them could he make a profit. He was upset, but it was the only offer they had. But George wouldn't shortchange the writing. He knew that he and Gracie could deliver good lines, but if there was one crucial lesson he had learned from vaudeville, it was that they needed the right lines to deliver. He therefore paid his writers $3,500 of the money. It took a full year before they were economically able to recover.

Just three days after George received his suspended sentence, *Honolulu*, their final motion picture together, was released on February 3, 1939. The incredibly poor timing of the film's release was a symbolically fitting end to a film career that never really did take off.

Honolulu has a tired premise of switched identities. Robert Young plays a film star who meets a plantation owner. The two look alike and decide to switch roles. Eleanor Powell meets the screen star. One more hackneyed romance doomed Burns and Allen's film career. Sadly, Gracie is still very sharp. That is, ironically, Burns and Allen's film career didn't fail because of Burns and Allen except in the sense of the material in which they agreed to appear, although it's hard to imagine they had much say about it. They were, like Eleanor Powell, mishandled by their studios.

As far as George Burns was concerned, after *Honolulu* he would no longer make motion pictures. And for decades that conclusion seemed more than reasonable. And so for almost two decades, Burns and Allen found fame and fortune doing what they did best — talking on the radio. They tried every available venue. Here, for example, is an exchange from a 1933 recording. The title is called "Comedy Skit" and it was released around the time when Gracie's missing brother was a key to their success.

GEORGE: Well Gracie, I'm sorry to hear about your missing brother.

GRACIE: Oh, that's too bad, George, because my brother's missing, too.

GEORGE: Well, the only difference between me and you is that I have the power of mind over matter and you have no mind, and it doesn't seem to matter.

GRACIE: Oh, I bet you tell that to all the girls.

GEORGE: I still would like to know how is your brother?

GRACIE: My brother? Well, I think they ought to open up all the prisons. It would help prosperity.

GEORGE: Wait a minute. That's the wrong answer.

GRACIE: No, that's the right answer, but you asked me the wrong question.

GEORGE: Uh....

GRACIE: Now, look, it costs the government 70 million dollars to feed all the prisoners.

GEORGE: Yes.

GRACIE: And when they're out they only steal 60 million dollars a year.

Gracie and George, here playing around in a Paramount photograph, made a series of films for the studios, often with famous stars, such as W. C. Fields in *International House* (1933) and Bing Crosby in *The Big Broadcast of 1936* (1935). But their film career as a team ended with *Honolulu* (Loew's/MGM, 1939).

GEORGE: Well.

GRACIE: Now, that gives the government a ten million dollar profit right there, don't you think so?

GEORGE: I think so. I'll see you later, Gracie.

GRACIE: Now, take my brother Harry.

GEORGE: You take him.

GRACIE: Well, they got him.

GEORGE: They got him?

GRACIE: He's ruining Sing-Sing. He eats them out of house and warden.

GEORGE: House and warden?

GRACIE: Yeah. And my older brother, Willy, well there's an appetite for you. He bit Harry.

GEORGE: Without ketchup?

GRACIE: No, with ketchup.

GEORGE: Yeah, it's better with ketchup.

GRACIE: Yeah. Willy goes to San Quentin.

GEORGE: He *goes* to San Quentin. He takes his books and he goes to San Quentin.

GRACIE: Yeah. Well, I'll never forget when my brothers got out. How proud my father was. As they left the gate, my father was standing, waving from his cell.

GEORGE: Your father waved from his cell?

GRACIE: Yeah. He said, "Good-bye kids."

GEORGE: Hmmm.

GRACIE: And they hollered back, "Good-bye, Pop."

GEORGE: Nice family.[17]

The notion of making fun of Gracie's extended mythical family was a staple of the Burns and Allen humor across the decades. They noted that Gracie's mother could read lips and so tell when her father was lying. He was lying when he moved his lips. Bessie, the sister, had the capacity to see with her tongue. She could see, for example, if the soup was too warm. Then there was Gracie's cousin Audubon Allen, a bird doctor. He improved an owl's grammar by teaching it to say "whom." He taught hummingbirds to sing the words. Her supposed Uncle Otis ran for the San Francisco City Council with a promise to improve the city: he would move to Los Angeles. Gallup Allen, her pollster cousin, conducted a survey to determine just how many people had telephones in their homes. He concluded that all the people he called had a phone in their home. Her cousin Rush Allen was a bus driver with an enviable safety record. Unfortunately, he took all his safety awards and pasted them to the windshield of his bus so he couldn't see and so had an accident.

Families were still relatively intact in America, and everyone had relatives. None quite like Gracie's, but audiences could identify the exaggerated examples of their own extended families. In a way, Gracie's odd relatives with their faults and foibles made it easier for listeners to tolerate real relatives. During the Great Depression, this was crucial because economic hard times had put pressure on the families, but if George and Gracie could find humor in Gracie's wacky relatives, maybe the listeners' relatives weren't so bad after all.

The idea of relatives extended to other jokes:

GEORGE: Gracie, were you the oldest in your family?
GRACIE: No, silly. My mother and father were older.
GEORGE: Gracie, do you think I should go over to the hospital and see how old Mrs. Taylor is today?
GRACIE: Well, you can visit her if you want, George, but I don't think she'll tell you how old she is![18]

Their radio comedy also relied on Gracie misunderstanding a given event. For example, on one show George had received an invitation to sing for the Army Air Force and, in preparation, he was going to receive some vaccination shots. The way that information filtered through Gracie's mind, though, led to her conclusion that the Army Air Force wanted to shoot George for singing.

Other shows focused on some problem George had, a problem Gracie was determined to help solve. On one show, George was running for the Beverly Hills City Council. Gracie decided it would help George if she got the support of her club, the Beverly Hills Uplift Society. Gracie went to Lana Turner for help.

GRACIE: Lana. I need your help.
LANA: What is it?
GRACIE: Well, you see, I'm married to George Burns....
LANA: Oh, you poor kid.[19]

The theme of Gracie or someone else making fun of George was always irresistible. On another show, the couple recalled going to Al Jolson to ask for a job. Somehow, Jolson came to believe that Gracie was a ventriloquist and George was the dummy.

GRACIE: But he's not a dummy. He's a real man. He's George Burns.
JOLSON: Are you trying to tell me that he has blood and muscles, and that he walks and talks and makes love like other men?
GRACIE: No. I'm trying to tell you he's George Burns.[20]

Gracie's eagerness to help extended beyond George to include various guest stars. For example, she once decided that she should adopt Mickey Rooney because, she was convinced, he had not received an adequate education. Mickey argued with her, explaining that he had degrees in geometry and Latin.

The unflustered Gracie responded, "Oh yeah? Say something in geometry."

Unsure how to answer such a question, Mickey thought about it for a second and said, "Okay, Pi R Square."

That convinced Gracie she had been right. "Oh yeah? There's proof you haven't had a good education. Everybody knows pie are round."[21]

Besides her husband and guest stars, the writers developed characters on the show with whom Gracie could interact. There was, for instance, Tootsie Sagwell, who was notoriously overweight and unattractive to men. Gracie was determined to help her achieve her long-sought goal of finding a husband. On one program, she suggested that Tootsie run for Queen of the Fleet against Hedy Lamarr. Gracie had the two stand side by side, looked them over, and announced her conclusion:

> GRACIE: Just as I thought. There's no difference in your faces. Your eyes and
> ears and nose and mouth are the same.
> TOOTSIE: Really?
> GRACIE: Yes. I counted them carefully.[22]

In radio, the announcers were an integral part of the show. They were characters, not just announcers who presented commercials. Burns and Allen started with Bill Goodwin who presented himself as a romantic, often affectionately flirting with Gracie. Ronald Reagan — then simply a good-looking actor — appeared on the show and got into a supposed tiff with Goodwin about their comparative attractiveness. Guess who they turned to in order to solve their dispute? Reagan found Gracie, and said:

> REAGAN: Now, forget you're married to George Burns.
> GRACIE: But it takes time to forget something like that.
> REAGAN: Well....
> GRACIE: That's long enough.
> REAGAN: Ah, Gracie, you're lovely. Beautiful ... enchanting. I kiss your hand.
> [He loudly kisses her hand several times.]
> GOODWIN: All right, all right. Now it's my turn.
> GRACIE: You'll love it, Bill. It tickles.[23]

George and Gracie developed enormous skills. They had bound books of gags that contained thousands of comedy routines and one-liners. An accompanying index listed the subject matter of each entry. (Many comedians had such collections. Milton Berle's collection was perhaps the most well-known among comedians.) Their writers would pick a subject and then just go to the index to find available jokes and supplement them, perhaps with a timely comment about a person or event in the news. For example, there were ten routines just under the heading of "Department Stores." Here is a routine they used on their March 28, 1932 show:

> GRACIE: I'm going into the department store business. I made up my mind.
> GEORGE: What mind?
> GRACIE: Somebody told you to say that. I'm going to open up about five or six department stores. Of course, that's only for a start.
> GEORGE: No doubt in a few months, you will have several hundred department stores.
> GRACIE: Well, I don't want to count my chickens before they're department stores.[24]

It was George who worked closely with the writers. Those writers, over time, included such people as John P. Medbury, Paul Henning, Harvey Helm, Sam Perrin, Frank Galen, Keith Fowler, and George's brother, Willy Burns. They were the ones responsible for thinking like Gracie and then writing the lines. George would meet with all the writers on the day after a program ended. They would discuss what the next show should be about, tossing around general subjects and idea. Then each of the writers went home and separately wrote scripts for the whole program. They would then reconvene in a suite of rooms at the Hollywood Plaza and listen to the various ideas, pulling together a script from the individual attempts. There were a lot of fights during those sessions. Writers nurtured affection for particular lines and didn't willingly give them up for the sake of another writer's pet line. On Mondays and Tuesdays (that is the typical day before a show aired and the actual day of the show), Burns took the writers to the coffee shop in the Plaza and they ate and fought it out. Maybe being in a public place restricted the profanity and anger.

Once the completed script was prepared, Burns and Allen followed it carefully. George had to memorize it because of his dyslexia. Gracie just read it. But neither did any ad-libbing. The script was nearly sacred.

The Burns and Allen joke index had 30 jokes dealing with the Great Depression. It was a tricky subject for comedians. On the one hand, they couldn't avoid it because it was the subject of every dinner conversation. On the other hand, a comedy show's purpose was to help people forget their troubles and woes. Therefore, an ongoing problem was to determine how to confront economic problems. This was easier for Jack Benny, who had a well-known and shrewdly developed character as a skinflint. Laughs from his stinginess only heightened because so many listeners could identify with his feelings.

For Burns and Allen, though, the comedic task was not so easy. They had to get listeners to laugh at their own pain. Laughing at Gracie's loopy logic was one matter. Audiences were taken into a separate world when they did that. But the Great Depression was in the real world. The Burns and Allen trick was to apply Gracie's mind to the economy and let listeners laugh just as they would about Gracie's unique perceptions of any other subject. But these economic references had to be "hammocked," that is, like a hammock that had to be tied to two strong trees, the economic jokes had to be tied to strong jokes of a more common Gracie Allen type. Another tactic was to wait until some economic matter became prominent beyond the ongoing crisis. For example, there was a banking crisis in 1933. Gracie might say the crisis had reached their home, that their baby's bank had failed. Or her mind would be put to work dealing with the unemployed:

> GRACIE: George, I've got the most marvelous idea for settling this unemployment situation.
> GEORGE: Do you mean to say you have an idea ... that's good?
> GRACIE: Well, I've decided to put all the men in the world on an island in the middle of the ocean. Then soon everybody will be working.
> GEORGE: You don't mind if I get this straight. [*He repeats her idea*].
> GRACIE: That's right.
> GEORGE: In the same ocean? ... And they will all be working? What would they be doing?
> GRACIE: Boat building.[25]

In real life, Gracie was a very private person. With the famous guests they had — Clark Gable, Betty Grable, Lucille Ball, Shirley Temple, Cary Grant, Frank Sinatra, and many others — and even with the regular cast and crew of the show, Gracie held back. She didn't let her personal side show. She was kind and decent always, but she fiercely guarded her privacy. Maybe it was shyness. Maybe it was self-doubt about her success (although that remains difficult to comprehend, with the enormity of the attraction to her by so many across the decades).

She never got over that mike fright, either, on radio or later on television. It is entirely possible to conclude that she intensely disliked success after wanting it so much and working so hard for it for so long. Once she had it, once she grasped how completely it devoured her soul, she only then realized the price of success. George gladly paid the price — the subordination of his character to Gracie's, the suppression of his ego, the industry chatter that without her he would be revealed as talentless. He loved what he got in return. The money was great, of course. But George needed the applause, the constant approval. He needed the identity of "star." Gracie not only didn't need it, she didn't want it. Fame scared her. She worried in the wake of the Lindbergh kidnapping that someone would snatch their young children. She worked with both of them, trying to train them to yell, "Police, police," if a stranger grabbed them. Gracie completely lost her privacy. Everyone knew her from all the publicity. A crowd gathered around her wherever she went. She was always "Gracie Allen" and could never be her true self outside the home. Gracie seemed so open and kind on the show that listeners just assumed she wouldn't mind if they chatted with her. They'd go right up to her front door and ring the doorbell to say they were visiting in town and had to meet her. Sometimes people just wandered around the house into the backyard.

But however uncomfortable Gracie was, she knew fame had set its trap and that trap had been sprung. Her husband needed her. She knew the fans wanted to hear her. She stayed for many years after she truly wanted to depart.

Radio should have been the easiest medium for George Burns. After all, he had writers to prepare the jokes. One might assume that all he had to do was show up, read the jokes off the page, collect his paycheck, and go home. But life was never going to be easy for someone with such reading difficulties. George constantly worried that his undiagnosed dyslexia would cause incredible problems on live shows. He was concerned that, as he read the script, he would have trouble with individual words. Burns and Allen's comedy depended extensively on timing and on his control of the pace of the lines. If he was concerned about whether he would be able to read the lines, that anxiety would interfere with his comedic control. To combat such a potential problem, George began memorizing all the lines in the script. He did this later on, in television and in motion pictures. Armed with a memorized script, George could relax and focus on the comedy delivery.

Despite its seeming ease, radio did have its challenges. During one program, for example, the studio lights went out. George could have kept on going because he knew the script, but Gracie read from the pages. They had a problem. On another occasion, Gracie dropped the script pages on the floor, and they scattered all over. Accidents happen, but on live radio with stars talking to a national audience, such incidents were potentially disastrous. Luckily in both cases, Burns and Allen had the experience not to let disturbances fluster them. George simply said, "Gracie, how's your brother?' and Gracie quickly followed up with part of their vaudeville act. When the pages fell, she reacted to George's question by saying that her brother had joined the navy. He had trouble, though, because every time there was an order to put all hands on deck, he followed the orders and people kept stepping on his hands.

As good as Burns and Allen were, then as now audiences wanted novelty. Of course there were new lines and music could always be added, but all audiences loved guest stars. The writers could add interesting situations as Gracie dealt with the stars or talked about them with George. James and Pamela Mason, two British actors with a fondness for cats, were guests on the show, and the writers adapted that interest and James's good looks into the script:

> GRACIE: My husband is a cat fancier, too.
> PAMELA: Oh, really. How many do you have?
> GRACIE: Just one. In this country we're only permitted one husband.
> PAMELA: Well, what is your method of raising cats?
> GRACIE: Same as yours. Put both hands under their belly and lift.
> JAMES: Mrs. Burns, I appeal to you....
> GRACIE: You certainly do, but I still don't want any more cats.[26]

Given the limitations faced by comedy writers — their inability to use provocative language or discuss banned subjects — it is unsurprising that they relied on language as a natural source of humor. This is important because in a wilder medium freed from the sponsors' restraints, a humor dependent on language would have been seen as more corny. Within radio's confines, no team was better prepared to use language as humor than Burns and Allen. Without the restraints their competitors would have put up much more of a challenge. The humor required on radio fit Burns and Allen perfectly, and no one could top it.

Gracie's language confusion was complemented by the then-common use of puns. Hearing some of the great radio comedians now induces groans of disappointment from audiences used to more modern comedic styles, but during its heyday, much radio comedy was highly dependent on puns.

Because of this, Burns and Allen employed puns on their show, perhaps most famously in a 1938 program with a bit featuring stage and screen star John Conte, based on city names:

> GRACIE: You see, I tell the story of cities and towns.... Now, for instance, Tony Martin is a Richmond who's been Macon a lot of money in Georgia, but he needs a few more Dallas to pay his Texas. Get it?
> GEORGE: Well, that's not Hartford me to understand....
> JOHN: Am I in this musical number, Gracie?
> GRACIE: Well, I should say you are, Johnny. You're the little Boise that I'm in love with.
> GEORGE: But maybe Johnny doesn't love you.
> JOHN: Oh, that's all right, George. I'm glad to Yuma her....
> GRACIE: ... The scene Ipswitche-es now to a town in Montana. But I can't mention the name of it.

GEORGE: Why not?
GRACIE: Well, George, you're not allowed to say Helena radio.
GEORGE: Well, that was really a Butte.
GRACIE: It's very funny Anaconda made it up myself.[27]

As clever as such humor was, the writers and the audience were evidently unaware of how it undercut Gracie's fundamental character. Her humor rested on her seeing language literally or in her own way. She doesn't have a strong command of language; she just sees it from another angle. The puns in this routine have Gracie with a mastery of geography and a mastery of the language. Had such efforts been repeated more frequently, they would have made audiences question Gracie's "normal" mind.

That points out a dilemma. The character was so clearly defined, so identified by audiences that it was explosive to tamper with it. And yet times changed. Tastes differed. Burns and Allen matured. The task for the comedians and the writers was to juggle all this.

The dilemma came to a head around 1939, when the show's ratings started to decline. Until this time, their show had always been in the Top Ten. It's true that there weren't a lot of comedy teams on radio, but Burns and Allen had to compete against the wide variety of programs that made up American radio. Ironically, had the ratings suffered a steep decline there would have been less cause for concern because the drop would have been ascribed to a particular event that week, such as a presidential speech. What was most troubling was that the decline was steady, a half point or a point each week, reaching a low of 14.9 in 1941. This meant that not only weren't Burns and Allen keeping their audience, but also more and more of that core audience no longer tuned in the following week. Unless steps were taken to halt the slide, George knew, he and Gracie were headed for cancellation.

There were various possibilities for the decline. Perhaps the audience members were tired of Gracie's character. If that were true, it couldn't be fixed because Gracie's character was the basis of the entire act.

The alternative was to accept that some aspect of the show — rather than Gracie — wasn't working any longer. Forced to that conclusion, George asked his friends for advice. Some said Gracie should laugh more. Some said she should laugh less. Some said the microphone needed to be replaced. Others said it was fine. Some said the writing had become stale. Others defended the high-quality writing.

The decline had no effect on Gracie. In many ways, she probably wouldn't have minded at all if the show ended. She would have more time to spend at home with her children. She had always been surprised by their success and assumed it couldn't last. Anyway, the couple had enough money. And Gracie was never driven by fame or ego.

In contrast, George had many sleepless nights. Spinning with contrary advice from friends and comedy legends, George knew he himself had a shrewd comedy mind. He was determined to figure out the problem and fix it.

Finally, in the middle of another sleepless night, George turned to his wife and began to shake her.

"Googie, are you awake? I know what's wrong."

"That's nice, Nat. What's wrong with what?"

"The show. I know why our ratings are dropping. Our jokes are too young for us. Everybody knows that we're really married and have the kids. But on the show you're still flirting with everybody. Let's tell them we're married."[28]

George was certainly correct about Gracie's role on the show. She did flirt with the announcer. They did have boyfriend and girlfriend jokes. He insulted her the way he might insult a girlfriend, but not a wife. Their radio truth was separate from their real truth. Had the audience not been familiar with their real lives, Burns and Allen might have continued as they were. But audience members were always reading about the couple's private lives, or at least a highly controlled version of their private lives. The audience, George perceived, saw the dissonance before the stars or the writers had. The audience thought Burns and Allen were not being honest. They were still doing their street-corner flirtation act. When the audience knew Gracie was a mother as well as married, they were upset that in the show Bill Goodwin flirted with Gracie on the show.

And they worked Gracie's attraction to other men into the show. For example, at one point they saw a Charles Boyer film. Gracie fell for the charming actor.

GEORGE: Gracie, could you walk a little faster?
GRACIE: If you wish, Charles.
GEORGE: Gracie, I'm George Burns, your husband. Remember? I'm not Charles Boyer.
GRACIE: Oh, well. That's life.
[*They walk into a store, and Gracie buys some magazines with articles about Boyer. Then they return home and retire to their bed for the night.*]
GRACIE: This article I'm reading now is fascinating: "Charles Boyer's Ten Rules for Being a Successful Lover."
GEORGE: Turn out the light.
GRACIE: That's the first rule.[29]

The successful transformation that occurred required them to keep the character types they had labored so hard to develop and perfect but to adapt the types to a new situation — married life. Once they did that, they developed the formula that would carry them through the rest of their joint career, with George the harried and frustrated husband dealing with the convoluted intricacies of his wife's seemingly illogical mind. This method worked. Gracie's mind continued to work as it did, but the writers came up with domestic conflicts. Here's a typical routine, done in 1947, as Gracie seeks money to get a new dress.

GEORGE: Good morning, Gracie. How about some breakfast?

GRACIE: All right. Would you like the table by the window?

GEORGE: Yeah. It's the only one we've got.

GRACIE: Now, what would you like to eat?

GEORGE: I'll have a glass of orange juice, a slice of toast, and a cup of Maxwell House ... coffee.

GRACIE: Yessir. [*Calls out*] Squeeze two, burn one, and please the sponsor.

GEORGE: What are you doing?

GRACIE: I'm a waitress. I'm calling your order to the kitchen. You wouldn't give me $85 for a dress, so I'm running this house like a hotel to earn the money.

GEORGE: This isn't a hotel, and you're not the waitress.

GRACIE: I'll prove it. Here's a glass of water. I'll bring the food two hours later.

GEORGE: Cut out the nonsense and bring me my breakfast.

GRACIE: You'll have to pay in advance. You haven't got any luggage.

GEORGE: Look, Gracie. You're my wife. I would pay you only if you were employed by me. This hotel deal is too much. I won't give in. I won't agree, and I won't cooperate.

GRACIE: You left out one thing.

GEORGE: What?

GRACIE: You won't eat.[30]

Whatever the nature of Gracie's illogical mind in the act, in real life she was generous and never forgot an old friend. When they had a new show (that began on October 4, 1939), Gracie made sure that Mary Kelly was in the cast as her friend "Bubbles." Kelly's was a sad show business story. Once the girlfriend of Jack Benny, and Gracie's roommate, Kelly's career in vaudeville had ended badly. She had saved some money, but, like many actors, had lost it all in the 1929 stock market crash. She tried marriage to Ray Myers, the booking agent who had helped George and Gracie. But the marriage fizzled and Mary became a telephone operator. She worked at the Academy of Vaudeville Artists in New York City, evidently to remain as close as possible to show business, but her life was in shambles. Mary Kelly, widely once known as "Pretty Mary Kelly," was no longer so pretty. She had put on an enormous amount of weight.

It would have been easy for Gracie to forget Mary Kelly, to consider her merely as a rung on the ladder to success. But Gracie wasn't like that at all. Over the years she had kept up a correspondence and visited Mary when she and George were in New York. To help her friend get back into the industry, Gracie got her a part. And it seemed to help. Mary was a success on the show. She appeared on other programs, including Jack Benny's. She had a few parts in some films. Her life had apparently turned around. But it was not to be. On June 7, 1941, Mary Kelly died in her sleep. She was 46 years old.

Burns and Allen meanwhile kept going through such personal tragedies. Although they continued to create laughs, their personal lives were separate. People rarely saw them kissing. As his writers knew, George entertained a string of young women in the area adjacent to his office. George, of course, had always loved women, but there was an edge to these relationships. George needed Gracie. Without her he had not been a success, and, he must have assumed, if he left her for another woman his success would disappear. He loved her and partially resented his needing her. And it was more than that. Burns and Allen had a national image as a couple deeply in love. If Burns were caught in a romantic entanglement or if he fell in love with another woman, the public would not be forgiving. All his dalliances, then, were truly flirtations with danger because each one threatened both his marriage and his career. The most famous tale of his infidelity, one he repeated in private and later in public, was that Gracie discovered his cheating. He supposedly didn't say a word to her but bought her a gift. The exact nature of the gift varied with the stories, but those stories always ended with Gracie saying she wished George would cheat again because she needed a matching gift.

In spite of George's infidelities, Burns and Allen stayed together. They not only performed, but they knew they had to do more than just do their show to remain successful. They tried a variety of publicity stunts. After the successful "search" for Gracie's brother, Burns and Allen knew such stunts equaled high ratings. Probably the three best-known, and certainly the three most successful ones that came after Gracie's brother, involved Gracie having an art exhibition, Gracie's concert tour, and, most of all, Gracie's run for the presidency.

The first of these was undertaken in 1938, just when surrealist art was causing a stir in America. Salvador Dali and other surrealists created master-pieces that didn't seem to conform to "real" reality. They were "super" real, the products of the imagination and dreams where events were not limited by the physical laws of reality. Since surrealism didn't make sense to the general public, Burns and Allen figured that was the sort of painting Gracie could produce. And produce them she did. George then arranged for a one-woman show at the Julian Levy Gallery on East 57th Street in Manhattan. The admission price was a quarter, and all the profits were donated to the China Aid Fund.

Gracie had to come up with wacky titles, though two of the paintings mercifully remained untitled. The others included such titles as "Behind the Before Yet Under the Vast Above the World Is in Tears and Tomorrow Is Tuesday" and "Gravity Gets Body Scissor on Virtue as Night Falls Upside Down."

An expert looked them over and declared them works of art. Gracie protested, saying she had painted them herself. At a party a reporter asked if the paintings were for sale. Gracie said they were as long as he didn't charge her too much.

The exhibition lasted for three months and then toured the country, eventually reaching 50 cities. In Los Angeles, someone stole one of the paintings — but returned it the next day.

In contrast to her purported painted abilities, Gracie was, in fact, quite a gifted musician. Like Jack Benny on his violin, she was good enough to pretend to be bad. At one point, Paul Whiteman was the musical conductor on the Burns and Allen radio show. His arranger prepared what became popularly known as "The One-Finger Concerto." It worked like this. Gracie played the musical scale using her index finger solely. She would get all the notes right except for the last one. The bit continued with the orchestra playing again up to the moment of Gracie's solo. She repeated the scale and the mistake on the last note. The process was repeated until Gracie hit the correct final note. The orchestra then stood and applauded.

The bit became popular and, much to Gracie's surprise, she began to receive invitations to perform the concerto in public arenas. She played the Hollywood Bowl and several smaller venues before reaching music's pinnacle: Carnegie Hall.

What the audience never knew — even at the famed music site — was that Gracie was never playing the piano. Her musical skills were not advanced enough, so a pianist backstage did all the playing at the concerts.

Gracie Allen was not the first celebrity to make a mock run for the presidency of the United States. Eddie Cantor and Will Rogers had made satirical races for the White House. But, like much else in the Burns and

Allen comedic whirlwind, once the idea began it took on an extravagant life of its own.

The gag started simply enough. George and the writers wanted to come up with an idea of how Gracie would spend her spare time. George was discussing the problem with his writers, when one of them noted that Gracie had done just about all there was to do except run for president. George was immediately taken with the idea. While in real life the presidential election in 1940 pitted Franklin Roosevelt against his Republican challenger Wendell Wilkie, Gracie decided that she could beat both canidates. The original idea was for the "race" to last for two weeks. So Gracie appeared on the first of the shows and noted that she had been laughing at presidential candidates for years, so she decided she should run. She said she was running on the Surprise Party ticket. Her father was a Republican, she explained, and her mother a Democrat. She, though, had been born as a surprise. Her slogan was "Down with Common Sense. Vote for Gracie." Audiences liked the bit, and so the writers added it to a few more shows. Soon, just as with the missing brother gag, Gracie was visiting other programs as a surprise guest star.

Just then another publicity stunt crossed with Gracie's. To celebrate the release of a movie titled *Union Pacific*, the real railroad arranged for a festival celebrating the Old West to take place in Omaha, Nebraska. The men of Omaha had grown beards and everyone joined in the fun by wearing old western costumes. Omaha had enjoyed such success with the effort that they wished to repeat it — with Gracie. Union Pacific Railroad agreed to provide Gracie with a campaign train with the idea that she would arrive in Omaha for her convention.

George loved the idea, but Gracie didn't want to do it. She intensely disliked making speeches, and this effort called on her to make a series of train stops, starting in Los Angeles and ending in Omaha, and making a speech at each stop. Finally Gracie's sister Hazel and Mary Kelly agreed to go along, and so Gracie accepted the idea.

George soon realized a problem. Neither he nor Gracie followed politics. They didn't support candidates. They didn't make political jokes like Will Rogers. Maybe, by venturing into politics, they could alienate a large portion of their audience.

But the whole nation seemed to want Gracie to run. First Lady Eleanor Roosevelt invited Gracie to Washington. Gracie got a campaign song and "wrote" a campaign pamphlet. At her first press conference Gracie promised to solve the simmering border dispute between California and Florida. She was asked about the Neutrality Bill and demanded that we should pay if it we owed it.

The train was due to depart for her tour on May 9, 1940. On that same day in Europe, the Nazi army started its attack on Belgium and Holland. There was some talk of canceling the trip because of the seriousness of world events. But, finally, comedy would assume the same role it had when dealing with the Great Depression. The jokes helped to relieve national anxieties.

And so the tour continued. There were hairdressers and costumers to take care of the wardrobe. There were PR people and, of course, there were writers. The train reached Riverside, the first stop, and Gracie again decided she simply couldn't go through with it. Trying to calm her nerves, all her friends sat with her and George assured her that if the speech didn't go well, he'd cancel all the other speeches along the way and the train would simply go directly to Omaha. Armed with what was probably an insincere promise on George's part, Gracie stepped in front of the crowd of three thousand people. They loved her from the start. She said she wanted more women in Congress because they were the ones who really knew how to introduce bills into the house.

Thousands of people greeted Gracie at each stop. There were parades. Babies just needed to be kissed, although Gracie insisted she wanted to wait until the male babies reached 21 before she kissed them. George and the writers had to scramble after each stop to create material to be ready for the next speech.

In total there were 34 campaign stops. The audiences cumulatively were estimated to exceed a quarter of a million people.

There were 15,000 people waiting to greet her (even in a light rain) when she arrived in Omaha. NBC radio was there to broadcast her arrival speech nationally. Dan Butler, Omaha's mayor, said that she should call him Dan. Gracie refused, noting that it was not permissible to say "Dan" on the radio.

The nominating convention was held on May 17. Eight thousand cheering faus were present to support Gracie. She announced to them that she did not have a vice-presidential running mate because she did not want to have any vice on her presidential ticket. After the official nomination, 20 bearded men carried Gracie, sitting on a chair, onto the floor of the building.

After the convention's conclusion, Harvard University announced that it was endorsing her. The reaction of President Roosevelt, a Harvard alumnus, was not recorded.

On Election Day, Gracie received several thousand write-in votes. The good people of Menominee, Michigan, nominated her for mayor, but noted that she couldn't serve unless she was a resident. Gracie wrote back that she was upset that she had to be a resident to serve as mayor because she couldn't live in two places at once.

Despite the overwhelming fact that Gracie's run was satirical, there were complaints that she was mocking the highest office in the land. After the campaign, therefore, Gracie made a serious speech saying she meant no disrespect.

And while Burns and Allen generally stayed completely away from all things political, George stayed away from discussing the rise of Hitler in Europe. He developed the same emotional strategy he had used since childhood: simply ignore the bad as though it weren't there and focus on the good. That strategy had helped him first survive, and then thrive.

But there was another element at play. George was in a particular generation of American Jews who were anxious about proving they were genuine Americans. Their parents spoke primarily, sometimes exclusively, Yiddish. Many in that generation were sometimes ashamed of their parents. When young, George and his generation felt they had one foot outside American culture and one foot inside. They didn't want to be different. They wanted to be accepted. They changed their names, whether legally or not, to enter the culture. They felt uncomfortable about people who were too Jewish because those religious Jews made these Americanized Jews uncertain about their true identity.

In George's case this can be most clearly seen by a visit he made to Poland before the war in Europe broke out. As he told an interviewer for the American Jewish Committee:

> GEORGE: I went through the Jewish section. Everybody wore those alpaca suits, everybody had a beard, everybody wore a hat, and I said to myself when Hitler came in and they killed all these Jews, it was so easy to find them, it was so easy to locate them. All they had to do ... half of them would have been saved had they taken off their hats, but they died with their hats on.
> INTERVIEWER: So we do share a sense of blame by being—
> GEORGE: Too Jewish ... I think the Jews sometimes get a little too cliquey, too ... too Jewish ... If everybody was like I am—now, this might not be true, maybe I'm taking bows for nothing—I don't think we'd have the kind of problem that you have in the world today."[31]

To a post–Holocaust ear, this statement has a tinge of self-hatred, but such an analysis misses the historical context, the sort of society in which

Natty Birnbaum grew up. He saw blending in as a means to self-protection. On the other hand the ultimate blending he did — an interfaith marriage, the separation from the organized religious Jewish community, and so on — is a recipe for Jewish disappearance, not Jewish protection.

Interestingly, the same interviewer asked Burns about Israel, about whether it was important for Jewish survival that Jews be secure in their own country. The response is revealing: "Well, I think it's very important for all the Jews. Israel must survive, just like any other country must survive. It's very important to be able to have a homeland."[32]

That is, George didn't think it was in any way undermining his American identity if the Jews had Israel, where they could provide some defense. Perhaps in a national identity George saw the Jews as having an identity comparable to his own as an American. That kind of identity, as opposed to an explicitly religious one requiring specific apparel and behavior, was more acceptable. Perhaps it is no surprise that George attended Israel Bonds events and made contributions. He was generous to Israel in other ways as well.

In truth, George Burns never surrendered his Jewish identity. He exemplified the struggles, particularly of Jewish males of his generation, and found his own way. His response was not religious but some cultural and national form, even as it was very private.

But before there could be an Israel, the Jews, and the Americans, had to endure the Second World War.

Like other radio shows, the Burns and Allen Program began to incorporate news about the war into their broadcasts once America officially joined the fight after the bombing of Pearl Harbor. The writers developed a routine of ending their show with a call for sacrifice or effort on behalf of the war. George and Gracie called for audience members to buy war bonds or plant a victory garden, to save paper or similar materials. The couple also broadcast from military installations and performed at war rallies.

Gracie worked on an effort to recruit volunteers for the navy. She appeared on a show broadcast on the Armed Forces Radio network in support of those who did volunteer. And Gracie worked on other shows with other stars to help the war effort. Here is part of a sketch about rationing she did with Eddie Cantor and Jack Benny:

CANTOR: Gracie, haven't you heard that gasoline is being rationed?
GRACIE: Well of course I know gasoline is being rationed! My goodness, what do you take me for, a dunce? I've read all about it. You're only allowed one cup a day.

CANTOR: Gracie, that's coffee.

GRACIE: Eddie, don't be silly. A car won't run on coffee.

BENNY: No, no, Gracie. I don't think you understand. You see, cars run on gasoline, so at this point gasoline has to be rationed.

GRACIE: But why? There's plenty of gasoline.

CANTOR: I know, but the real reason for cutting down on the amount of gasoline we use is to save rubber.

GRACIE: Really? That's very interesting. I had no idea gasoline was made from rubber.

CANTOR: It isn't. You see —

GRACIE: I had the impression that gasoline came out of wells in the ground.

CANTOR: That's right.

GRACIE: And I've often thought how convenient it was for the filling stations that these wells were always found under the busiest street corners.

CANTOR: Jack, you try it.

BENNY: Gracie, look. What they're really rationing is mileage. The less we drive our cars the more rubber we save. And the rubber we save is vital to essential industries, and to the army.

GRACIE: The army? Uses rubber?

BENNY: Sure.

GRACIE: Gee, wouldn't you think with all the modern weapons that soldiers wouldn't have to use sling shots.[33]

Burns and Allen's popularity soared, not only because of their efforts undertaken exclusively at their own expense, but also because once again their comedy was desperately needed. They provided a momentary escape from a seemingly mad world. For a few minutes the audiences sitting in their homes could surrender their fear of losing a loved one and could just relax. Burns and Allen provided a great gift to an anxious nation.

It was not easy. Many writers were drafted. The shows had to be very careful about the raw nerves of their listeners. New characters were introduced. These included, most importantly for their future, Blanche Morton, their next-door neighbor. She was a character (played by Bea Benaderet) who would migrate with them to television. Other new characters included Tootsie Sagwell and Herman the duck.

Despite their personal success, George Burns knew the end was coming. He had witnessed the collapse of vaudeville, a form of entertainment he assumed would last his lifetime. He had been quick to try both film and radio, and learned to succeed, at least in the latter medium. He therefore carefully watched in the post-war world to see how technology was developing. He looked at television shrewdly. Most entertainers at the time assumed television was a gimmick. They thought Americans would be reluctant to give up their radios. But, as had happened so often before, the audiences were ahead of everyone else. In the 1949–1950 season, radio had given up a fifth of its audience to television. It would take a while—and Milton Berle's show, *Texaco Star Theater*—for there to be a mass exodus from radio to TV.

George Burns was no fool. He loved radio as he had loved vaudeville, but he was hardly ready to stay on a sinking ship. He had developed a lifestyle and a circle of friends. And keeping his world intact meant staying on top of the entertainment world. That meant taking a hard look at moving to the new medium.

The world he loved outside performing revolved around a small number of matters: parties, friends, events, and his club.

George and Gracie liked to attend and give parties. The small parties consisted of playing cards, business chat, or watching movies. Scrabble was popular at such parties, but George didn't much like it. Big parties were often held in tents in the back yard. One of George's biggest problems with parties had to do with arriving on time. Trained in vaudeville, he and Gracie often arrived early. In Hollywood, late was characteristically early, so they were considered to be very early.

George liked parties. He liked the schmoozing. He liked the entertaining; he could sing when he gave parties. He liked industry gossip. And always he liked the recognition he received as a star, the recognition that was a bottomless need. For Gracie, though, parties were a burden. She didn't care at all about the business. She was exhausted by the social requirements of chatting and often returned from a party with a migraine headache.

Of course, as celebrities, George and Gracie were invited out to a lot of dinners. They got a chance to dine with people they admired, although sometimes the evening turned out to be a disappointment. Charlie Chaplin, though laughing politely at the right moments, was not very funny at dinner. And neither was Al Capone. The gangster issued an invitation to George and Gracie, Eddie Cantor, and George Jessel, among others, to come to his house for dinner. They all decided it would be a prudent move to accept his invitation. After the dinner, he asked if anyone wished to entertain. They all raised their hands. No one wanted to turn down Capone's gentle request.

George had many friends.

Eddie Cantor had given George and Gracie their start in radio and had constantly been supportive. Eddie came from the same scrappy Lower East Side Jewish background as George, so the two knew each other at a deeper level than most show business acquaintanceships. Cantor had boundless energy. George wasn't quite sure about the nature of his talent, but audiences loved his pep, his pop eyes, his stories and songs. Cantor was known for being especially tough on writers. George yelled at his writers as well. All the stars were nervous. They couldn't take their nerves out on their spouses without serious consequences, so all the anxiety was unloaded on the poor writers. Ed Wynn and Milton Berle were also challenging for writers. Only Jack Benny was constantly kind to writers, often awed at their ability to come up with great lines. And like all the others, Cantor relied on his joke file.

George liked George Jessel and Al Jolson as well, even though these two were bitter rivals since Jolson had gotten the part Jessel thought he deserved in the groundbreaking film version of *The Jazz Singer*. George had a way with friends. Jolson, for example, was, to put it kindly, not a kind competitor. When someone else was onstage, George claimed that Jolson sometimes ran the water in his dressing room so he wouldn't hear the laughter and applause. He was widely accused of stealing jokes he liked and threatening the original joke teller, saying it was his original material. But George thought, for good reason, that Al Jolson was the greatest entertainer who ever lived. So they got along. And George liked his old friends from vaudeville, including those whose fame had evaporated in show business history, people like Blossom Seeley and Benny Fields.

George and Gracie were also friends with Ronald Reagan and his then-wife, Jane Wyman. The attachment was close enough so that for the single time in her career when Gracie's migraine headaches were so severe she was unable to perform on the radio, George asked Jane Wyman to fill in that evening.

Most of George's friends in show business were glad to be offstage. They didn't want to dress up in costumes. Some didn't want to perform. Others, like Milton Berle and Phil Silvers, were so reflexively funny that they were always "on." They needed to perform, for an audience, at a party, or even for a cab driver.

In Hollywood, George and many of his comedian friends met for lunch at the Hillcrest Golf and Country Club. Entertainers had joined together to form the Friars Club in New York City. The comedians, actors, and singers needed privacy from adoring fans. They needed a place where they could be themselves. They wanted to be around people who understood them, people who had gone through, were going through, or would eventually go through exactly the sorts of problems they were encountering. Jewish entertainers had a special problem. Gentile social clubs frequently excluded them. Hillcrest was meant as a Jewish alternative, a place where Jews could go.

And so the comedians began to meet at a table at Hillcrest. It was a West Coast version of the Algonquin Club in New York. Harpo Marx was the connection; he frequented both settings. In the Men's Grill at Hillcrest there was a large, round table that would seat 12 people. There, at around noon each day, the comedians would gather. Frequent participants included George, Jack Benny, Al Jolson, Eddie Cantor, George Jessel, the Marx Brothers, the Ritz Brothers, Danny Kaye, Milton Berle, Lou Holtz, and Danny Thomas (who was not Jewish). The comedians struggled to get the next joke into the conversation. They kibitzed about which shows were doing well, what parts were becoming available, as well as the tortures imposed by critics and fans and audiences. They made a point of listening to one another's programs. They wouldn't say they didn't like a program, but in the very act of avoiding a discussion of it, the star of the program got the message of disapproval.

George prided himself on getting along with other performers, as he had his whole life, but he did have a mental list of people he didn't like. For that matter, so did Gracie. She especially didn't like the actress Myrna Loy, who interrupted her at a party given by William Randolph Hearst.

The comedian Frank Fay was also on her list, but more for his treatment of George. As George recalled, "We were headlining a bill with him, and at the end of the show, the three of us came onstage to take a final bow. I was standing between them, and Fay made several complimentary remarks about Gracie's talent, but then, as both of them leaned forward right in front of me, he said in an exaggerated stage whisper, 'But where'd you find the man?'"[34]

But, despite George's attempts to be nice, a rivalry developed between him and Groucho Marx, one that had sharp edges. Groucho had at one time dated Gracie. That might have been part of the problem. Later in their lives, during one season on television, Burns and Allen would be opposite Groucho's hit show, *You Bet Your Life*. But the heart of the rivalry rested on Groucho's perception of himself as the world's greatest comedian. George thought Chaplin was the greatest comedian — at least onscreen. Groucho got so mad at this that for a while he didn't talk to George. Groucho couldn't stop himself from trying to top everyone else's line. At one point, Groucho started to play tennis at the Beverly Hills Tennis Club instead of Hillcrest, so the people who ran Hillcrest asked Groucho to send a formal letter of resignation. That prompted one of the famous letters in show business. Groucho wrote the letter saying he was resigning because "I don't want to belong to any club that would have me as a member."[35]

The most famous George-Groucho dispute while Groucho was at Hill-crest involved, of all matters, fish. One day George, who liked fish, ordered sea bass for lunch. Groucho invoked a Sophie Tucker song titled "If You Can't See Mama Every Night, You Can't See Mama at All" and at the table said a variation of the line involving sea bass. It wasn't perhaps a classic Groucho line, but people at the people laughed politely. But George liked the sea bass, and every time he ordered it, Groucho would annoyingly repeat the line to George. This went on for many years. At one point when they weren't talking, George used to order the sea bass just to glare at Groucho who, unwilling to speak, was not able to offer his standard line. Another time, when they were talking, George thought he could fool Groucho. George indicated for the waiter to bend over and in a whisper ordered the sea bass. Unfortunately for

George Burns had many close friends in the entertainment business, but Groucho Marx was not among them. Perhaps the animosity started because Groucho had dated Gracie before she married George. Whatever the reason, George and Groucho argued about comedy and much else. Here's Groucho with Margaret Dumont in *At the Circus* (MGM, 1939).

George, the waiter had heard Groucho's response so often that he felt compelled to repeat it to George.

George and Groucho remained friends, but the friendship was a cool one.

Of all of George's friends, Jack Benny was, without doubt, the one he felt closest to, the one who deserved the title of "best friend."

Jack Benny made a career out of a few well-defined supposed characteristics. His persona was that of being the world's cheapest man, perpetually 39, and a terrible violin player. Combined with brilliant jokes, utter courage in allowing for extended silences, and razor-sharp timing, Benny became extraordinarily popular. Everyone knew him. Asked to throw out the ball at a World Series game, Benny stood up, held the ball, and then put it in his pocket and sat down. The crowd roared. Once he approached the White House gate, carrying his violin case. The marine guard stationed at the

George and Gracie adopted two children, Sandra and Ronnie, and raised them as Catholics. George, who remained Jewish, was pleased that Gracie could bring up the children in her religion. Here is the family setting off in August 1938 for a three-week vacation in Hawaii. (Wide World Photos).

entrance stopped him and asked what was in the case. Joking as usual, Benny responded that it was a machine gun. The marine smiled, and responded, "You can pass then. For a minute I thought it was your violin."[36]

Jack and George were justly famous in Hollywood for their friendship. At the heart of it was that Jack thought George was the funniest man who ever lived. George could do something that to an outsider, might seem trivial, but to Jack it was hysterical. In a characteristic move, Jack would laugh so hard that he would collapse onto the floor and begin pounding it. Having such an advantage, George used to provoke such reactions when the two were in public. George didn't tell jokes. It was the ad-libs combined with the two men's sense of closeness that made Jack laugh. For him, George was a laugh prompt. Once at dinner, for example, he just started laughing, seemingly for no reason at all. George wanted to know why his friend was laughing. After all, George hadn't uttered a word. Jack said, "I know. But you didn't say it on purpose."[37]

At another time, at Hillcrest, Jack said to George, "I didn't sleep at all last night."

George responded, "How did you sleep the night before?"

"Oh, the night before I slept great."

"Good," George said, "Then try sleeping every other night."[38]

At a Jeanette MacDonald recital, George warned Jack not to laugh. No sooner did Jeanette open her mouth than Jack became hysterical and they had to leave. At the fights, George handed Jack a drink and told him to pass it down the line. Only when the last person in the row started to return it did Jack realize that no one had ordered it. If George was driving and spotted Jack, George would stop the car, roll down the window and signal his friend to come over. When Jack reached the car George would roll the window back up and drive away. Jack was such a sucker for the joke that George used it on him eight times. Famously, George always hung up on Jack mid-sentence when they spoke on the phone. At a party he gave, Jack complained that the event was dull. George suggested he go upstairs, take off his pants, put on one of Mary's hats, and walk back down the stairs playing the violin. When Jack was upstairs, George told the 150 guests exactly what was going to happen and that they should ignore Jack. Jack was astonished by the lack of reponse, but soon realized what happened, and began pounding the floor again.

They constantly joked with each other. Once Jack came into George's hotel room after sending a telegram that he would arrive there. He found George — naked, standing on the bed, holding the telegram. When George sent a similar telegram, Jack was ready. He, too, was naked, standing on a bed, and wearing a lampshade over his head. George sent in the maid.

While George and Gracie adored Jack, they did their best to put up with his wife, Mary Livingstone. George thought Mary was jealous and insecure about being Jack Benny's wife. She had, after all, been a sales clerk at the May Company in Los Angeles when the two met, not some vaudeville star. They married not long after George and Gracie. George was convinced that Jack simply wanted to pair off as his friends had done. Mary's jealousy came out in her desire to have whatever Gracie had. Gracie didn't like that at all, but was willing to tolerate it for the sake of Jack Benny. But Mary could never have all that Gracie had, because Gracie was a nationally beloved star. Mary was not and could never be. She didn't have very much talent. Gracie sometimes had fainting spells, and people always rushed to help her. Whether faked or not, Mary then fainted.

George and Gracie had a good life, filled with family and friends and laughs. But they weren't lazy. They knew only hard, constant work, including the publicity which kept them in the public eye. And they knew that history never stood still.

World War II ended, and with its successful conclusion came a new America. The sweet, restrained landscape of radio comedy no longer worked, especially for younger audiences. And technology kept moving forward. Television was about to conquer American entertainment.

Looking back at the incredible radio career of Burns and Allen is not easy. The era called for a completely different humor than today's audiences demand. For all the quick repartee, the ingenious writing, Gracie's utterly disarming character, and the other elements that made them famous, their show was excellent but not ground-breaking. Jack Benny's program, on the other hand, changed the landscape of comedy. He developed the format for situation comedy with a larger, more complex cast.

The relationship between George and Gracie — the warmth, the tolerance of the eccentricities found in George, the acceptance of the determined logic found in Gracie — carried them across the decades in entertainment. They weren't just funny. That would not have been enough. Audiences had to find them endearing otherwise they would not have been repeatedly invited back into their living rooms each week to hear more of their loony interplay.

It's not clear that audiences fully understood the psychological gifts that Gracie was giving them. She did not obey the rules of her husband's linguistic world. Her rebellion as a woman fit perfectly into the era's rising sense that women should be, and could be, independent. Gracie's great success was that, in disobeying George's rules, she wasn't confrontational. She was funny. She gave women permission to be rebellious and demonstrated a tactic that engendered sympathy and comfort, not confrontation and hate.

But as the radio career of Burns and Allen was reaching its natural end, they found a way to migrate seamlessly into the newly emerging medium of television. George Burns was never a quitter. Through good times and bad, he would not stop. He even developed a joke about it: "If I get a laugh, I'm a comedian. If I get a small laugh, I'm a humorist. If I get no laughs, I'm a singer. If my singing gets big laughs, then I'm a comedian again."[39]

CHAPTER FIVE

Burns and Allen and the Magic Box

The stars of radio, including Burns and Allen, didn't worry at first about television. Radio was so popular, they concluded, and the new invention was so small and grainy that it posed no serious challenge. And radio was so convenient for actors. They were used to reading their scripts on air even though George was rare for memorizing them. But they all knew that on television they would have to learn the scripts. For someone with long, complex lines, someone like Gracie, the prospect was not a pleasant one. The idea of doing a weekly show — planning it, writing it, memorizing it, rehearsing it, and then performing in it — seemed utterly impossible.

But a few years after the war, television screens grew. Now the viewer could see the picture. And the picture was clearer. It all happened so fast that radio performers were astonished. People gathered in friends' houses or in bars or in front of stores to watch the new and dazzling invention. George, ever sensitive to audiences, knew the inevitable was coming. He had jumped from vaudeville to film and radio as vaudeville was fading. The team's film career was over, so that was no longer an option. It was time to jump from radio to television.

George gently approached Gracie with the idea. She was appalled. Learn the lines? Dress up? Impossible. She said she would not do it. George knew his wife. He knew he had to proceed carefully. So he told her the truth: television was a permanent new medium. He asked her to make one test, and he said that if she didn't like it they wouldn't do a television program. Although she was, as always, reluctant, Gracie agreed. She realized the unspoken truth. If she didn't go ahead, George couldn't, either. It was widely assumed by just about everyone in show business that the audience was only interested in Gracie. Yes, George was a great straight man, a brilliant guy behind the scenes.

But Gracie was the money. Gracie knew she would be perfectly content in retirement, focusing on her family and friends. George, though, still had an aching desire to perform. He could not leave show business. Gracie, no doubt, was concerned about what would happen to him if his career faded. But she also had another thought. In his mid-fifties, George was not used to the physical strains required by television. Because radio was so simple for performers, the sheer physicality television needed could be difficult. But, despite all her concerns, Gracie knew what George needed. And so, as she always had done before, Gracie agreed to George's request.

With the decision made, George had to find a format for the show. His only solace was that every radio performer had the same problem. All they had been doing for a decade or more was standing at the microphone speaking lines. That was not going to be possible on a visual medium.

But whatever problems he faced, George had a magic potion named Gracie Allen. The audience wanted Gracie. They knew her character. They knew his character. In the movies, Gracie played characters. She didn't play the same character from film to film in the way she did on the radio. Gracie, it was clear, shouldn't be "Grace Smith" or some other character that's a bit daffy. She needed to be Gracie Allen, wife of George Burns. The problem, then, wasn't in coming up with new characters; it was, rather, to provide an appropriate transition of the characters from one medium to another.

George had seen a production of Thornton Wilder's great play *Our Town*. In that play the Stage Manager speaks directly to the audience all the while commenting on the action. George liked the idea. He spent a week with his writers discussing all his options, and they all agreed on the simplest one: George and Gracie would be a married couple living at home. Gracie would get into trouble. And George would both talk to the audience and go back into the story.

George met with William S. Paley, CBS's chairman, and eagerly described the show. Paley said, "George, I understand you make a lot of speeches at stag dinners. Why couldn't you do a little monologue on the show?"[1]

That's when George knew he could introduce to Paley the novel idea of breaking the fourth wall and speaking directly to the viewers at home. Paley agreed.

Ralph Levy was hired as a director. The pilot was made and bought by the Carnation Company. More importantly, Gracie was pleased with the pilot and agreed to make the show. Later, the B. F. Goodrich Rubber Company joined Carnation and came on as a co-sponsor. For two years Burns and Allen did a live show every other week, but starting in the third year they put the show on film and performed weekly. Although it much harder to produce a high-quality show every week, George Burns knew audiences. A show every two weeks gave audiences a time to forget to watch, an emotional distance from the characters. In contrast, a weekly show became a habit with just enough time away to allow for the growth of anticipation to see what Gracie would do next.

On May 17, 1950, Burns and Allen broadcast their final radio program. It had been a long and extraordinary run. But show business was a cruel business. Just because they had been successful in vaudeville didn't guarantee they would make it in radio. And just because they had been radio stars didn't guarantee they'd make it in television. Just ask Fred Allen, a major radio star, who couldn't succeed on television. It was a huge challenge.

Starting in the summer of 1950, George and Gracie stayed at the Algonquin Hotel in New York to prepare for their program. They aired their first live show from the Mansfield Theater in New York at 8 P.M. on October 12, 1950. The Mansfield was not far from the Palace, the site that symbolized the start of their great success in vaudeville. Perhaps they hoped the proximity would bring them luck.

As the show opens, George is standing by himself in one corner of the stage. He begins with a monologue and an introduction, delivered while he holds his trademark cigar:

> Hello, everybody. I'm George Burns, better known as Gracie Allen's husband ... I've been a straight man for so many years that from habit I repeat everything. I went fishing with a fellow the other day and he fell overboard. He yelled, "Help! Help!" so I said, "Help? Help?" And while I was waiting for him to get his laugh he drowned.[2]

After the monologue, the curtain parts — like in a play or a vaudeville show — and the audience can see the set. The show takes place in a suburban home. There is a small living room and a kitchen. The living room has a large, rock fireplace. What looks like a cloth used for picnics is on the kitchen table. There are many chairs, presumably to let visitors have the option of sitting or standing as the plot requires. The windows look out on trees in the backyard. George uses a simple device. When he is taking part in the show itself and wants to leave to talk to the audience, he steps over some bricks. When he is outside (but still in the show), he uses the front door as his narrative base.

Originally, the house in the show had no TV set. After all, in 1950, television sets were hardly universal. Gracie helped design the living room in the set's house.

Besides George and Gracie, the cast included Bill Goodwin as the announcer, and Bea Benaderet and Hal March as the neighbors, Blanche and Harry Morton.

Benaderet had a long career in radio. She had played Millicent Carstairs in *Fibber McGee & Molly*; Gertrude Gearshift, the telephone operator (among other characters for Jack Benny); and had appeared on many other programs. Most importantly, she had played Blanche Morton on the Burns and Allen radio show. Audiences were familiar with her voice, and the cast, writers, and crew found her easy to work with. Hal March had been part of a comedy team called Sweeney and March.

The shows were organized around a plot problem. With so strong a character as Gracie, George didn't feel the need for guest stars, so the writers instead focused on problems that Gracie could get into. The early shows would mimick radio by having a musical number interrupt the story. In the first show, for example, Gracie and Blanche are fighting with their husbands about where to go out for the evening. The women want to attend a movie; George and Harry think the fights would be more interesting. George decides to make Gracie angry so the women will go to the movies alone; he sets up a card game thinking Gracie won't be able to play, and, feeling frustrated, she and Blanche will go to the movies unaccompanied.

Instead of interrupting this story line for a commercial, Burns and Allen integrate the advertisement directly into the show. The announcer, Bill Goodwin, rushes into the living room looking upset. He relates a harrowing incident while flying his plane. He put in a call to the air traffic control tower to ask if they used Carnation Evaporated Milk because, he claimed, whenever a microphone was in front of him, all he could think of talking about was the sponsor's product. When Goodwin finishes, he makes a mistake. He starts to leave the set not by the front door through which he had entered, but over a ledge on the set's front. George stops him and tells him to leave the same way he came in, telling the audience he wants to keep it all realistic.

Naturally, the writers had to establish Gracie's identity in this first show. But they faced a fundamental problem. It was clearly going to be difficult if they had to establish her character in a way that was tied to the particular plot point in the script. Instead, they exemplified Gracie's surreal point of view by having her logic used in ways that often were irrelevant to the story.

Audiences didn't mind at all. The stories were not intricate or brilliant. They were serviceable. What audiences wanted were generous samplings of Gracie's mind at work. To expedite this, the writers simply ignored the story. For example, in that first episode an encyclopedia salesman makes the mistake of trying to sell a set to Gracie:

> SALESMAN (pointing to a picture of George): These books would make a wonderful birthday present for your father here.
> GRACIE: That's not my father. That's my husband.
> SALESMAN: Oh, forgive me.
> GRACIE: Oh, my father wouldn't mind, although he's a much younger man.
> SALESMAN: Younger than your husband?
> GRACIE: Yes, when I met George he was 30. But when I met my father he was only 24.[3]

When the story line continues, it turns out that Gracie intuitively grasps this card game immediately, wins, and the women end up at the movies with their husbands.

At the story's conclusion, George and Gracie step in front of the closed curtain. They are holding hands. George turns to her and says, "Say good night, Gracie." She does.

It is a common error, understandable given her character, to believe that her response was "Good night, Gracie." But the real response is a simple and demure "Good night."

The critics were all generous. Most of them admitted that the lines, in themselves, were corny, that is, without the benefit of Gracie delivering them. In this post-war America the same kind of bland jokes that had been accepted by pre-war audiences were beginning to sound dated. But Gracie saved every joke. John Crosby of the *New York Herald Tribune* had the most interesting comment. He thought George talked too much. That was fine on radio, when talk was all there was, but television was a visual medium and Crosby didn't think George had taken adequate advantage of—a euphemism for not understanding—how television could work. But the ever-loyal Burns and Allen radio audiences, as well as their new fans, were not thinking about the subtleties of television. They wanted their weekly dose of Gracie.

The operation worked smoothly and well. There were some cast alterations. The popular radio announcer Harry Von Zell replaced Bill Goodwin. George and Gracie's son, Ronnie, suddenly popped up on the program as an already-grown 18-year-old. Ronnie injected youth into the show and was an attraction, especially for young women. His role in the show frequently involved his covering for Gracie. Here's a typical exchange between Ronnie and George. Ronnie is in his room studying when George enters:

RONNIE: Hello, Dad. What brings you here?
GEORGE: Just visiting.
RONNIE: That's nice ... Er, anything you want to talk to me about?
GEORGE: Just visiting.
RONNIE: If it's about the dent in the fender, I did it when I hit the avocado tree this morning.
GEORGE: Just visiting.
RONNIE: If it's about your new blue suit that's missing, well Mother didn't send it to Uncle Harvey, I did. Is that it?
GEORGE: Just visiting.
RONNIE: If it's about your electric razor, I'm the one who peeled the potatoes with it. Just visiting?
GEORGE: Mmmmmmmmm.
RONNIE: If it's about the Mortons' car, it was my idea to drive Mother downtown in it this morning.
GEORGE: End of visit.[4]

Besides Ronnie, the biggest cast change involved the character of Harry Morton. No fewer than four actors played the part. They included (in addition to Hal March) John Brown, Fred Clark, and Larry Keating. George had learned a lot from his radio experience of simply announcing to the audience that he and Gracie were now married. For example, when Fred Clark left the show and was replaced by Larry Keating, George made a comparable introduction. In that case, Blanche was waiting to hit Harry over the head with a telephone book. George walked into the scene, explained to the audience that Clark had left the show and introduced the new "Harry." Then he introduced Larry Keating to Bea Benaderet. The two actors bowed, George said the show should continue, and it did. Bea hit Larry Keating over the head with the phone book.

George kept the show in New York for the first six episodes. In those days, New York was the national media center for television, and a show got much more publicity if it was made in New York than in Hollywood. But the cast and crew missed the warmth and the familiar surroundings of their California homes. They yearned to head back west. The live performances in New York also led to another problem. A 16mm camera was set up in front of a monitor displaying their live show. This produced a kinescope of the program. Copies of that kinescope were then shipped to California to be shown two weeks after the live show. In addition to the poor quality of the reproduction, East-Coast comedians could hear the lines and use them before the show aired on the West Coast. This infuriated George who demanded that such behavior end. But the theft of jokes, hardly an uncommon practice, was another incentive to return to California.

The writers knew their work was hard. Gracie's lines were demanding. The writers started by meeting in one of the Algonquin's suites and trying to find a premise for the show, some one-sentence idea on which to base the script. Once they agreed on that premise, they divided up the work. George liked to work on his own monologue, often getting help from his brother Willy. The other writers worked on the dialogue. This was followed by a reading of the entire script. That was the time when bad lines stuck out, when George was known to raise his voice now and then. Writers had hard jobs, he knew, but he and Gracie were the ones in front of the cameras. Audiences didn't blame writers for bad lines — they just didn't laugh. And after enough experiences of not laughing, they would stop watching the program.

By the end of December 1950, the show (and the happy cast) returned to the West Coast. They now broadcast at CBS Studios in Hollywood, and from then on it was New York that would have to wait for the two weeks to see the show. This situation lasted until the October 11, 1951 show which was the first broadcast on a coaxial cable, so that the entire country could see the show at the same time.

This was a great technological advance, of course, but it had the effect of multiplying the pressure on the actors. They responded as the professionals they were. Gracie, especially, never flubbed a line, an incredible achievement for a complex, weekly script she had to learn and perform in front of a mass national audience. Additionally, they performed the show live, as though it were a play. Perhaps this helped the actors forget about the people outside the theater. And most actors thrived on immediate laughter and approval. At first, it seemed like a good idea to have the show's dress rehearsal, done a day before the show, in front of a different audience. But hearing the rehearsal audience made the actors expect to have the same reaction to the same jokes for the same amount of time at the real show. That didn't happen. Rehearsal audiences invariably reacted differently; no two audiences are ever quite the same. To avoid such confusion, the show simply stopped using rehearsal audiences.

Beyond the pressure of recalling each line perfectly, moving correctly and carefully so as not to trip or knock over some piece of the set, the actors had to be precise in their timing. The show could not go over its allotted time limit. This was an incredible task. Because the actors were never quite sure how the audience would react, they had to constantly adjust to keep within the time limits. Ultimately, George — ever the straight man — had to control the end of the show. A stage manager stood nearby telling George how much time was left. George had jokes that varied in length, and he simply adapted as needed. When there was no time, he just said a quick good-night. He made it look a lot easier than it was.

The Burns and Allen show was a mirror of sorts. Like any other successful piece of the mass media, it both represented and symbolized what was going on in the wider culture.

Post-war Americans were tired of restraint. They, after all, had lived through the Great Depression and a horrific war. From 1929 until 1945 Americans had to surrender their sense of self. They had to accept less, dream smaller dreams, restrain their desires, live in fear of death overseas and hunger and poverty at home. After the war, they wanted change. They wanted an economic and a psychological liberation at home just as there had been a political liberation of Europe.

The veterans came home. They got married, and they started families right away. They got jobs or went to college and got training. The dawn of the Baby Boomers led to a need for new houses. Desperate to raise their children away from the dusty, crime-ridden, crowded urban streets, the parents of the Baby Boomers used their G.I. loans to buy houses outside of cities in the suburbs. And when the houses were built, the new homeowners needed roads and gas stations to get to work. They needed furniture, refrigerators, and stoves. And they increasingly felt they needed a new product, that technological marvel, that magic box known as television. In the beginning of television's assault on American culture, people were unsure about the new medium. They loved the idea of pictures and sounds being delivered for free. In theory, television was radio with pictures — an awe-inspiring possibility. But televisions were relatively scarce at first, and in order to see this new advice people went to bars, to friends' homes, or they stood in front of windows of stores that sold them. In 1950, 9 percent of American homes had televisions. By 1955, 64.5 percent had a set. As these numbers show, it didn't take long for television to conquer the family home.

The American belief in families seemed to fit perfectly with television. Tired fathers could come home and get free entertainment without rising from their chair. Children could be amused. Some parents began to use television as an electronic babysitter. There were few channels, and families were forced to gather together to watch programs, thereby uniting the family in the evening — even if artificially and temporarily.

For a while, it must have seemed as though the families were creating a Dream America, a perfect place to raise a perfect family. There were situation comedies to reflect that, including *Ozzie and Harriet, Father Knows Best,* and *Leave It to Beaver.*

But suburban life had its darker side. Women, used to freedom during the war, suddenly found themselves at home during the day without a car and far from the activity they came to know. They were trapped in velvet prisons. They focused on their 2.1 children, but neither their spouses nor their children were delighted with this new suburban paradise. The husbands were grouchy and tired, under enormous economic strain to pay for the car, the new house, and all that went with it. No one wanted to slide backwards on the economic scale. The children were bored, trapped in neighborhoods with no escapes.

The touches of revolt against suburban life began to creep in. Language was part of that revolt. Gracie fit in so well because she was part of that need for linguistic liberation. But she didn't challenge the limits of the language. That would be for comedians like Lenny Bruce to do. Gracie continued utilizing her radio personality, one of soft revolution. And that is exactly what television sponsors wanted: clean, wholesome, inoffensive material that somehow would appeal to a mass audience. And convincing product endorsements, either in separate commercials or embedded in the shows themselves, endorsements that would lead viewers to buy products.

In a way, Burns and Allen fit well with the family shows, with their nice suburban home with a pool, no less (not a real one, it was faked on the show). But Burns and Allen had no young children. And audiences seemed either to not notice or to not care that George and Gracie very rarely kissed on the program. Father hardly knew best. Burns and Allen were, that is, in their own television universe.

That universe depended on Gracie's unique interpretation of reality. Her view might be seen as being only loosely tethered to the real world, or as a child's view. Many viewers might have been uncomfortable if they thought Gracie was psychotic or neurotic. But Gracie was endearing. As George noted about her, "She is completely earnest about what she is doing and saying, and I think it is the fact that she is so kind to the rest of the world for its lack of understanding of what is perfectly clear to her that makes people love her. She is right and everybody else is wrong, but she doesn't blame them — she just gently tries to explain to them, patiently, and puts up with everybody."[5]

That's an important insight, but it doesn't explain why the audience tol-

erates, and loves, her interpretation. In any other adult, such behavior would
have been considered inappropriate. But if Gracie were seen as someone who
needed to be protected, someone encased in a permanent child's mind, audiences would be charmed by the character.

There is a sociological question, however, that remains. Why did audiences want an adult character with a child's mind? And Gracie, by the way,
was hardly alone. After all, Jerry Lewis had been extremely popular after the
war. And on radio, Fanny Brice's Baby Snooks was a popular character. She
was an adult who literally played the part of a child. Lou Costello was a childlike comedian.

During the Great Depression, audiences felt challenged, diminished as
wage-earners, even as human beings. They needed to escape, and part of that
escape included receding into a childlike past. After the war, they needed the
liberation discussed above. Having had to act like responsible adults for so
long, even with their occasional and desperate need to escape temporarily,
after the war they wanted to vent emotionally. It took a while for such an attitude to work its way through the culture, but Gracie fit that need.

The writers were clever. They could even rely on audiences to almost
read the literalness of Gracie's mind. On one show, for example, Gracie has
visited her mother in San Francisco and is on the train going home. She chats
with other passengers, a Mr. Garland and a Mr. Lindstrom:

> MR. GARLAND: Yeah, it's going to be great, sitting in my own easy chair with
> my dog at my feet, reading my paper and smoking my pipe.
> (*Everyone waits for Gracie to say something, but she doesn't.*)
> MR. LINDSTROM: Mrs. Burns — aren't you going to ask him why he lets his dog
> smoke his pipe?
> GRACIE: Of course not. If his dog is smart enough to read the newspaper, why
> shouldn't he smoke the pipe?[6]

Part of Gracie's charm was her utter innocence. She wouldn't hurt anyone.
She intends no harm. She wanders though the world without a clue. She's
like some innocent lamb that stops to rest on some railroad tracks. Here,
again, it is instructive to consider Gracie's social appeal. Economic deprivation
and war had combined to take away much American innocence. Soon much
more would be taken away — Hugh Hefner produced the first issue of *Playboy*
in 1953, and the birth control pill was approved in the United States in 1960.
But even as the world was changing slowly in the 1950s, there was a sense of
a lost Eden. Perhaps the rush to suburbia was, in part, an attempt to recapture
it. People felt different.

George and Gracie came from the past. Even without vaudeville, Burns and Allen continued to be a talking act. They were, in different guises, vaudeville performers for their entire careers. They adapted well, but their material would not have lasted into the 1960s. For the 1950s, though, they were perfect. Gracie was the audience's more innocent self, even their better self. As such, Gracie was an atypical comedian. The usual comedian tells a joke and we laugh at it. Sometimes we laugh at a character. But that's not the nature of the laughter surrounding Gracie. It's a laughter encased in a protective cover, as though the laugh itself was fragile. When we smile at a child's cute saying, we're laughing with the child, never at him or her. The laugh comes from the inherent cuteness of the statement combined with our caring about the child. That's how audiences felt about Gracie.

Sometimes writers used other characters to describe Gracie. They couldn't use George, who had evolved from his early radio and movie character when Gracie's behavior exasperated him, to a gentler, understanding nature. So the writers might, for instance, use someone associated with the nature of Gracie's mental mishaps. Take the case of Vanderlip, the banker, who is speaking to George:

VANDERLIP: Tell Mrs. Burns a check is intended only as a means of transferring money from one person to another. Not recipes and song lyrics, the latest gossip or ten-day diets.
GEORGE: She writes all that on her checks?
VANDERLIP: Not only that, she signs them "Guess who?"[7]

Gracie is good with household chores. She puts salt in the pepper shaker and pepper in the salt shaker so that people who are always mixing them up will be right. She makes out her laundry list after the laundry is returned from the cleaner, and in that way she never loses any clothing. She calls the operator and asks her to put all the day's calls through at that moment because Gracie is working near the phone.

These innocent, childlike behaviors were also grounded in gender stereotypes. Women were idealized as innocent, zany, incompetent at male tasks. It might then be thought that Gracie put a brake on an accelerating notion of women's desire for independence. But the situation was more complicated. Women were testing out new roles, and Gracie provided an unusual role model for them. As Patricia Mellencamp has noted,

Garbed in dressy fifties fashion, set in an upper-middle-class milieu of dens, patios, and two-car garages, constantly arranging flowers or making and serving coffee but not sense, Gracie equivocally escaped order. Despite being burdened by all the clichés applied to women — childlike, illogical, crazy, nonsensical, with their own peculiar bio-logic and patronized (and infantilized) accordingly — in certain ways, she was out of (or beyond) men's control. Unlike the ever-loyal and bewildered Harry Von Zell, this series and the story's announcer, and other characters in the narrative sketches, neither she nor her neighbor and best friend Blanche (who loved and understood Gracie) revered George or was intimidated by his cleverness; in fact, Gracie rarely paid attention to him or any authority figure. She unmade decorum, she unraveled patriarchal laws.[8]

It was on television that, given the long history of the character, Gracie's humor became complete. Television was, after all, a visual medium. As much as Gracie hated the demands it made, TV, by definition, forced her and the writers to go beyond the confines of radio. Gracie's voice had to be perfectly complemented by her appearance, as did George's. The house had to look like the house Gracie would live in and decorate.

And the humor had to be precise. Gracie's stories developed as comments on other stories or as the driving story itself. The side stories relied on the tried-and-true Burns and Allen routines, frequently about Gracie's relatives, who — in a bow to radio's gift of forcing audiences to employ their imaginative powers — never appeared onscreen. The stories that drove the narrative were of a different type. They depended on the interrelationship of Gracie's perception of reality and reality itself. She would claim an event to be true, and the show was about the very claim, which inevitably was true in its own way. Gracie's perceptions, that is, were a finer guide to ultimate reality than the sensibilities of the more "realistic" characters or the seeming reality we experience.

Consider the classic episode involving Gracie's accident:

GRACIE: Thanks for driving me home, Dave.

DAVE: As long as I towed your car in, I didn't mind at all, Mrs. Burns.

GRACIE: There's some coffee on the stove. Would you like some?...

DAVE: I've been wondering, Mrs. Burns. How are you going to explain this little repair job to your husband?

GRACIE: I'll just tell him what happened. I went shopping and bought a blouse and on my way home I stopped to watch them put up the tents and this elephant came along and sat on my fender and smashed it.

DAVE: He'll never believe it.

GRACIE: Of course he will. He knows a fender isn't strong enough to hold up an elephant. George is smarter than you think he is.[9]

Gracie has the new blouse to prove she went shopping. With this premise, the episode expands on the story as Gracie tells it to Blanche, who in turn tells it to Harry. Gracie keeps repeating the story to different characters.

George is around, as the ironic and detached narrator, to comment on the scenes. For example, he notes of marriage: "Married people don't have to lie to each other. We've got lawyers and friends to do that for us."[10]

The show concludes with a scene in a courtroom with everyone agreeing on Gracie's story. George was just not going to win that argument over reality, and neither was anyone else. Gracie's vision was the one that triumphed. Her ability to recalibrate reality to her needs, combined with her literal comprehension of language and utter confusion that others didn't take language in a similarly literal vein, made Gracie a force of nature and a vital character. Many listeners just assumed that they liked her because she was cute and funny. But Gracie's power, as seen in this episode, lay precisely in her ability to remake reality in her own image, a magic power audience members no doubt wish they had. This power may also be interpreted as a wife's power over her husband at a time when men controlled money and much else in the marital union. Gracie offered a mighty weapon to the women in the audience. And it was a weapon wielded with success week after week, with never an exception. Gracie always triumphed. Gracie's version of reality prevailed.

But her triumph was deceptive. George always understood it. He accepted it. What audiences may have missed is that Gracie's reality was accepted because George allowed it to be accepted. The triumph of the woman in the marriage still was dependent on the man who had ultimate control. George let Gracie's reality win. George was really in control. He could talk to the audience at home when other cast members couldn't. He could see all that was going on, while other characters were limited in their view by direct experience. He offers winks and nods and wry smiles to show that he's the showman, the ringmaster. Gracie may be in the center ring, but if he wanted, George could change the show. The simplest illustration of this fact is the signature sign-off. It is George who says, "Say goodnight, Gracie." And Gracie meekly follows his rule. At the end, George is the one who controls reality.

There is, in this interplay, a conflict model established for a stable marriage. The husband must be wise enough to let his wife's view of reality prevail even though he understands it is at variance with real reality. At the end, the wife must follow her husband. Both win, and the marriage endures. That was the 1950s model of success, one already being undermined by Lucille Ball and others, but one that was comfortable for Burns and Allen in real life, and for many in their audience.

No one who watched Burns and Allen's television show and who wrote about it thought George was the more important to the two characters. By design, the entire show seemed to revolve around Gracie and her narratives. But, by his ultimate power, George is as crucial as Gracie. His role has been consistently underestimated. George was the audience's guide to Gracie's mind. He was the string that pulled her back to reality. Without such a string she would have wandered too far from us. We, in the audience, always know George is there to make sure she doesn't wander too far.

George's character, like Jack Benny's, relied on a few simple self-definitions. If Benny was eternally 39, cheap, and a bad violin player, Burns was a cigar-puffing, aging (and this was when in reality he'd be living another four decades), and always looking for a place to sing.

The writers put in a lot of age jokes:

> I can't understand why I flunked American history. When I was a kid there was so little of it.
> Tennis is a young man's game. Until you're 25 you can play singles. From 25 to 35, you should play doubles. I won't tell you exactly how old I am, but when I played, there were 28 men on the court — just on my side of the net.
> I remember the first time I voted. How could I forget it? It was the first time anybody voted. It was raining that day, and on my way to the polls I saw a kid standing in the rain flying a kite with a key on it.

And Gracie jumped in on the kidding:

> DECORATOR: This is a beautiful lamp.
> GRACIE: My husband bought that.
> DECORATOR: Early American?
> GRACIE: Oh, yes. He's one of the earliest![11]

It may be surprising that George let himself be the butt of age jokes, but the very age allowed him a distance from the events and gave him a presumed wisdom. That is, the idea of his being old fit perfectly into the character he had constructed. Someone younger would be more impulsive, less forgiving of Gracie, more willing to challenge and fight with her. George's temperament, grounded in long years, let him accept her and, in so doing, let the audience enjoy her without worrying that her shaggy-dog stories would ever endanger the marriage.

George's singing voice, which no vocal teacher would describe as enviable, was nonetheless a focal point of his identity as an entertainer. The gravel-voiced Burns didn't so much sing the songs as speak them in a rhythm. But there was a special combination of skills George employed. He picked particularly obscure songs. This simultaneously let audiences know that he was familiar with the traditions of vaudeville. And his song choices had the added advantage for George of knowing audiences had never heard the songs before. They couldn't compare his renditions to alternate presentations of the songs; they had never heard the songs sung. It would be inaccurate to describe the songs George chose as clever or witty or of lasting musical value. Their charm lay in their very obscurity, of the fact that they were an artifact of entertainment history that would have remained (perhaps deservedly) undiscovered if not for George's determined efforts to let people hear him belt the songs out. The humor was not inherent in the songs, but it was George Burns singing them. The speedy delivery, in an almost deliberately unvocal singing voice, allows George to phrase the songs and present them so they're funny. None of them seemed likely to be successful, or remembered, but George did what he did best: use timing to make language funny. "I'll Be Waiting for You Bill When You Come Back from San Juan Hill," or any of his many other songs, were not choices for any other singer of the era. George owned them.

A running gag on the show was George's desire to sing these chestnuts, and everyone's resistance, except Gracie's. As he did at parties he gave at his own house, George wanted to sing in his fictional television house. And, as in real life, it was Gracie's character who loved his singing and never grew tired of it. Gracie always supported him:

GEORGE: Maybe I'm getting too old to sing.
GRACIE: Why, that's ridiculous. Good things improve with age. Your voice is like rare old wine. It's like ripe old cheese.[12]

George was determined, though: "At 12:30 I said I was going to sing a few songs, and all the guests formed a circle around the piano. By the time I broke through I was too tired to sing."[13]

Besides his age and voice, George's lightly drawn character included his use of a cigar. He told the *Palo Alto Times* why the cigar was so crucial: "It's a handy timing device. If I get a laugh with a joke, I just look down at the cigar or twiddle it a little while I'm waiting for the laugh to die down. If I don't get a laugh, it's nice to have something to hang on to. When a joke calls for a delayed laugh, I exhale my smoke slowly. If the laugh never comes at all, I swallow."[14]

The quotation aptly illustrates not only George's grasp of the intricacies of comic timing but also his understanding that, in performance, he is in a constant dialogue with the audience. His explanation is valuable, but incomplete. He doesn't give himself enough credit. All Jack Benny had to do was to walk onstage with a violin for the audience to laugh. So it was with George's cigar. It was, by itself, a laugh prompt. George used the cigar for timing, but his use of it also made the audience laugh at it as a supplement to the line uttered. Perceptive audience members might have noted that George kept his cigar in his left hand. His right hand was frequently in his pocket. He didn't know what to do with it. The cigar, that is, was more than a device. George needed it emotionally. Maybe he thought of it as a lucky charm, as a link to past success. If all else failed he had a good smoke. George needed the cigar. He was more confident with it, more in control. It was like an orchestra leader's baton; with it he conducted the show.

Even with his history of success, even with these audience-tested aspects of his identity, even with superb writers, George remained determined not to take it easy. He remained a professional. He continued to memorize the lines, relying on an aide to prompt him if he forgot one. Steve Ferry, who assisted with props, always memorized the lines as well and stood by in case George forgot his line. And George was always on the set early, often showing up a couple of hours before he was scheduled to be there. It was a habit he retained from vaudeville. He wanted to be ready. He had breakfast with the workers in the studio. In turn, they would work extra hard for him. He could work on his monologue. There was plenty of time to put on his make-up. When the time came to perform, he was ready.

As he had done since the vaudeville-success days, George remained willing to be the butt of jokes. It is less clear that he was as genuinely self-effacing as Jack Benny. George's decision to be made fun of by Gracie was a correctly calculated business decision. It was what worked. Over time, any hurt feelings were mollified by the public love, by the money, by the enormous success. His long-deferred dream of being the comedy lead had been covered over with a sweet crust of success. And Gracie didn't let up on her seemingly unintentionally less-than-gracious evaluations of him.

GEORGE: Would you ever think that such a beautiful mink coat would come from such an unattractive little thing that looks like a weasel.
GRACIE: Oh, George, you're just fishing — you know I think you're handsome.[15]

These lines are interesting because, after George's line, the audience can pretty well guess how Gracie is going to interpret him. Her line is not funny by itself. But within the context of her character and with her delivery it's a funny line, even if it is expected. Indeed, the very expectation adds to the pleasure because audience members could more fully identify with Gracie and be rewarded with their cleverness by having their expectations met.

George and Gracie's personal and professional relationship seemed happy and pleasant on the outside. The tensions were all inside. Gracie didn't like show business and never talked about it. George lived and breathed it. It was the core of his identity. They presented themselves as a perfectly contented couple, a model for the rest of America to emulate. And the people around them seemed to verify their compatibility with carefully constructed explanations. For instance, Ralph Levy, their producer and director, presented clues to their success:

> George and Gracie never rehearsed together. I don't think they ever read their lines together till they came to the studio, and that way they never had any domestic spats over what was funny or what they did or didn't like. On Saturday and Sunday, a secretary from my office would go out to work with George in the morning on his lines. Then she would work with Gracie in her boudoir in the afternoon on her lines. But when they met onstage, they had never worked the lines together. That way there was peace in the family at home, and it was very fresh when they got onto the stage. It was important in keeping a happy relationship as a team.[16]

But this is more revealing than it seems, and also does not provide the complete picture. The fact that they didn't run lines together can just as easily be interpreted as friction in the relationship as a way of providing peace. That they couldn't rehearse together means they might have fought over each line. There were comedy teams in history whose members didn't talk to each other off stage, learned their lines separately, collected the checks, performed, and went their separate ways. It's impossible to tell to what extent George and Gracie wanted separation or how much they had it, but Gracie was more insistent on the right lines than this indicates.

Going back at least to radio, Gracie was adamant about certain jokes. And George was not always polite to her. Paul Henning, one of their writers, recalled sessions between them: "We'd have a reading, and Gracie would say, 'Natty, I don't like that joke about Pasadena'—or whatever—and George would just give her hell in front of everybody. 'Googie, goddammit, that's the best joke in the whole script'—and so forth. Then we'd break up for that day. Next morning, George would come in and say, 'You know, I was thinking about that joke about Pasadena—I kind of think we ought to lose that.' Pillow talk."[17]

It seems likely that their public spats forced them to rehearse separately, as Levy described. Private rehearsal meant that Gracie would feel less compelled to change lines. But Henning's observations are vital in understanding the relationship between George and Gracie. Ultimately, in his perception, he had to please her. The kind way to look at this is that he cared for her and loved her. A less charitable interpretation is that he was desperate. He truly believed he would be a failure without her and so, whatever he thought of her skills at evaluating jokes, ultimately, he had to allow her to triumph.

Of course, such an evaluation may simply miss the sweetness of George. He was a good person, frequently driven to yelling about lines, especially at his brother Willy and Gracie. But he was a good boss to work for. Writers may not have been as fond of him as they were of Jack Benny, but he was not, ultimately, a tough man to write for. Like Benny, George's generosity came out in various ways. Starting in radio and continuing into television, for example, he always made sure that everyone in the cast got laughs, not just him and not just Gracie. He reasoned that it was a way to prevent audiences from getting tired of him. But that strategy had backfired in their films because they were rarely the stars. As the stars of the radio and TV show, sharing laughs made more sense and it worked.

Beginning on October 9, 1952 — at the start of their third season — the program became a weekly broadcast. It was at this time that the show left CBS and settled in at the General Service Studio lot at 1040 North Las Palms in Hollywood. Stage 1 became the home of the show. George formed McCadden Productions to distribute the filmed show. ("McCadden" was the name of the street in Hollywood where Willy Burns lived.) The new filmed show was enormously important to Gracie. She was no longer under the intense strain of a live broadcast. She might well have quit without the change.

The filmed show had a set routine. Such a rigorous approach was required to make sure the show was ready. On Mondays, George met his writers at eight A.M. Together, they developed a story line for the show. If possible, they attempted to keep two or three shows ahead in case of a problem. As with all creativity, sometimes the ideas came almost unbidden and other times there was much angst in the room. It was a prison of sorts; they couldn't leave without a story line. Gracie, meanwhile, spent Mondays in wardrobe, very carefully selecting what she would wear on that week's episode. She then took a nap, and in the evening learned her lines.

Tuesday was rehearsal day. George and Gracie arrived at nine in the morning. Shots were blocked out. Each line was rehearsed. On Tuesday and Wednesday, George always ate his lunch at Davey Jones' Locker, which (as its name implies) offered great seafood — but George just ate scrambled eggs and salami, toast and coffee. The poor owner of the restaurant had to go each Tuesday and Wednesday to a nearby delicatessen to get the salami, but that's what George wanted.

On Wednesday, the program was filmed. It usually took half a day, often up to seven in the evening, to complete the filming. They would go to one set, rehearse the scene, shoot it, and shoot any other scenes on that set. They would then go to the next set and rehearse and shoot all the scenes which were set there. Gracie was utterly exhausted by the end of the day. Her character was typically featured on thirty of the script's 40 pages.

On Thursday, George met with the writers again. They worked with the story idea they had developed on Monday. (This was a work day, so lunch was intentionally at a dive; they didn't want to be distracted by good food or even a pleasant atmosphere.) After a brief lunch, they were back at work until late in the afternoon. Gracie had the day off. She had to schedule any personal matters for Thursdays because the rest of the week provided her almost no free time.

Friday was again set aside for writing. There were no breaks, no small talk. The work had to be done. Gracie spent the day in wardrobe.

Although George and Gracie were wealthy by almost any standard, George could not slow down, not even on the weekends. On Saturday he was up early collecting all the written material done during the week. Afternoons were devoted to spending time with his friends at Hillcrest. It was a rare moment of relaxation, but George inevitably used the time to chat about business matters, seeking gossip, news, and advice. His mind was never far from his show, because his career was his life. The script arrived at his house on Saturday night, but it always ran long and he would have to cut it by taking out the weakest lines, making sure there was continuity to the rest, and leaving it the right length for a shooting script.

Sunday was also busy. A secretary took George's notes on the script. His director arrived at ten to talk over the script and discuss problems that might arise before the filming. Gracie was required to be there for those discussions precisely because the show invariably revolved around her character. George used Sunday evenings to watch television. For most people such an activity might be termed relaxation, but for George it was a form of work. While George was checking out the competition, Gracie was working on her script. It was, of course, hard to memorize any script. But Gracie's lines were especially difficult: there were a lot of them, and they changed each week. It was an enormous undertaking to learn those lines well enough to appear to be speaking spontaneously. Rehearsed spontaneity was a key ingredient for successful actors, and it was a grueling process when it had to be repeated week after week.

For George, such a schedule was energizing. He seemed to be always planning and working. His attraction to young women, his parties, his time at Hillcrest — all supplemented his work. Upon closer examination, there was an oddity regarding George's social life. Gracie was Catholic, and the children were being raised as Catholic. George professed no religion. And yet Hillcrest was a Jewish club. The social circles in which George and Gracie moved in Hollywood were almost exclusively Jewish. Jack and Mary Benny, their best friends, were Jewish. In a later book entitled *All My Best Friends*, George mentions Benny, Eddie Cantor, Georgie Jessel, Al Jolson, and others. All of them were Jewish. Of course, most comedians at the time were Jewish, and comedians share an affinity as only another comedian can appreciate the challenges of that demanding craft. Still, George found his friends particularly among his co-religionists. If an observer just looked at the people with whom George socialized, they were exclusively Jewish. Gracie didn't seem to mind this. George's friends were inevitably kind to her, and they entertained her. And perhaps the friendships

George considered Al Jolson the greatest entertainer who ever lived. Jolson had starred in *The Jazz Singer* (1927), which marked the beginning of public acceptance of sound in film. In the movie, Jolson played a cantor's son who can't follow his father's Jewish faith. Burns had seen the original play, recognized the story was about his struggle as well, and cried.

were the way in which George balanced out Gracie's religion. His friends were proof to him that he had, in fact, never really surrendered being Jewish. He remained proud of his heritage.

Perceptive viewers observed the subtle way in which Gracie's appearance changed across the years. The dresses, the fact that she maintained her weight, her carefully kept blonde hair were continuous. Television, like film, demanded that her natural hair color be lightened. But during the run of the show, technical improvements in make-up and lighting enhanced Gracie's appearance. She seemed almost younger at the end of the show's run than at its beginning. But that was all show business. Underneath the make-up Gracie was no longer young. She kept her real age a secret, and her heart condition as well. She kept taking pills, and they seemed to work. She was like the picture of Dorian Gray: she looked great in the picture, but her real self was aging. She had a heart attack sometime in the early 1950s, although it wasn't a very serious one. When the doctor told her she had angina he also told her that she needed to quit the program. For whatever reason, whether because of her own determination or George's pleas, she continued. And she continued without public whining. She didn't tell people about her condition. On the set, though, people noticed. There was talk, from 1954 on, that she could not continue past that season.

Perhaps it buoyed her when her son Ronnie joined the cast, on October 10, 1955. Ronnie was youthful, thin, and good-looking. And Gracie was working with at least one of her children. That must have pleased her immensely. But Ronnie offered another advantage. There were now story lines that revolved around him, releasing Gracie from carrying all or most of every show. Carefully, George and the writers were slowly trying to reduce the immense weekly pressures on her.

While Gracie's role on the show was reduced, she was, of course, still its center. But Ronnie's involvement had another effect. Gracie's character began to appear more maternal. It was a third stage in the team's evolution. Burns and Allen had started as a flirtation act, as though they were two young people playing around with each other's emotions, testing out the limits of their mutual attraction. When, during the radio years, George realized they were too old to continue with such an act, they went from playing single characters to playing married characters. But without children, the stories and lines that fit their more mature status were still sufficiently zany to have a direct continuity to their flirtation act. However, once Gracie had a grown son on the show, once she was a mother and not just a wife, the character could no longer sustain the same level of zaniness. Parenting required more responsibility than being childless. There was a subtle shift in Gracie's character, one some critics noted with disapproval.

But through all the changes, all the medical problems, the daily and weekly rigors of production, the writers were heroic. They kept going. They knew their characters, and they knew what they had to produce. Writing for Gracie was deceptively simple and never easy. Most of all writers had to keep a simple rule in mind: "Gracie" really believes what she says. She doesn't have an iota of deception or manipulation in her. Writers had to learn to listen to the language the way Gracie did, trying to hear the literal meaning of the words, as in this exchange:

> BLANCHE: I have to stop at Sears and Roebuck. We don't have a garbage disposal.
>
> GRACIE: Isn't that a long way to take your garbage every day?[18]

It is difficult to hear the language that way, and writers had to be good in order to do it. They had to think with Gracie's patented illogical logic, thinking logically about the illogical and illogically about the logical. In a way, Gracie's grasp on the language is a mystery. Just as audiences watch mystery shows to find out how a murder will be solved as they look for clues themselves about who did it, so, too, did audiences wait to figure out how Gracie was going to take the language they all used and misapply it. Of course, many in the audience did not understand how the show was put together and so thought Gracie made up all the lines she spoke. Such audiences were enchanted and looked forward to being surprised by Gracie's mental and linguistic gymnastics just like they looked forward to being surprised by the revelation of the killer at the end of a mystery.

Gracie, for her part, was careful about which jokes she told. She refused to allow any jokes about mice because she didn't like them. She also refused to do any jokes about people with disabilities. But she did like jokes about relatives. These were the most popular running gags on the show. The running gags were used by writers as sort of a reward

George poses with Jack Benny, whom he considered to be his best friend. Benny became famous for supposedly being cheap, eternally 39, and unable to play the violin. In fact, he was a generous man, aged well, and was an excellent musician.

for faithful viewers. They had heard jokes about the same subjects before. It was like they were part of a club of insiders. The relative jokes, of course, were straight out of vaudeville. It's interesting that they held up so well on television, and serves as a reminder that the subject of family was a perennial one in humor. Here are a couple of typical jokes about Uncle Harvey, for example:

> GRACIE: Uncle Harvey never needed a watch. He always told time by his wallet.
> GEORGE: Uncle Harvey told time by his wallet?
> GRACIE: Yes. Every night he'd go down to the corner bar and keep looking in his wallet and when it was empty he'd say, "Well, it's time to go home."

And

> GRACIE: Uncle Harvey loves crowds. Crowds and ice cream. That's what he loves. Now, once Uncle Harvey was walking along Main Street eating

When George made a friend, he kept that friend throughout his life. Here are four famous entertainers, all Jewish, all who started performing when they were children. They are (from left to right) George Jessel, George Burns, Eddie Cantor, and Jack Benny.

ice cream. He had two ice cream cones in each hand and suddenly his belt broke.

GEORGE: That must have been terrible.

GRACIE: It was. After he finished eating the ice cream, he had to walk back two miles and get his pants.[19]

Given the requirements of the show, given the time frame in which they had to produce, George and the writers deserve great credit.

Paul Henning was a principal writer on the show. Henning had begun writing for Burns and Allen in 1942 during their radio days. George was particularly impressed by Henning because the young writer was able to come up with the key concept for many of the shows. Unsurprisingly, then, Henning followed Burns and Allen into television. George, with Jack Benny as a model, made sure Henning was happy with large raises each year. But, in 1952, Henning had been given a chance to produce and so ended his ten-year relationship with the Burns and Allen show, although he was involved with other efforts by George's production company.

Sid Dorfman had also followed George and Gracie from radio. Dorfman was prized because he (along with Harvey Helm, another writer) was capable of coming up with the twisted logic that Gracie's character applied to language. Dorfman was on the television show for its first three years before leaving. He later wrote for such programs as *M*A*S*H*.

Harvey Helm had begun his association with George by selling jokes when Burns and Allen were still in vaudeville. Helm then went on to work on the radio show; he wrote for the television show for its entire eight season run. Helm was noted for his inventive mind. He would sit, cigarette dangling, and flip through decidedly unfunny magazines staring at the pictures and waiting for some wild idea to hit him.

Willy Burns had an unenviable task. He was the scapegoat. George didn't want to anger his writers. He may have feared they'd leave or that they wouldn't produce their best work. George had seen other comedians mistreat writers, and he didn't want to repeat the mistake. George yelled plenty, but he often directed his outburst at Willy, his younger brother. Everyone in the room knew the game; George would get over it, Willie learned to take it, and the other writers knew the anger meant they all had more work to do. Willy, though, had an inventive mind. He kept throwing out ideas, playing off lines, keeping the other writers nimble.

After Paul Henning left, George hired two younger writers: Jesse Goldstein and Nate Monaster. But they were only on the staff for a year. Both had successful writing careers, and it is not clear why they left the show, although it is the case that the Gracie character was notoriously difficult to write, especially for less-experienced writers.

George hired Keith Fowler for the 1953 season. Fowler had worked on the radio show along with Paul Henning, so at the very least he had an intimate sense of the characters George and Gracie created. Norman Paul was the last of the writers on the show. He was the journeyman, the man whose mind was always on his work.

Dorfman and Helm were the early arrivals at the office, with its extended couch, its oversized desk, its chairs, and its bookshelf. There were photos of the sets to keep the writers anchored. Helm was there at five in the morning. The two men wrote together for three hours until George arrived, and they could then show their efforts to him.

Norman Paul followed George and Willy, who sat at the desk. Paul filled the couch.

Tommy Clapp, who served as secretary of the all-male group, sat at the typewriter, trying his best to get all the lines down on paper.

Because of the success of the show, it is easy to underestimate the restrictions under which the writers and George worked. They couldn't use any material in the news because the scripts were prepared so far ahead of time. They didn't want to offend anybody. For both those reasons, there was no overtly political material or specific social satire. Of course, given the era, all the comedy had to be completely clean. There was no swearing, no suggestiveness, no provocative story lines.

More subtly, Gracie did not do physical comedy. Her principal female competitors, Lucille Ball and Joan Davis, both excelled at such comedy, so Gracie and the writers were, from the start of the writing of a show, at a disadvantage. Gracie was elegant. Not only were there no pies, no pratfalls, no tripping over couches, but Gracie couldn't wear any disguises or wild costumes the way Lucy did. Additionally, the writers had to guess every week whether their material would or would not work. George and the writers all knew that a line or a whole script could be very funny as they sat around and wrote it, and yet the audience might not like it. They had to trust their instincts. George had the perfect ear. He knew what audiences liked. He was part of them. In an odd way, it is probable that George's lack of an education helped him in show business. Without higher education, he was at the same level of learning as the vast majority of his audience. His mind was fast and clever and funny, but it wasn't beyond the reach of the audience. Still, the words had to be produced without a break.

By the time the series concluded, the writers had produced a total of 299 shows and had to adhere to these restrictions, facing all the potential barriers imposed by the new medium. It was quite an accomplishment.

The plots usually revolved around marriage and family, but the writers were also subject to the prejudices of the time. Because the humor was essentially one of recognition, the writers had to create situations that the audiences had or might have confronted in their own lives. Unfortunately, the all-male, California-based, well-off writers occasionally relied on stereotypes. This was particularly true in their connection of women and bad driving.

The scripts were unusually complex. Even with all the rehearsal it was especially difficult to memorize such difficult lines. For that reason, the show was among the first to use cue cards. Because Gracie was so professional and worked so hard, she had a chance to determine beforehand which lines would be troublesome. When she found a particular line that she struggled with, she would write the line on an index card and paste it somewhere on the set that couldn't be seen by the camera, such as inside the sink. Because the lines weren't logical, it was an enormous strain to learn them. But Gracie insisted that she learn the lines, even with the available prompts. It seems impossible to imagine that the enormity of such a weekly task didn't add to her anxieties and cause her headaches. For 39 weeks out of every year, for the full run of the show, Gracie had to be constantly working. Writing the lines was painfully hard, but memorizing and performing them was infinitely harder.

Of course, the show took up most of the team's lives, but not all of it. And while Ronnie eventually appeared on his show, his sister, Sandy, did not find show business so appealing. This meant that George and Gracie could not always be around while either of their children were growing up.

Thus they were shocked when at the end of the first season they came home to discover that Sandy had eloped. The adventure began when Sandy phoned her good friend Joan Benny, Jack's daughter, and asked her to come over to the Burns home. Joan arrived at seven in the evening. George and Gracie had gone to dinner and Sandy was at the house with her boyfriend, Jim Wilhoite, a good-looking blond surfer type. The couple was engaged. George and Gracie and Jim's parents had agreed to the engagement, but then Sandy and Jim had called it off. Now young love had returned, and they were back together — and eager to get married. They were eloping to Las Vegas, and they wanted Joan Benny to accompany them. Joan, who had entered into more than one adventure with Sandy, was ready.

Marvin Mitchelson — later a nationally famous divorce lawyer — was Wilhoite's best friend, and, in this case, the couple's driver. He had also dated Joan Benny. His convertible made it to Vegas in five hours, but it was already after midnight. That didn't much matter in Las Vegas, where all-night wedding chapels were available. Without money, without plans, without telling her parents, Sandy went through with the wedding. It was August 8, 1953.

Meanwhile, George had returned home and was concerned. He kept waking Ronnie, who was not part of the conspiracy and so couldn't provide any useful information.

The four-person wedding party was driving aimlessly. Suddenly, they spotted Tony Martin's name on the Flamingo Hotel's marquee. Martin knew Sandy and had been a frequent guest on the Burns and Allen radio show. They roused the singer just as he was preparing for bed. He opened the door of his hotel suite.

> "What are you doing here, Sandy? Joanie?" the confused singer asked
> "Well," Sandy said, "I'd like you to meet my husband."
> "I'm calling your parents right now."
> "*Please* Mr. Martin. Can't we talk about this for a minute?"
> "Look, come on in, all of you. Call room service and get something
> to eat. But I've got to call your parents."[20]

George refused to speak with his daughter, so Gracie took the receiver and ordered Sandy to return home immediately. Jack and Mary Benny then came over — in their bathrobes and slippers.

The young couple, supplied with Tony Martin's money, stopped on the way home to get breakfast. They didn't get home until ten in the morning.

George kept his anger under control, but Gracie did not. She lit into her daughter about getting married in such a manner. But the anger subsided in time, and Sandy was married.

Meanwhile, the show rolled on. It wasn't as revolutionary as *I Love Lucy*, but it reflected a part of the times. Gracie was where women were in the society; Lucy was where they were going. Many in the audience were caught. They didn't always like the velvet traps of their suburban lives, but they were scared about leaving it. Gracie provided comfort that the old ways were fine. They'd laugh; they'd be the real victor in the husband-wife struggle, despite the fact that the man had the money and the job. Lucy challenged her husband.

She wanted to push. She wasn't satisfied to stay and home and look pretty. She relied on her wits to attain her goals.

There were similarities between the two women. Both had female friends. But, because of the inherent limitations of Gracie's character, it was Blanche who had to come up with the ideas that were wild. Gracie thought all her ideas were normal. And the plots weren't that wild. They typically involved schemes like trying to get their husbands to take them to an expensive night club or to buy them a new mink coat. In contrast, it was Lucy who usually dragged Ethel along on the adventures, and the adventures were genuine adventures, stepping outside acceptable behavior. Gracie wouldn't have been drunk doing a commercial or stomping on grapes, as Lucy famously did.

If ratings are an indication, Lucy beat Gracie. Burns and Allen, despite winning their time period, were rarely among television's great successes. Only once, during the 1953–1954 season, did they crack the list of television's top 25 shows, based on A.C. Nielsen's numbers. During that season they reached number 20, and had a 32.4 rating. In contrast, *I Love Lucy* was the number-one rated show. It had a rating of 58.8. A perceptive sociologist might come to the conclusion that as American women made their choice of staying in their traditional roles or stepping out of them, those women were about to make history. And indeed they would do so, especially in the coming decade.

But George and Gracie accepted their success as a "safe" show, that it was a continuation of their radio program. No complex plots. No gag that was difficult to understand. Everyone could "get" Burns and Allen. George wanted the audiences to sit back and laugh. He wasn't out to provoke. He wasn't out to get them to think or examine society. He wanted to provide some laughs after a hard day. If the jokes, in retrospect, are mild, then that had been the plan.

If George wasn't busy enough, his friendships, and his eagerness to prove how good he was, how successful a man he could be, led him to expand McCadden Productions' efforts.

When Paul Henning left the Burns and Allen writing staff, he approached George with an idea for a program starring the actor Bob Cummings. MCA (originally the Music Corporation of America, and now defunct) distributed television programs and included both George Burns and Bob Cummings among its clients. But executives at MCA were very hesitant about the new show. Henning asked George to help, and George did. McCadden Productions now had its second show, and George was the executive producer, often visiting the set to observe the dress rehearsals and, now and then, providing advice. George could have been an annoying figure, but he was not. He didn't stomp and demand that his suggestions be taken. He just made them. George, universally recognized as one of the great masters of comedic timing, always noted when two jokes were told too close together. Audiences needed a pause, and Rod Amateau, the show's director, recognized a valuable suggestion when he heard one.

Love That Bob (also known as *The Bob Cummings Show*) was on the air from January 2, 1955 to September 15, 1959. Bob Cummings played the part of Bob Collins, a Hollywood photographer who had more than a passing interest in attractive young women. The character was also a reserve officer in the Air Force. The series was successful enough to help the future careers of many associated with it, although not for Bob Cummings himself.

George's support of Paul Henning was clearly justified. Henning went on to produce such television successes of the 1960s as *The Beverly Hillbillies*, *Petticoat Junction*, and *Green Acres*. And if Cummings and co-star Rosemary DeCamp didn't go on to future hits, the show nevertheless was a launching pad for others. Ann B. Davis played "Schultzy" on the show and won two Emmys for her performance. She went on to play Alice, the housekeeper, on *The Brady Bunch*. More minor cast members made an impact. Nancy Kulp went on to play the memorable Miss Hathaway on *The Beverly Hillbillies,* and the very attractive Joi Lansing — sometimes dubbed television's Marilyn Monroe — who played the model Shirley Swanson — went on to have a recurring role in *Hillbillies* as well. Finally, Dwayne Hickman played Bob Collins's nephew. Based on his popularity, he was cast as the title character in *The Many Loves of Dobie Gillis*.

Because Henning's writing successor, Harvey Helm, was so successful, and unique, in channeling Gracie's character, George found himself able to focus on producing other shows. And George was wanted. He had been represented by the William Morris Agency, but he had left them. They wanted him to return, and so they came to him with an idea. Actually, the writer Irving Brecher had the idea, but Morris wanted to acquire George's services. They pressed Brecher to ask George to be his partner. Brecher didn't need a partner, or a partner's $27,000, but he did need the Morris people to represent him. And so, Irving Brecher cut his deal. He would approach George to be his producing partner and Morris would represent them both.

When Brecher approached George with the idea for *The People's Choice*, George and Willy were in their office at General Services Studio. Brecher and the man from the Morris Agency came in. Brecher and George knew each other from Hillcrest, which was a good start. George leaned back, put his hands behind his head, and said, "I hope we can do something together. What do you have in mind?"[21]

Brecher mentioned the title, but said it wouldn't make sense without an explanation. George said he wanted such an explanation.

"In the pilot, Sock Miller is the name of the character. He's working for the National Bureau of Wild Life. He works in the woods, looking after the interests of wildlife, especially birds. As he walks through the woods, he's followed by a dog with long ears — a basset hound. He stops at a tree and he carves a heart into it, with initials. "And the dog looks at it and says —" George was never slow. "The dog *says*?" Brecher responded, "That's right." George looked at his brother and said, "Give him the money."[22]

Brecher, understandably disgruntled at what he saw as being pressured, thought George didn't contribute much to the show beyond a few comments. George, no doubt with a very bright vaudeville shine, later summed up his contribution to the show:

> I would read a script and know something's wrong. But I don't know how to fix it. So I go out to Hillcrest. I wander around the clubhouse until I spot some $250,000 comedy writer. I tell him the story. I say it's great. He looks at me like I've got two heads. Now I've got $250,000 worth of comedy brains for nothing. I go back to the office and call Irv Brecher. I tell him how to fix his script, but I don't say where I got my ideas. And everybody tells everybody what a genius I am.[23]

The People's Choice ran from October 6, 1955 to May 29, 1958. The plots of the show revolved around Sock Miller as a city councilor having arguments with the mayor, John Peoples. The twist on their constant bickering was that Mandy, the mayor's daughter, was Sock's girlfriend and, later in the series, his wife, although they kept the marriage secret for a time because of the mayor's objections. Cleo, the talking basset hound, spoke to the audience, not to the other cast members. Her comments were inevitably wry and humorous. The actress Mary Jane Croft was a perfect voice for Cleo; Croft also appeared as Betty Ramsey on *I Love Lucy* and Clara Randolph on *The Adventures of Ozzie and Harriet.*

McCadden Productions was thriving. They were filming commercials (such as spots for Carnation and U.S. Steel) and pilots. George, though, was never fully satisfied. No matter what he accomplished, part of him remained the young man who had lost his father and who had been a vaudeville failure for so long. He feared a slide back down on the fame ladder. Every waking moment (and, no doubt, some moments in his dreams) was dedicated to making sure that his career would not falter. Unfortunately, part of that effort included convincing Gracie to stay with the show and with the commercials and other efforts necessary to boost the show. Gracie's migraines were getting worse. Her heart was weakening. Clearly, George was incapable of fully grasping the extent of her health problems. His own emotional needs were so powerful that they blocked out perceptions that he might otherwise have had. This is not at all to suggest that George knew he was endangering Gracie's life. First of all, he loved her. He knew, or profoundly believed, that his success was directly tied to Gracie. If he thought he was pushing her toward disaster, he would have stopped. But he could not see what he was doing.

And why wasn't Gracie more insistent sooner? She loved George. She had her own insecurities. She was very conscious of her scarred arm and deeply appreciated the fact that George didn't mention it, ever. Perhaps she believed no one else could love her the way he did — despite his habit of dalliances with young women. Gracie suffered her headaches and her heartaches without public complaint, only stopping when she literally couldn't go on.

If Gracie wouldn't appear in movies, George could try. He did provided the narration for the 1956 Judy Holliday comedy, *The Solid Gold Cadillac.* Gracie had adamantly refused to appear in the film and George without Gracie was a narrator, not a star.

If film stardom still eluded him, George found another outlet: books. It must have been a particular and private pleasure for him to write a book given his immense problems with reading.

Nevertheless, in 1954 George co-write *I Love Her, That's Why!* with Cynthia Hobart Lindsay. Her husband, Lou, was an agent at MCA, so she knew show business. The book sold reasonably well when it was published on October 30, 1955. It eventually reached the eighth spot on the *Los Angeles Times* best-seller list. Unsurprisingly, the book was mentioned in the show when Gracie and Blanche went into a book store. Perhaps because George intended this to be his only book, its stories ring truer than in some subsequent works. The vaudeville shine was never gone, but George found an emotional core, letting the early Lower East Side part of his story especially ring with truth. Once Gracie entered the story, however, the George Burns mask is on again. Indeed, it is remarkable how many contradictory stories are told in his books, even as he recites many of the same tales as though, book by book, he is constructing a life narrative that pleased the person he had become.

It's fair to say that, in many cases, it is not clear what the truth is. Beyond public documentation, some of the crucial events in George's life occurred privately. Even though he was in front of the public for virtually his entire life and famous for almost 70 years, like everyone else, George's internal life can only be pieced together by watching his behavior and interpreting him carefully. It is not that his books should be considered fiction, but neither should they be considered accurate. *I Love Her, That's Why!*, however, merits the attention of people interested in George's life because it, at least, sounds the truest, particularly concerning his early years.

Like other stars, one of the problems George had was dealing with television reruns. If the producers, directors, writers, and performers were exploring the limits and borders of this new medium, so was the audience. And the audience did not like shows being rerun in the summer. During the summer of 1953, George had tried to mollify the audience by coming out before the repeated show and announcing openly and honestly that the show had been broadcast earlier in the season. That didn't help.

George decided to try an experiment. During the summer of 1954, he determined to reach his audience in a different way. He thought they reacted badly to the word "rerun," so instead he called the repeats "encores." Cartoon characters of Burns and Allen appeared, as did a billboard announcing that the show was, in fact, an encore presentation. In addition, some original shows were broadcast during the summer.

Television technology didn't stop to wait for everyone to catch up with what had already been done. Programs began experimenting with color. And George, ever vigilant about progress in the industry, ever ready to explore the new so as not to fall behind, looked into using color. On October 4, 1954, the Burns and Allen show's only color episode was aired. Gracie was uneasy about this new development. She struggled hard, and successfully, to hide her true age. But she couldn't hide the headache and heart problems from herself. And she didn't like color. It was simply too intrusive.

Around this time, she and George became grandparents. Sandy's first daughter, Laura Jean, known as Laurie, was born in 1954. Sandy would have another child, Lissa, in 1956. Her marriage to Jim Wilhoite eventually ended, and on September 2, 1959, she married Rod Amateau, the third director of George and Gracie's television show.

With two grandchildren, health problems, trepidation about television's intrusiveness, and the constant need to memorize difficult lines, Gracie finally could take no more. Of course, her desire to retire had been known before. Indeed, she had raised the issue for the first time as early as their radio days.

But George had always talked her out of it. At some level, he simply didn't believe her. He couldn't conceive that *anyone* would voluntarily would choose to leave show business. As his life after Gracie indicates, he thought there was no real alternative in life. Show business people didn't retire if they didn't have to because audiences would no longer listen to them. But George's persistence in insisting that Gracie stay had another source. He felt desperate, sure that he could not succeed without her, and she felt that desperation. Gracie's love and devotion to her husband had been her motivation to stay with the show.

But time finally caught up to Gracie in the early 1950s. She had her first heart attack. They were on the train. Gracie, in the lower bunk, called up to her husband that she was having chest pains. George, who knew Gracie's every mood, realized this was serious. Gracie did not complain. If she was saying there was a pain, George knew it had to be a serious pain. (The couple understood heart problems well. Gracie's mother had died of a heart condition.) George jumped down off his bunk, held his wife, and assured her all would be okay. The pain went away, but once they were home, Gracie immediately went to her doctor, who delivered the news that she had suffered a mild heart attack. Gracie instructed George not to tell anyone. She didn't miss a rehearsal or a show.

But the attack was a sign of what was to come. During the next few years she had several more minor attacks. Still, she was a trouper. She always went on with the show. Her doctor prescribed nitroglycerin pills. He said that, when she had an attack, she should place a pill under her tongue. These pills were commonly prescribed in Hollywood, and performers looked at taking the pills as part of the high-stress life of show business.

Soon, George and Gracie adopted the same attitude. The pills were there, so there was nothing to worry about. Gracie might have some mild attacks, but she'd be all right. The two soon developed a ritual. CBS would renew the show. George would be excited. Gracie, whose cooperation ensured the show's success, wanted it to stop. Each season George had to coax her to continue. Eventually, however, George couldn't deny that the end was near. He noticed that Gracie had increasing problems with her lines. She took longer breaks and seemed more tired.

On one particularly hot day, Gracie and Ronnie were filming a scene. Suddenly, right in the middle of the filming, Gracie said, "Excuse me, I'm sorry. But I just can't see the card."

The man holding the cue cards immediately responded, "My fault." He put the cue cards together and moved closer. But everyone on the set, including George, knew that he had been standing where he always stood. He had been gracious about accepting responsibility, but it wasn't his fault.

George said, "Let's take a break."[24]

Incidents like that soon became more common. George, sensitive to audiences and sensitive to Gracie's feelings, took some time to admit the truth to himself. And on top of what George noticed, Gracie's doctor had become insistent that she retire. Finally, some months after the cue card incident, he and Gracie were at home on a Sunday night. They sat in their den, watching a television show. George turned to her and said, "You really want to stop?"

"I really do," Gracie responded.[25]

And so, George accepted reality. On February 16, 1958, the two called relatives and close friends and informed them that on the following morning Gracie was going to announce her retirement. There was some disbelief, but George was startled because no one attempted to persuade Gracie to continue. Perhaps, George thought, they knew this was coming and had accepted it before *he* did. He remained convinced, even after she retired, that when a few months passed she would be bored and return to the show. He couldn't imagine leading his own life apart from show business, and he couldn't imagine her doing so, either.

Either consciously or not, George had been preparing for a solo career during the program. His efforts were easy to miss. He opened every program with his monologue. Even if the audience anticipated Gracie's appearance, they were already attentive. Whether the viewers knew it or not, they were getting used to George standing up and telling jokes without Gracie at his side. Additionally, George constantly stood alone during the show, commenting on the program itself or on television generally. That is, the show was not what it might have been: simply a situation comedy in which George and Gracie were always directly in the show itself. If the show had been like that, George would have had much less preparation for appearances apart from Gracie, and audiences would have felt much less accepting when she eventually did leave.

Perhaps George finally felt confident enough. This confidence, added to Gracie's now undeniable health problems, allowed them to announce that Gracie was leaving.

Gracie and George decided that Louella Parsons, the gossip columnist, would provide the right forum for the announcement. Parsons told the world that Gracie was going to retire at the conclusion of the 1957–1958 season. Parsons wrote:

Gracie ... leaves a vacuum that cannot be filled in the entertainment world. The hold that Gracie, the fluttery rattlebrain, the queen of the non sequitur, has on her public has never been equaled by any woman in show business. Without her cheerful inanities Monday night just won't be Monday night on TV.[26]

Gracie told the columnist, "At first I'm going to sleep for six months. I'm going to invite people in to dinner and visit my grandchildren. And I'm going to clean out my bureau drawers."[27]

Some people were shocked. After all, Gracie's public age was fifty-one; in reality she was 62.

Gracie's announcement was not without its uses for the show's writers. Freed from having to keep up the character, the writers concocted a two-part show in which Gracie shows her intellectual side. Gracie meets a British hypnotist and thinks he's a French designer of fashionable dresses. He hypnotizes her into brilliance. With such a premise, they could have her say completely uncharacteristic lines, such as to neighbor Harry Morton (by then an accountant in the show): "I think you'll find the discrepancy in your figures was in your failure to amortize the depreciation in the value of steamships over a ten-year period."

Harry responds, "Who is this?"[28]

Finally, the hypnotist removes Gracie's genius by taking her out of the trance. "Repeat after me. My mind is a perfect blank, ready to accept any suggestion."

And so she repeated, "My mind is a perfect blank, ready to accept any suggestion."

"You are now the old Gracie Allen."

And the writers came up with the perfect line: "My mind is a perfect blank."[29]

The show's final episode was filmed on June 4, 1958. It wasn't a concluding script. The show concerned Ronnie, who was worried that a good-looking foreign exchange student would attract Ronnie's girlfriend. There was no mention that this was the final show of the series. The show would live on in reruns, and George wanted to let Gracie's world go on and on like that. Closing it seemed inappropriate.

As the filming of that final episode concluded, Gracie received loud applause and a standing ovation from the crew. There was champagne, though in paper cups. Everyone remembered the remarkable moments they had shared with Gracie.

And that was the last time George and Gracie would ever work together.

The program was popular, but not immensely popular. Neither the show nor (shockingly) Gracie won awards. The principal reason for this was that the show was too safe. Compared to the wild, unexpected antics of Lucille Ball, Gracie was — in a word that seems not to fit her but does — restrained. The jokes were safe, aimed at the wide audience, and often old. The humor's origins lay in vaudeville, and the whole American world was changing. Audiences had grown up with George and Gracie, and the familiar was part of what they clung to as that world changed.

And while most critics enjoyed the show, none could truly say that the humor was revolutionary in its narrative structure. George wanted success, and he got it. He wanted security, and he got it. But he paid a price. It was the daring shows that got the awards and a more prized place in television history.

But the show's format was perfect for Burns and Allen. George always flirted with reality as he told his stories. And the show reflected that. Being stars in a show supposedly about their private lives kept him in the public eye, but because the show didn't cut too close to the truth, George and Gracie were simultaneously able to maintain their privacy. There was no talk of health problems, or of George's infidelity, or of any other personal matter.

George had no real public identity apart from his stories; his stories were his life, and the show let him tell them in any way he wanted. Even friends often couldn't tell when he was being sincere and when he was acting. His public and private selves meshed into one for him. The show was, in a way, an ongoing dialogue between Burns and Allen about their lives. Maybe they needed the fantasy life of entertainment to paper over the real problems that they otherwise might have had to face.

But it seems unfair to leave the discussion of the show with a recitation of its shortcomings. It's far more appropriate to end the way George and Gracie ended their shows, with one of their famous double routines. Their dialogue had nothing at all to do with the show the audience had just seen. Here's an example:

> GEORGE: Well, Gracie, any news from home?
> GRACIE: Yes. I got a letter from my little niece, Jean.
> GEORGE: What did she say?
> GRACIE: She didn't say anything. She didn't phone. It was a letter, and she wrote it.
> GEORGE: I mean, what did she write?
> GRACIE: It's Spring again, and my family is putting on a backyard circus ... admission was free ... my cousin Barney was the sword swallower, and

what a performance he put on. The kids would cheer when he put a sword four feet long down his throat.

GEORGE: Could Barney really swallow a sword?

GRACIE: Oh, George, don't be silly. It was a trick. You know the scabbard that the sword fits into?

GEORGE: Yeah.

GRACIE: Well, before the show he would stick that down his throat.

GEORGE: I see.

GRACIE: Then when he'd slip the sword into it....

GEORGE: ... everybody thought he was swallowing it.... Say goodnight, Gracie.[30]

CHAPTER SIX

Goodnight, Gracie

George Burns was 63 years old. He and Gracie had been a team for over three decades. George was wedded not only to Gracie, but also to work. His profound and bottomless need for approval remained ever strong. He knew he had to keep going.

Gracie, meanwhile, was content in retirement. The angina continued unabated. The chest pains bothered her and the migraines didn't stop. But now she had to time to be with her family, to shop, to redecorate the house. She had time — for the first time in her entire life — to be normal. She had servants to get her what she wanted. She had led a hectic life in show business, and just stopping was pleasurable in and of itself. Gracie's sole regret about retirement was that she was no longer privy to industry gossip. George didn't have much to tell her. He was all about the business. But she found her sources. And, until a more serious heart attack in 1961, she spent many evenings in one theater or another. She enjoyed being there, especially because she wasn't the one who had to perform.

And Gracie gambled, with friends, at the racetrack, in Las Vegas. She was not a talented or lucky gambler and consistently lost money. Despite Gracie's continual habit of losing money, gambling was an escape from her problems.

Time was closing in on her family. Her sisters Hazel, Bessie, and Pearl, each in turn, had to be put in nursing homes because of senility. They didn't recognize Gracie very often, but she kept going to see them regardless. Quietly and without complaint, Gracie continued life as usual, but George knew that she was concerned about her own mental health. She feared that she would one day end up like her sisters.

And while Gracie kept busy in her own fashion in retirement, George did what he feared most: he began to fail. In 1958, McCadden sold the Burns and Allen telefilms to another company, Screen Gems. What that meant was that McCadden's main business was gone, and so the company started a downward spiral.

In a desperate move, made in part to allow Gracie to come back as he hoped she would, George immediately began work on his own program, appropriately titled *The George Burns Show*. In the new series, George was a producer, and instead of the Burns home the show was set in an office. Ronnie Burns, Harry Von Zell, and the Mortons (Bea Benaderet and Larry Keating) all worked for him. Blanche was his secretary and Harry Morton his accountant. The program premiered on October 21, 1958. George tried to fill Gracie's place with a variety of guest stars including Jack Benny, who appeared on the second show. Plots were thin, revolving around a producer's problems such as temperamental actors. When audiences didn't respond, George altered the format to include a variety show inside each episode. That didn't work either. There was no getting around it: audiences simply missed Gracie. She had been the center of the show, and though the writers struggled mightily, they had no crucial organizing principle from which to work. As George so perceptively put it:

> It didn't take a genius to figure out what was wrong. Sure, we had the same people, but any minute you expected Gracie to come through the door. It was like having dinner; we had the soup, the salad, and the dessert, but the main course was home playing with the grandchildren.[1]

George realized too late that he shouldn't have kept the cast because every one of them reminded the audience of the missing Gracie. And if George thought Gracie, seeing his agony, would ride in to rescue her husband, he was mistaken. Gracie had reached the Promised Land of retirement, and she was not going to leave it. And so George had to accept television's cruel ruling. The show was not renewed and broadcast its final episode on April 14, 1959.

Every fear that George had, every insecurity, returned like a nightmare. Time must have disappeared for him. There he was again, without Gracie, naked before the audience so that they could see that he couldn't succeed in show business on his own merits. No doubt George presented a joke or two about his condition when he went to Hillcrest to lunch with friends, but neither is there a doubt that his pain was profound.

After decades of productivity, George Burns, the great George Burns, was out of work. Adrift, his fears confirmed by a failed show, George turned to his writers. Television didn't offer him a chance to act. He would soon return as a producer, but George needed an audience like he needed air.

With a film career that hadn't worked, his kind of radio defunct, and an inability to get a television show, George took the only available road. He would go on the nightclub circuit. He could tell some jokes and stories, woo the audience with his idiosyncratic singing of obsure vaudeville songs, and generally just be George Burns. He opened at Harrah's in Lake Tahoe, Nevada, in June 1959.

George continued to reveal his insecurity. He had heard a record of Bobby Darin singing, and without ever meeting or hearing him in person, he hired the young singer. George heard what others did, that Darin had a narrative power and energy that was catching. And George, with his ear, knew that Darin, like Frank Sinatra, knew how to phrase a song well. After the signing, Darin came to the office and George saw in him a talented, 23-year-old symbolic son. Darin joined two other musical acts with George in the show, the DeCastro sisters and Brascia Tybee. George remained afraid that audience wouldn't accept him alone.

Gracie was there sitting directly in front, the first time George walked out on stage. George introduced her, and the audience, as it always did, gave her a standing ovation. George did his act, and then, later that evening, asked Gracie her opinion. She said she liked Bobby Darin a lot. He pressed her, and she said, "Well, Nat, I think you're reciting your monologue. You know how you always say that honesty is the most important thing onstage, and if you can fake that you can do anything? I don't think you're faking it very well. And if you don't believe what you're saying, how do you expect the audience to?"[2]

George could recognize the truth when he heard it, especially about show business. He slowed down, trying to sound sincere, even if he really wasn't. From Harrah's George went to the Sahara in Las Vegas for four weeks.

George was part of the nightclub circuit until 1964. Additionally, he began to spend more time at Hillcrest or at the Friars club with other entertainers, swapping jokes and stories.

The more Gracie watched him, the more she was concerned that there was a crucial part missing from the act. George agreed. He needed a partner whom he could play off. He was, after all, a straight man. Gracie thought about a suitable person. Neither she nor George thought it possible for someone to substitute for her, but they could, perhaps, find someone with talent and some unique comic quality. Gracie hit upon the idea of using Carol Channing, who had, like Gracie, one the most distinctive and recognizable voices in show business. Channing was married to Charlie Lowe, who had represented Carnation Evaporated Milk, Burns and Allen's longtime sponsor. By that time, Channing was already a star on Broadway, most famous for singing "Diamonds Are a Girl's Best Friend" in *Gentlemen Prefer Blondes*. George and Carol had worked together — in his living room, playing to an audience of family and friends.

Channing agreed, and Gracie began to school her in the art of the two-act. Channing had great natural talent. Gracie stressed the importance of looking good. She knew that if an actor looked good it added to the humor when the actor did an odd or unexpectedly funny bit. Gracie made Channing get new glasses and a new hairstyle.

Gracie explained what might seem obvious but wasn't. What was crucial, she noted, was that the routine must seem natural. George and Carol had to appear to be having a simple conversation. It couldn't sound either forced or rehearsed.

Channing was tall — several inches taller than George — and, in that sense, wholly different from the diminutive Gracie. They went on for the first time in Lake Tahoe. They were such a success that they decided to go on tour. Channing was professional and accomplished. But no one could replace Gracie. At some level George knew that it took years for a team to perfect their timing and find their mutual comfort level. It was profoundly unfair for him to expect either Channing or anyone else to serve as a comparable, even if different, partner. And, just as inevitably, the act ended.

George worked with a variety of other female partners, including Jane Russell, Connie Haines, Dorothy Provine, and Beryl Davis. He also played a key role in Ann-Margret's career. She got a call that George was auditioning women singers for a spot in his show. She was part of a group and was concerned about her partner, but he was promised a spot in the show if she did well. By then George's ability to make stars was well known and young performers were anxious to work with him.

In November 1960, Ann-Margret met George for the first time at his office. He was, of course, puffing on his cigar. She was wearing black toreador pants, shiny and tight, and a wool sweater. George didn't keep a piano in the office so they went to a nearby soundstage. She did three songs, ending with "Mack the Knife." George, who, unknown to her, had only agreed to see her as a favor, was impressed. He immediately asked her to be part of the show.

She asked him, "Are you joking?"

"Not unless you're paying me," he snapped back.[3]

Ann-Margret was delighted. She and George did one of the "sand dances" that he had done with Gracie. The two rehearsed at his home, and Ann-Margret was very perceptive about Gracie's role: "What really impressed me about Mr. Burns was his relationship with his beautiful and gracious wife.... Whenever he wanted an honest opinion, he called Gracie. Hers was indeed the final word. He trusted her totally."[4]

This is a crucial observation. George might yell at Gracie in front of writers in his office. He might tell his pals at Hillcrest that he understood show business. He might accept every last perk that show business had to offer, including available and beautiful women. But underneath it all, he was insecure. He had trusted his mother, and then he trusted Gracie. That provided guidance in his life.

As George and Ann-Margret prepared for the first show, he became troubled. He asked if she was going to wear the new outfit she was wearing, a red-orange velvet pants suit. She had just purchased it. George wanted to know what happened to the tight pants and tight sweater she had worn to the audition. He told her, "People don't only wanna hear your voice. They wanna see where it's coming from."[5]

She immediately turned around, went to her dressing room, and put on the old outfit. George was happy. Ironically, several days later, George approached her and asked if she had a dress she could wear. Gracie had heard from some people and thought perhaps the tight outfit would send the wrong message. As always, George advised her to follow Gracie's suggestion.

Meanwhile the ever-busy George was continuing to work as a producer. Arthur Lubin, who had directed several Abbott and Costello films and a series about Francis, the talking mule, approached George with a series idea about a talking horse based on a series of short stories by Walter R. Brooks. For Lubin, this idea, titled *Mister Ed,* was, of course, just a variation of the Francis series, and George had enjoyed Cleo, the talking dog of *The People's Choice.* He agreed. They produced a pilot, but it didn't sell. They knew they had to make some changes, and started with the horse. They replaced the original horse with one named Bamboo Harvester (1949–1970). They also needed a new script one that focused on the relationship between Mister Ed and the human with whom he spoke, Wilbur Post, an architect who worked from home. When they began to look for an actor to play Wilbur, it was George who observed, "I think we should get Alan Young. He looks like the kind of a guy a horse would talk to."[6]

With Young signed, the show's creators sought a wife for him. They found the perfect actress in Connie Hines, who had the unusual blend of a sweet and innocent face and voluptuous physique. She didn't have much of a role, and she seemed better than Wilbur deserved, but that added to the subtle charm of the show.

Of course, Mister Ed's voice was crucial. They hired Allan "Rocky" Lane. He had been in many westerns, but he had trouble finding work at this time in his career. Still, he was proud. He wasn't sure he wanted to have his career devolve into speaking for a horse. He needed the money, though, and so a deal was struck. He would accept the job provided that his name was not used in the credits for the show. Unsurprisingly, Lane was not happy. Everyone could understand if not appreciate his reluctance in doing the part. Once the show became a hit, Lane did want credit, but the producers would not give it to him.

The pilot was filmed, though Lubin was out of the country. One of George's distant relatives did the directing. He did not have George's talents. Young and George and all the key people involved assembled to view the complete show. It was a mess. As Young recalls,

> The pace was off, the scenes were labored, and the camera angles missed much of the comedy. There were no laughs in the screening room.
> When the show ended, the lights went up. Everyone sat silent. George Burns was in the first row, with his back to us all. After a moment or two, he rose and turned to the assembly.
> "On behalf of me and my ... family, I want to apologize to you all. This was terrible."[7]

True to his word, George worked with Lubin to make sure it was a different show that audiences saw when it premiered on January 7, 1961. *Mr. Ed* was a midseason replacement, indeed the first show ever to open in such a spot. Both critics and audiences reacted positively. The program stayed on the air until February 6, 1966, and has been in reruns ever since.

Finally, George decided to do another television program. To no one's shock or surprise, he was still trying to duplicate the Burns and Allen show format. But fewer than three weeks before his new series, *Wendy and Me*, aired, tragedy struck.

On Thursday night, August 27, 1964, George came home from working on his new show. He and Gracie had dinner. The Democratic Convention was then taking place, and there was a tribute shown to President John Kennedy, who had been assassinated the previous November. Gracie cried as she watched the story of the fallen president. When the show was over and there was a commercial, George turned off the television and went downstairs.

As always, he had work to do on a script. As he worked, he heard the television go back on. He shouted up to Gracie to turn off the TV and get some sleep, but she said she was enjoying a Spencer Tracy movie that was near its conclusion.

Only a short time later, Gracie called out to George. She was struggling to breathe. The breaths came only heavily, and she began sweating profusely. They had a settled routine. She had the pains; she took some pills; she got better. But the pills didn't work this time. George was deeply worried and knew this was more serious than usual. He gave her another pill, but the pains only got worse. George called Gracie's doctor; he immediately came to the house, listened to her heart, and told George that she needed to get to the hospital. While they waited, George called Ronnie, Sandy, and his brother Willy. Then he held Gracie's hand and tried to console her.

The ambulance arrived at around ten. The attendants reached down to put her on the stretcher, and she apologized because she was all wet. The doctor directed George to sit in the ambulance's front seat. They rushed towards Cedars of Lebanon Hospital, with the attendants giving Gracie oxygen. The red lights were flashing, the sirens blaring, and George simply sat, stunned. He who was so careful to avoid hearing bad news, who had worked so hard to insulate himself from pain, struggled with the reality of it all. The ambulance arrived at the hospital at around 10:25 P.M. Gracie was rushed upstairs. George could do no more than stand in the hallway. Ronnie, Sandy, and Willy and his wife, Louise, all arrived.

The doctor stepped out to see them at around 11:15 P.M. George looked at the doctor's face and knew. The doctor said that Gracie was gone, that she couldn't be saved. The doctor then asked if George wanted to see her. George walked into the room and looked at Gracie, lying still and at peace. He leaned over, kissed her on the lips and told her he loved her. Then he walked out of the room, alone for the first time in almost 40 years.

Jack Benny, who had been performing in Lake Tahoe, hired a limousine and, by dawn, was on his way back to Los Angeles. He arrived at five in the morning. Jack stayed at George's house.

Guests started to arrive the next day. It was an odd assortment of people, mostly comedians whose only way of dealing with pain was to tell jokes. George remained alone upstairs, coming out of his room only on Sunday night. The house was filled. George went into the library and came out. He wasn't wearing his toupee. Most of the people collected had never seen him without it; some weren't quite sure who that man was emerging from the library. George walked over to Carol Channing and Charles Lowe. He hugged them, as though to provide a symbol that he was struggling to get back to life. Everyone turned to look at George, and he responded in the only way he could. He began to tell stories about Gracie and her family. He talked about life on the road. He recalled old acts he had seen in his youth such as The Cherry Sisters, widely judged to be the worst act in vaudeville. He sang the old songs he loved. He spoke without stopping for about five hours, entertaining the crowd. Telling stories was his routine, his reflexive reaction to the pain of life.

The funeral took place at three P.M. on Monday, August 31, at Forest Lawn Memorial Park in Glendale. More than four hundred floral tributes arrived. George gripped Jack Benny's arm. The services were conducted by Dr. Kermit Castellanos of the All Saints Episcopal Church. Gracie, of course, was a devout Catholic, but as Forest Lawn is not a Catholic cemetery, George suggested an Episcopalian service as a substitute.

George Jessel was among the speakers. He said, "The act is over, the bow music has faded, the billing will have to be changed. The next stage manager will have to be told 'George N. Burns, in one alone.' So be it. The passing of this sweet girl who never seemed to grow older is again something which cannot be challenged. The hope of mankind must be in the faith that the play is never over — when the curtain falls, it rises again." Jack Benny then rose to speak: "I was afraid I might not be able to say these few words. I was afraid it might be too difficult ... but I was encouraged by George ... Mary and I have lost one of our two closest friends.... The whole world loved Gracie ... all of us will miss her so very, very much.... We'll never forget her, ever."[8]

Gracie's bronze coffin was adorned with red roses and shell-pink carnations. Jack Benny, George Jessel, and others served as the pallbearers. With the public service completed, there was a ten-minute private service. Willy had arranged for the crypt, and Gracie was placed in it. George could take no more. Jack Benny and Ronnie had to help him leave.

After the funeral, all of George's friends came back to his house. There were no jokes this time. George simply remembered coming home each night to Gracie, lying in bed with her, holding hands and enjoying a television show.

Perhaps that is why, after Gracie's death, George could not fall asleep easily. Because of Gracie's heart condition, the couple had twin beds. One evening George slept in Gracie's bed rather than his own. After that, he could sleep without trouble. There was still the warm embrace of Gracie's memory in that bed.

George struggled. He began his weekly visits to see Gracie's crypt. He went to work. He kept to his routine, as though that would somehow enable him to get through this pain. He, no doubt, was convinced that he was living but not alive, that his career in show business had been dismal to non-existent before Gracie and would be the same after her.

If George was concerned, his outlook wasn't helped by the new show, *Wendy and Me*. It premiered on September 14, 1964. In the show, George co-starred with Connie Stevens, a bubbly, attractive actress who had become well known because of her role in the TV series *Hawaiian Eye*. Burns wanted to hire her, but she was under contract to Warner Bros. In return for being allowed to cast her, George had to agree to produce another series, *No Time for Sergeants*. Indeed, on the day after Gracie's funeral, George had gone to the office to work on that show.

In *Wendy and Me*, George played the owner of an apartment building in Southern California. Stevens played a tenant married to an airline pilot. Unsurprisingly, Stevens's character, Wendy Conway, is a bit of a ditz, somewhere between Gracie and Lucille Ball. As he had previously done, George spoke directly to the camera as the show's narrator. The show lasted for one season, 34 episodes. Connie Stevens was one more talented actress who was not Gracie. Of course, it was not fair to her to ask her — or the previous actresses who had tried to do so — to fill Gracie's delicate shoes. *No Time for Sergeants* also lasted only a year. Another effort, *Mona McCluskey*, didn't even make it that long. The downward spiral continued.

It seemed as though a turning point was reached in early 1966, after Ronnie was married at the Bel-Air Hotel. Unfortunately, Willy Burns drank too much at the reception. When he returned home he took too many sleeping pills. Ronnie and his wife had just arrived in Hawaii when they got a call to return immediately. Willy Burns was dead at age 63. It was January 20, George's 70th birthday. Some observers thought Willy had killed himself, frustrated by having to compete with his older brother, upset that George never fully appreciated all the contributions he made, anguished about what his life might have been had he not been George Burns's brother. The more common conclusion, however, was that the death was an accident. Willy's wife, Louise, blamed George. As for his own beliefs, George remained quiet. He knew Willy had a drinking problem. He knew that he had to yell at Willy because that was the only way he could make Willy understand. If George felt any guilt about the death, he didn't say. Any anger, resentment, or guilt was contained. But it surely must have struck him that, after Gracie's passing,

After Gracie retired, a restless George began to look for substitute partners. Here he is with Connie Stevens in the show *Wendy and Me* (Natwill Productions/Warner Bros. Television), which lasted only through the 1964–1965 season.

Willy's death was another reminder that George Burns the comedian was at the end of his professional career. He now, it seemed, had only to await his own death. But George Burns had a spirit that could not be beaten down by the world. He had an inner strength, an ability to take a hit and get up off the canvas, a fierce determination that he could and would keep going. He had a glint in his eye as a child, and he never lost it. It was as though he saw the world as one long joke and wanted to let the rest of humanity in on it.

In 1966, Americans were in the midst of a youth revolution. The young had conquered the culture. A Berkeley student named Jack Weinberg had caught the spirit of the age by suggesting that his generation would not trust anyone over 30. The singers were young and had long hair. George Burns was old and had no hair. But he still had that glint in his eye. It was then that George Burns made a decision. He would not hide his age at all. He would turn it into a virtue. George Burns would revel in old age. He'd use it as a source of self-deprecating humor. He appeared in clubs and on television shows, now as George Burns the funny old guy with the cigar.

But if George Burns was an old man in his act and even in the minds of his friends, he was not an old man in his own mind. Privately, he was still a man who was attracted to and who could attract beautiful young women. On December 30, 1966, the gossip columnist Sheilah Graham reported that it appeared as though George Burns, a few days short of his 71st birthday, was about to marry a woman named Kami Stevens, then 22. But George disdained the idea, saying, "My tuxedo is two years older than she. I still go out with girls who are young and some who are not so young. Some of them are even 21. I take them to a restaurant and sit in some dark corner so they can do their homework. I enjoy women, but I would never remarry."[9]

George did, however, jump headlong into the dating pool. An actress named Evelyn Keyes, who had played one of Scarlett O'Hara's sisters in *Gone with the Wind*, was the first woman he dated after Gracie's death. He also dated actress Lita Baron.

And despite his protestations about not marrying, George may have come close to marriage with Lisa Miller. She was 18 when they met in May 1967. She was then a member of a singing group called The Kids Next Door. There were 17 of them, and they opened for George at the Riviera Hotel in Las Vegas.

Miller enjoyed chatting with Charlie Reid, a vaudevillian who had fallen on hard times. To help an old friend, George gave Reid a job as his "dresser," making sure his shoes were shined and overlooking the wardrobe. Reid, who had been a dancer, began showing Miller some tap moves. The two were tapping one evening before the show when George heard them and came into the room. George saw them and asked Miller if she could do a traveling time step. Then he pushed her arm to show her how it was done. But Lisa Miller was no shy little girl. She twisted his nose to indicate she didn't like being poked. George talked to her, discovered a song she could play (the "Maple Leaf Rag") and heard her perform it on the piano.

Lisa Miller was five-feet-eight, very blonde, very California, very pretty. George Burns was none of these. He heard her sing and immediately asked her out to dinner. She didn't hesitate with her refusal. George said, in words that stuck with her, "Kid, you don't have to be so strong when you say no because I don't think anyone's ever going to make you do anything you don't want to. Besides, it just makes it that much harder when you want to change it to a yes."[10]

A few days later, one of her co-performers told Miller that George wanted to see her. George taught her a song and later sang it with her onstage. George, being as direct and persistent as he had always been with women, asked her to dinner again. She accepted and they began to have dinner together each evening. He arranged for her to have acting classes and for a joint appearance on Dean Martin's show.

Inevitably, George wanted Lisa to fill the Gracie role. They watched some of the old routines together on the road.

It was no doubt a heady time for both of them. Miller writes that it was then that they began to have discussions about getting married. According to Miller, George wanted to do so, but she realized it would not work. Still, she traveled with him and when they returned home, she moved into his house and attended classes at nearby UCLA.

It was around this time that George recorded an album. No one would confuse his voice with Sinatra's, but for George, the song was in the presentation and the pedigree. He chose old songs and developed a patter that made them come across as kind of a musical series of one-liners.

Burns and Miller appeared on one of Bob Hope's specials with Miller again cast in the Gracie role:

GEORGE: Lisa, this is Bob Hope.
LISA: Hello, Mr. Hope.
BOB: Hello, Lisa.
LISA: Oh, I'm so happy to meet you, Mr. Hope. And I must tell you, you look much younger since you shaved off your beard.
BOB: I never had a beard.
LISA: Well, that would be impossible. Then how could you shave it off?
BOB: I didn't shave it off.
LISA: Well, whoever did, did you a favor. You look much better without it.
BOB: George, if these are the right answers, I must be asking some pretty stupid questions.
GEORGE: Lisa, I don't think Mr. Hope understands you.

LISA: Oh? Mr. Hope, would you like me to talk slower?

BOB: Oh, no, no. I'll just try to listen faster.

LISA: Well, whatever makes you comfortable. You know, I watch you all the time on TV, and I love the finish of your show where you always smile at the audience and wave your hand and say, "God Bless."

BOB: Lisa, Red Skelton does that.

LISA: Well, he should be ashamed of himself. Now you'll have to get a new finish.[11]

George and Lisa came on a Hope special again in the spring of 1969 and continued where they left off:

BOB: It amazes me to see a man your age with such a young body.

GEORGE: Well, thanks, Bob.

BOB: I saw her backstage. Who is she?

GEORGE: You remember her. She was on your show last year. Her name is Lisa Miller.

BOB: Oh, yeah, she worked with you. That's the kid who's a little off-center. Is she still as flaky as ever?

GEORGE: No, she's changed completely. I was with her at a party the other night, and the hostess happened to mention she was fixing some lasagna with tomato paste. And Lisa said to her, "Why bother fixing it with tomato paste? If I had a broken lasagna, I'd throw it away."[12]

The lines are instructive. They're good lines, and they illustrate with incredible clarity just how much beyond the lines Gracie brought to the performance. First of all, audiences were familiar with her. That familiarity provided both recognition and comfort. Gracie was a laugh prompt. All she and George had to do was to walk out in front of the audience to get people feeling good. A substitute for Gracie, however talented, however well supplied with good lines, simply couldn't provide the history or the comfort. Indeed, the very attempt to substitute was simultaneously jarring and capable of causing resentment. Audiences didn't want another Gracie. They wanted Gracie.

Lisa Miller eventually married and moved away from George, but they continued to stay in touch. He knew how to treat young women. He told Lisa Miller that he was the nicest man she'd ever meet. He was right.

George was depressed. He stopped playing golf, concentrating instead on bridge. He began to exercise. He had already begun daily swimming. Now he began additional exercises, following the regimen of the Canadian Air Force. He showed up each morning at his office whether or not he had a project. He had a secretary to take down his good lines. He worked on a memoir or an article.

Relationships were fleeting. Visits to Gracie brought tears and some temporary comfort. His production company wasn't doing well. He couldn't find the right partner for an act. He was getting old in a young person's world.

He was taping Johnny Carson's *Tonight Show* in July 1974, telling one of his shaggy dog stories when his voice faltered. He struggled to find the right words. No one knew this, but George had been having fainting spells. On August 8 he was with Ronnie watching a concert when he felt intense chest pains. On August 9 he had triple heart bypass surgery.

Anyone taking bets would not have put money on the return of George Burns.

CHAPTER SEVEN

"I Can't Die. I'm Booked."

If George Burns seemed to be at or near the bottom, fate seemed to have better plans for Jack Benny. As George lay on his back in the hospital, a new movie was being cast. The movie was based on Neil Simon's 1972 Broadway comedy, *The Sunshine Boys*. Simon had completed the screenplay and director Herbert Ross had cast one of the lead roles. The principal characters are a pair of 70-something old-time vaudeville comics, "Lewis and Clark." In the screenplay the pair are angry with each other and, have not been on speaking terms for years. They then learn that a TV network wants to reunite them for a special on the history of comedy.

Bob Hope and Bing Crosby, famous not only individually but also for their many successful *Road* pictures, were the first choices. But Simon wasn't happy with that idea. He had written about two aging Jewish comedians, and Hope and Crosby clearly were not aging Jewish comedians.

Walter Matthau was eventually cast in the role of Willy Clark. Primarily because of Matthau's masterful performance in Simon's *The Odd Couple*, Matthau was seen as the consummate Simon actor. If Matthau was too young for the part at 57, make-up and acting would take care of that. Casting for Al Lewis was for more difficult. Woody Allen had originally been offered the chance to direct the film but turned it down because he wanted instead to play Lewis. It seemed as though every member of the elderly Jewish comedic community in Hollywood — not a small crowd — yearned for the part. Ray Stark, who produced the movie, wanted the non–Jewish Red Skelton for the part. But the screen test told them Skelton was no more suitable to play a small, Jewish vaudevillian than Hope or Crosby. Milton Berle certainly had the comedic skills, but his acting skills were judged inadequate. No one considered George Burns for the part.

But Jack Benny was another matter. He had his problems as well. At the test, Benny was told he spoke too quickly and was too sprightly for a 70 year

158

old. He calmly reminded them that he was 80. Jack Benny was set for the part.

On the day after George returned home from the hospital, he got a call from Benny. He told George that he had not been feeling well but that the doctors could find nothing wrong. George told him to get more tests — a complete examination.

In October, Benny was in Dallas preparing for a show when he began to feel dizzy. His left hand became so numb that he was unable to play the violin. For a while, despite the tests, doctors weren't sure what had happened.

By early December Benny had stomach pains as well. Again, a test proved inconclusive, and so an additional test was made. It was his second test that showed that he had pancreatic cancer so advanced that no operation could help. Benny spent his remaining days at home, with George and other friends stopping by to comfort him. Jack Benny died on December 26, 1974. George was in the house at the time. Mary Benny had come downstairs to tell everyone that her husband had died. George asked to be permitted to go upstairs to be alone with Jack for a few moments. Mary told him the doctors didn't want anyone there. George said he knew Jack longer than the doctors knew him, so George went upstairs. Jack was lying in the bed, his hands clasped as though he was ready for another comedy bit. His head was off to one side, engaging in one of his famous long pauses between lines.

George tried to deliver a eulogy at the funeral, but he broke down and was unable to

Here are Walter Matthau (left, made-up as Willy Clark), and George Burns (who didn't need old-age makeup to portray Al Lewis) starring together as battling vaudeville partners in *The Sunshine Boys* (MGM, 1975). Burns got the part when Jack Benny, who had been cast for the film, died.

continue. Now his best friend had followed his wife into death. George Burns could not have felt more alone. Gracie had died in 1964, and Jack Benny in 1974. It had been a horrible decade for George, and the prospects for the next one, if there was going to be a next one, did not look good.

But Jack Benny's manager, Irving Fein, had other plans. Fein knew that Jack was sick. It was a few weeks after that when Benny phoned Herbert Ross and said his illness would prevent him from taking the part. And Benny, true friend to the end, asked the director to consider George Burns for the part. And Irving Fein agreed. On that very day, Fein called George saying he should play the role. George, of course, thought the part was Jack's, that it didn't seem right for him to take it. Fein told him the truth, that Jack would want him to have the part. Fein, ever the manager, then put the script on George's desk and told George to call him the next morning. Eventually, he decided to accept. Some time later he had his audition.

Herb Ross lived in Beverly Hills, and George went to his home to do a reading for the part. George took his Cadillac for the five-minute drive. Ross was there with Ray Stark and Neil Simon. He asked them what lines they wanted him to say. The three were surprised because George wasn't carrying his script. George had memorized the entire script. He delivered his lines as an aging Jewish vaudevillian, which he most certainly was. The assembled group was impressed. George was even better in the role than Jack Benny. He just inhabited the part. And, most amazingly, George Burns wasn't playing himself. He was playing Al Lewis. He was acting. All the other potential actors were comedians who played themselves reciting Al Lewis's lines. But George, seemingly without experience in acting as anyone but himself, and away from movie sets for almost four decades, came fully prepared to play Lewis.

All seemed set. And then an executive stepped into the mix. MGM, the studio making the film, got a new head of production named Frank Rosenfelt. The new boss had an idea. He wasn't sure audiences wanted George, someone famous long ago but new old, tired, and without a fan base. Rosenfelt had what (on paper at least) sounded like a great idea. He wanted to bring in Jack Lemmon to play opposite Walter Matthau, as the two had done so well in *The Odd Couple*. But, as with Hope, Crosby, Skelton, and others, even a great comic actor couldn't necessarily be convincing as Al Lewis. Ross and Simon, having seen George, were determined. They said they would not make the film without George. Ray Stark supported their decision. Rosenfelt finally agreed.

George knew very well that not only was he an old vaudevillian, but he *looked* just like an old Jewish vaudevillian. In a way, he was embracing himself by taking the part. He understood Al Lewis in a profound way, and embracing the character brought him closer to an understanding of his Jewish self.

Ross was a superb director. There is one scene in which Willy Clark's nephew, Ben, played by Richard Benjamin, comes to talk a reluctant Al Lewis into agreeing to the joint appearance. Ross wanted George to play the scene without a toupee. George must have had great faith in the director because he agreed, and the scene is improved by the absence of hair. It is startling to see George without it, but for the character it is a moment of revelation. His baldness is a symbol of his lost vigor and fame. He is without it, but can put it back on for the show. Additionally, George without the toupee is a crucial reminder that actors play parts. Anyone who remembered George would know he was playing a part and playing it well. Some critics have noted that in that single scene the Lewis character doesn't have all his wits, a characterization not present later in the film. George is very careful about playing that side, and it is possible to see a subtle interpretation of his character by Simon, that without a job to go to, without a booking, the old vaudevillian was indeed slowly losing his mind but that this new part gave him a purpose again, and with it, an active mind.

The characters of Lewis and Clark were based, in part, on the real-life vaudeville team of Smith and Dale. Joe Smith and Charlie Dale were most famous for their sketch "Doctor Kronkheit and His Only Living Patient." ("Kronkheit" is a Yiddish word for sickness.) Dale played the doctor and Smith the uncertain patient. Here is part of the sketch:

SMITH: Are you a doctor?
DALE: I'm a doctor.
SMITH: I'm dubious.
DALE: I'm glad to know you, Mr. Dubious. [*Dale then tries to discover the illness.*]
SMITH: It's terrible. I walk around all night.
DALE: Ah! You're a somnambulist!
SMITH: No, I'm a night watchman.
SMITH: I got rheumatism on the back of my neck.
DALE: Ah, where would you want a better place than on the back of your neck?
SMITH: On the back of *your* neck.
SMITH: Doctor, it hurts when I do *this*.
DALE: Don't *do* that.
[The patient explains that he has already seen a doctor.]
SMITH: He told me I had snew in my blood.

DALE: What did he told you?
SMITH: He told me I had snew in my blood.
DALE: Snew? What's snew?
SMITH: Nothing. What's new with you?
SMITH (*reacting to Dale spitting on his stethoscope*): Doctor, what is that you're doing?
DALE: Sterilization.
DALE: The whole trouble with you is, you need eyeglasses.
SMITH: Eyeglasses?! I suppose if I had a headache, I'd need an umbrella.
[Dr. Kronkheit's fee is ten dollars.]
SMITH: Ten dollars! For what?!?
DALE: For my advice.
SMITH: Doctor, here is *two* dollars, take it. That's *my* advice![1]

When George and Matthau were preparing the scene, arguably the most important one in the film, George was upset. Both actors wore wild wigs. There were a lot of props including a tongue depressor called an "ah stick" in the sketch. It's not clear if George didn't like the writing. Neil Simon had gone beyond the Smith and Dale routine, mixing it up with a bit of burlesque, such as this line from the movie:

NURSE: Is there anything else you can think of?
DOCTOR: I can think of it but I can't do it.

But, generally, the lines were adequate. It was the props that bothered George. He leaned over to Matthau and said, "Listen, this sketch is not going to work."

"Why won't it work? I think it's fine."

"It won't work," George said, "because the props aren't funny. You see, you can't play funny dialogue against funny props. People won't know whether to watch the props or listen to the dialogue. You'd better tell Neil [Simon]."

"He's one of the most successful playwrights in American history."

"The sketch won't work. Tell him."

"Why don't *you* tell him?"

"Walter, it'll sound better coming from you."

Burns then called Simon over and said Matthau had some advice. Simon listened to Matthau repeat George's concern and said. "Walter, I don't buy that. The sketch stays the way it is."

George was no fool. He said, "I'm with you, Neil."[2]

But as it turned out, George was right. The scene is not as funny as the build-up for it promised. George's insights stemmed, of course, from his encyclopedic knowledge of vaudeville, the very entertainment being portrayed. Neil Simon, a product of radio and television, simply was too young to have such vaudeville experience. But George brought all the lessons of vaudeville to his part. As in his act with Gracie, George shrewdly looked around him and listened to his partner. He mostly kept his hands still. Gestures, like props, would focus an audience's attention away from the words. And, like any good straight man, George in vaudeville and George in the movie learned to show an appreciation for the insanity going on around him. He was at an aesthetic distance from it, looking at it, absorbing it. By stepping back from that insanity, George's character always gave the situation a heft that it might not have deserved on its own comic merits. Or, because Neil Simon was such a comic genius, in this case it added to the comic merits already present in the text.

And Burns and Matthau were terrific together in the film. In a sense, George had finally found another partner. In one scene, for example, Herb Ross thought George was being too serious. But Ross was not about to confront George Burns. Instead, between takes of the scene, Ross approached Matthau and told him that George seemed tight, that he needed to play the scene in a looser fashion. The scene was only of George. Matthau stood behind the camera, saying lines to which George would respond. Just as he spoke some of the lines, Matthau dropped his pants. George didn't miss a beat and continued with the scene, no doubt loosened up a bit.

The film was shot in eight weeks. Ross, in particular appreciated George's understated interpretation of the role. Matthau was given to exaggerated movements, and George's counterpoint played well. Ross put it this way, "Because of George's simplicity and directness and honesty, he set a tone for the picture ... and you had to play within that tone. It didn't allow for lying by an actor. It stripped away a lot of that 'stuff' which I worried about with Walter. He was being too bombastic, there was too much 'acting.'"[3]

The critics were impressed, and probably surprised, by George's performance. He was nominated for an Academy Award in February 1976 in the Best Supporting Actor category. He went to the award show with Lisa Miller, who by then had separated from her husband. The audience cheered as George accepted the award. Alluding to the fact that he had made his last film in 1939, George quipped, "I've decided to keep making one picture every 36 years. Getting this award tonight proves one thing: if you stay in this business long enough, you get to be new again."[4]

After the ceremony, some reporter asked him how he planned to celebrate. George was ready for the question. He said he was heading home for a bowl of hot soup.

George was getting offers to work in Las Vegas. And, although he had only planned on writing one book, he decided to do another. He would end up doing a string of them. Just as the Al Lewis role had made him appreciate his Jewish side more, so being alone after Gracie and having to come up with an act made him focus more on himself as part of the act. His life was the heart of the act and of the memoirs he wrote. In both cases, however, his constructed life was based on, but not identical to, his real life. His mind adjusted reality to make reality more palatable. So, too, his stories adjusted his own reality. All the stories were filtered through a strainer to make the result funny and touching and warm. Comedians always test out jokes, trying them out on new audiences between the sure fire jokes. George began trying out stories in the same way. He'd tell a story about his life and see how the audience reacted. If they liked it, he kept telling the story the same way. If they didn't like it, he didn't discard the story but retold it in a new way. Reality was determined by audience approval. George told his audiences and his readers he was doing this. He wasn't lying exactly, and he wasn't telling the truth exactly. That was show business to him.

His book *Living It Up (Or, They Still Love Me in Altoona)* was published in 1976. Taking no chances with an outsider, George wanted more control of the writing. He dictated anecdotes about his life to Jack Langdon, his secretary. After he completed enough stories, the notes were given to Elon (Packy) Packard who polished the narrative. The disjointed book was not a great success, but George enjoyed the process, and it was very easy money.

But thankfully George's movie career was not going to have to wait another 36 years. The story of the movie *Oh, God!* begins with the Avery Corman 1971 novel of the same name. Warner Bros. had bought the rights to the book, but it seemed as though no one wanted to make it.

Larry Gelbart, well known for his extraordinary work on *M*A*S*H*, had been given the job of writing the screenplay, and Carl Reiner, famous for his work on Sid Caesar's show but especially well known for *The Dick Van Dyke Show*, was asked to direct. Reiner had directed three films, but his previous one had not done well at the box office. At first, Reiner's great friend Mel Brooks was considered for the role of God, and Woody Allen as the grocery clerk God selects for a mission. Reiner declined the directing offer, noting that he and Brooks had done the "2,000-year-old man" routine and Brooks's playing God would be too similar to that. It looked as though the film would never be made.

At that point, Larry Gelbart went to see *The Sunshine Boys*. Just like everyone else, he was amazed by George's performance in the film. Everyone else saw Al Lewis. Larry Gelbart saw his God. Gelbart went to see Reiner who immediately liked the idea. Reiner, a master at understanding television, immediately noted that, in a sense, George had played God on the Burns and Allen television show by looking at scenes of the action from a distance and explaining them to the viewer. It was a keen insight.

George came to read for the part, and the writer and director knew their instincts had been perfect. George had grown into Al Lewis. His aim had expanded. He had now grown into God. He may have grown into the part, but he still wasn't a star. Despite his winning an Academy Award, George was not considered a guaranteed box-office hit, and so the money he was offered was not great by Hollywood standards. Irving Fein accepted the offer regardless. He knew his client wanted to be working and was nourished — perhaps even kept alive — by the new recognition he was getting. Fein might have been able to negotiate a higher salary, or George perhaps told him not to bother, but both men knew this part would be perfect for George and would enhance his reputation.

George was an older man who attracted an older audience. This new film was a chance to seek out younger fans as well. For all its comedic merits, *The Sunshine Boys* had been aimed at an older audience that remembered George. Now there would be a chance to introduce him to a younger audience that didn't know him. And, knowing that such a younger audience was needed for the film, the producers hired the popular singer John Denver to play the grocery clerk.

As he had before, George astonished the filmmakers by showing up on the first day with the entire script memorized. He didn't forget lines during the filming. He didn't need extra takes. George Burns, whatever his age, was a professional.

The film is about God paying a visit to Earth. He has a message but He needs a messenger. For that messenger He chooses Jerry Landers, an assistant manager of a supermarket. Landers (John Denver) is an average citizen. He's an honest, hardworking family man with a wife and children. Landers gets his first communication from God by a memorandum with the message, "God grants you an interview," and a location. Confused, Landers goes there, although the location — at a building on the appropriately named North Hope Street — is for the 27th floor. The building, Landers notes, only has 17 floors. But, for Landers, an elevator goes to the non-existent floor where God's voice (the very recognizable George Burns) comes through on an intercom. Later, Landers hears the same voice through his car radio.

It's interesting to note that audiences found George Burns believable as God. It's easy to understand why producers cast John Denver; he looks and sounds exactly like a Jerry Landers—an everyman—would look and sound. But George Burns's appeal is more mysterious. It's not familiar casting, as would have been the case with Mel Brooks. It's not a stunt bit of casting like Woody Allen. No one thinks of God as a stand-up comedian. And George didn't have the big-star appeal of the other actors whose names had been suggested. Indeed, by the time of the film he was not well remembered. He was routinely dismissed as having been lucky to be Gracie Allen's husband and unlucky that she had retired so that he had to struggle alone, only to reveal that, in fact, he really *did* need her. George Burns was a small, thin, old, Lower East Side New York Jewish God. But George had learned the greatest lesson needed by all straight men. He knew how to listen. In the film he really appears to be listening to Jerry, he seems to be kind, to care about people. George Burns's God, that is, was *exactly* the kind of God audiences craved, a Being who would listen to them sympathetically.

As God, George conveys his message to Jerry. He wants Jerry to let the world know that God still exists, that humans have what they need to do well on Earth, but they need faith. Eventually, the skeptical Jerry is convinced that he is receiving this message from God, and tentatively takes steps to convey that message to the world. Rarely is a prophet kindly received, and so it is in Jerry's case. Everyone doubts him.

One interesting scene occurs when a variety of religious leaders from different spiritual movements issue a challenge to Jerry. They will give him written questions in the ancient language of Aramaic. He is to be locked alone in a hotel room. If, the challenge goes, he is really in communication with God, he will know the answers and be able to respond. Jerry waits in a frenzy in the room, but God eventually appears (as a bellhop with a bottle of ketchup [the very seasoning George liked to put on all food in real life]) and provides all the answers. The questions and answers are the film's warm, simple theology. All religions are good. All spiritual seekers are good. But the film doesn't shy away from some tough questions:

> JERRY LANDERS: How can you permit all the suffering that goes on the world?
> GOD: Ah, how can I permit the suffering?
> JERRY LANDERS: Yes!
> GOD: I don't permit the suffering. You do. Free will. All the choices are yours.
> JERRY LANDERS: Choices? What choices?
> GOD: You can love each other, cherish and nurture each other, or you can kill each other. Incidentally, "kill" is the word. It's not "waste." If I had wanted

"waste," I would have written, "Thou shalt not waste." You're doing some very funny things with words. You're also turning the sky into mud. I look down, I can't believe the filth. Using the rivers for toilets, poisoning my fishes. You want a miracle? You make a fish from scratch. You can't. You think only God can make a tree? Try coming up with a mackerel. And when the last one's gone, that'll be that. Eighty-six on the fish, good-bye sky, so long world, over and out.

At one point, Jerry directly asks God if Jesus is His Son. And God has His ecumenical answer ready, with a George Burns twist at the end: "Jesus was my son. Moses was my son. Mohammed was my son. Buddha was my son. And so are you. And so is the guy who's charging you $18.50 for a piece of room service roast beef."

God only doesn't like one of the leaders, a TV evangelist. That is to say, the film strikes at an easy target and avoids alienating anyone else. The choice of targets is also a theological statement. The film shows a flawed, warm, kind God. This God is not the literal God of the Bible. This God does not have a group of followers on Earth with an exclusive path to the truth.

Jerry tells the TV evangelist's flock what God thinks of the preacher, that he is a phony, and the preacher in turn sues Jerry for slander. The climax of the film takes place in a courtroom during that slander trial.

Jerry is at first disappointed when God doesn't show up in the courtroom. The impatient judge is unhappy with Jerry, threatening him with a contempt charge for "what you apparently thought was a clever stunt." Undaunted, Jerry points out that as he called for God to appear, everyone turned to look for the arrival. And then God appears. At first He does some card tricks. To further prove His existence, He walks away from the stand for a few steps and then disappears in front of everyone with the final words: "It can work. Don't hurt each other. If it's hard to have faith in me, maybe it will help to know that I have faith in you."

Oh, God! was a mammoth success, although Larry Gelbart himself wasn't entirely satisfied with it, thinking the movie could have been more complex if he could have redone the screenplay. But the film had a huge impact on the public's perception of George Burns. George was no longer Gracie's partner, not even a successful Oscar-winning actor. George Burns was God. He relished the role, and for the remainder of his life, George did seem superhuman in his ability to transcend age. He was the living visitor of the lost past, a past without the frenzy of modern life. George was the kind, warm grandfather everyone wanted. He was the promise that everyone could lead an extraordinary life in old age. He was a fragile icon in an age that mocked heroes.

There were two sequels to the film, but neither captured the original's scope and charm. But that didn't matter. The sweet, kindly George Burns, the one hidden behind the straight lines and the jokes, had come out of hiding, and the public loved it. George became famous for being old and being nice. The jokes flowed from this persona. George literally had a second chance at life. At first hidden behind Gracie, alone or with a new partner, he seemed incomplete and lost. *The Sunshine Boys* proved he could act, but it was *Oh, God!* that was the beginning of the new George Burns, the one audiences embraced from that moment to the end of his life.

Refreshed by this new identity, George wasted no time. George wrote several more books. He had his own way of writing books. George was a schmoozer, a natural talker, so he didn't sit down behind a typewriter or with a pen and pad. Instead he decided to talk out his book. At first, he used a tape recorder, but George couldn't be George without an audience, and he was decidedly unhappy that the tape recorder never responded to any of his jokes. Instead he interviewed writers, claiming to choose the writer who laughed the loudest at his jokes.

He hit the road to appear in the best venues. He continued to appear in films. He kept up a whirlwind of promotional efforts from late-night television shows to the recording studio to state fairs to his regular Beverly Hills social circle.

In a way, this was the life George had always envisioned, with himself the center of attention and adoration. He knew his age made him a bit of a sideshow attraction, but he played to it. He embraced the new identity lovingly, bathing in the limelight and basking in the applause.

Such a pace might seem incredibly difficult for a man in his eighties. Indeed, George played shows even when he felt ill. He kept going. Irving Fein, his manager, knew the gold he had found accidentally after Jack Benny's death. It is a cruel interpretation, though, to claim that Fein forced George to go on the road and play so many dates. George could have stopped anytime he wanted to do so. Ronnie and many others had a more accurate understanding. Despite his fame and fortune, George had never felt like the money and attention came for him, but rather for Gracie. Now it was different. He was trying to cram a lifetime into those golden years. He loved all the work. He lived for it and probably because of it. The bookings became his reason to get up in the morning.

But Irving Fein did have an influence. There were fewer unpaid benefit appearances. George charged a lot of money (typically $50,000) to go to someone's house to appear at a party.

It would be an exaggeration to claim that, in his later years, George recovered a bit of his Jewishness, but he seemed to do so. Jan Murray invited a few of his fellow comedians to his house for a Passover Seder. Not everyone attended. Groucho Marx, for example, responded to Murray's invitation this way: "I appreciate being asked, but I'm an old man and I can't wait that long to eat. I have my dinner now at five-thirty. Besides, I went to a Seder last year, and it's the same material."[5]

Marx, like George, Jack Benny, Milton Berle, and Eddie Cantor, was not religiously observant. Jan Murray, on the other hand, was one of the younger Jewish comedians who took Judaism seriously. The younger comedians hadn't, like their elders, started in show business as children and spent their entire careers enmeshed only by show business. Despite his age and lack of Jewish observance in his life, George accepted the invitation.

Everyone at the Seder loved the stories and the songs, but one man, someone from outside the world of entertainment, shocked the crowd by asking the elderly comedian, "Mr. Burns, do you believe in the hereafter? I mean, do you think there's a heaven and hell?"

George was unflustered. He said, "I don't know what they've got waiting for me, but I'm bringing my music."[6]

Around this time George began to receive a series of letters from Catherine Carr, letting him know how much she liked his new book. As he did with all letters, George had his secretary, Jack Langdon, write a thank you note. But Carr's letters kept coming and kept going from a professional to a personal admiration for George. Finally, George added a note to the thank you letter. He invited Cathy Carr to call him so they could go out for a drink.

Cathy Carr was a wealthy socialite from Texas, a divorced mother of two with blonde hair flowing to her waist, and, not incidentally, 45 years younger than George Burns. She journeyed to Los Angeles and did go out to dinner with George. Given his charms, Carr continued to visit him and found him more and more enchanting. While she stayed at a hotel in Beverly Hills during the visits, it was clear to all observers that George looked forward to seeing her and she him. There were press reports that they planned to marry. Evidently, Carr wanted to do so. And she certainly didn't look like a young woman out to take advantage. She didn't want to be in show business, and she didn't need the money. It may have seemed, to outsiders, like an unusual or awkward relationship. But it worked well for both of them.

George was now an American institution. In the comedy world, there is no higher tribute than a roast, and George appeared as the roastee on the *Dean Martin Celebrity Roast* on May 17, 1978. His friends wasted no time in going after him:

> DEAN MARTIN: I don't want to say *when* he started singing, but that was the year the Top Ten were the Ten Commandments.... Did you ever hear a voice like his?
>
> RED BUTTONS: Ladies and gentlemen, the question tonight is why, why are we roasting this ancient comedian ... a man old enough to be his own father.... A man who embarrassed everybody at The Last Supper by asking for seconds.
>
> RUTH BUZZI [*in character as Gladys Ormphby*]: George Burns wasn't the same person you see today. He didn't even like the smell of those big, fat cigars. So I stopped smoking them.
>
> DOM DE LUISE [*playing a psychiatrist*]: George Burns came to me because after playing "God," he thought he was. So I put him on the couch and said, "Mr. Burns, you came to the right doctor. I can cure anybody. I once cured a man who thought he was a rabbit. Of course, I must admit not before he and his wife had 78 children.'"
>
> DON RICKLES: George, we're both of the Jewish world. Not that that matters to show business, but it matters to me. And on behalf of the Jewish religion, we want you out.[7]

George made two interesting films in 1979. The first of these was *Just You and Me, Kid* co-starring Brooke Shields. Shields played Kate, a teenager in foster care who is a runaway. She is being sought by a drug dealer for taking $20,000. She hides in a car trunk because the dealer has taken her clothes. Bill (Burns) an ex-vaudeville entertainer, discovers her in the trunk, wrapped in a tire, and decides to protect her. There are various sub-plots to the film, such as Bill's greedy daughter trying to have him institutionalized because he keeps giving money to his friends, and the relationship with his pal (played by Burl Ives) who is in an institution.

Much of the charm and strength of the movie depends on the relationship between Bill and Kate, as in this dialogue:

> BILL: Running away from home?
> KATE: I'm an orphan.
> BILL: What happened to your folks?
> KATE: They died. Went down with a boat. Sank. Forget the name of it. Big boat.
> BILL: *Titanic?*
> KATE: Yeah, that's it!
> BILL: Then your parents died 63 years before you were born!

KATE: Which is why I hardly knew them.
BILL: Yeah, well that ... that ... that makes sense.

Bill and his friends play cards, and Bill always loses. It is his way of giving money to his needy friends without forcing them to ask for it. Probably most of the members of the audience didn't know it, but in real life George was supporting people from show business, especially his friends from vaudeville. He took care of Blossom Seeley when her husband, Benny Fields, died. He first donated a million dollars to the Motion Picture and Television Home and Hospital in Woodland Hills, and he later bought land for the home. The land cost him half a million dollars.

Just You and Me, Kid is so sweet that it sometimes lacks any sting, but it was a good movie for George. There were frequent small nods to his career and to the pain of aging. Bill's house was equipped with an alarm clock that wakes him each morning to the roar of applause. At a later hour it plays "Swanee." And Bill keeps the jokes and one-liners coming. He is spry. He is a walking, talking argument against the idea that aging is, by definition, debilitating. Still his daughter, Shirl, is determined to remind him of his mental failures:

> SHIRL: Sometimes I think you don't realize what's going on, I think sometimes you're getting—
> BILL: Senile? That's the operative word nowadays, isn't it, Shirl? You know, it's funny. When I was young, I was called a rugged individualist. When I was in my fifties I was considered eccentric. Here I am, doing and saying the same thing that I did then, and I'm labeled senile. I wonder what my billing is going to be ten years from now?

The film, which has never been released on DVD, may by its nature appear to rely a bit on old George Burns stories, but it is as sweet a movie as George Burns ever made. George himself seemed to recognize that:

> I enjoyed making my other pictures, but there was something special about *Just You and Me, Kid*. Everything seemed to fall into place right from the beginning. Everybody liked everybody. The crew liked the actors, the actors liked the crew, we all loved the director, Leonard Stern, we were all crazy about the script, the words just seemed to fit everyone's mouth, even the food in the commissary seemed to taste better. One day on location we got caught in a cloudburst. We all looked up and exclaimed, "What a beautiful rain!" Another day it was 114 degrees in the shade, and nobody perspired. I don't know what it was. I'd say it was chemistry, but I'm not a chemist.[8]

The other George Burns film released in 1979, *Going in Style*, is about three elderly men, Joe (Burns), Al (Art Carney, Jackie Gleason's longtime co-star) and Willie (Lee Strasberg, the famous acting teacher). They have to share their Queens, New York, apartment because each is just getting by on Social Security. They're bored by their lives, much of which is spent in a nearby park where they feed pigeons, read newspapers, watch characteristically annoying children, and observe the world going on without them.

Wanting both a thrill and much-needed extra cash, Joe comes up with a wild idea to rob a bank. The three are excited, but there are concerns:

> WILLIE: What if we get shot?
> [*silence*]
> JOE: What's the difference?

And so they determine to go through with their plan. Al secretly borrows pistols from his nephew, Pete. The three elderly bandits don Groucho Marx glasses for disguises and succeed in stealing $35,000 from a bank. Willie is overcome by all the excitement and gets a heart attack the very same day as

Three comedy legends dressed in disguises are here shown in a scene from the film *Going in Style* (Warner Bros., 1979). The actors are (from left to right), Lee Strasberg (the famous acting coach), George Burns, William Pabst as the surprised guard, and Art Carney (famous for teaming with Jackie Gleason).

the robbery. It is at his funeral that Al and Joe determine that Pete and his needy family should get most of the money, though without telling him its source. Al and Joe decide to spend the rest on a trip to Las Vegas.

While they are having fun, the police, hounded by the media which loves the story of this unique trio of thieves, make a concerted effort to find them. Al and Joe, win even more money, but Al dies in his sleep as soon as they return from their trip.

Joe is arrested on his way to Al's funeral. The film closes with Joe in prison talking to Pete. As Joe is being led away, he turns to Pete and says that "no tin-horn joint like this could ever hold me." It would have been fascinating to see a sequel to the film in which Joe tries to escape from the prison.

George's appearance is one interesting aspect of the film. As he later wrote,

> It was a challenge for me because I had to play an old man. I had to learn how to walk slow, how to drop food on my tie, how to remember to forget things.... It took time for the makeup man to put on wrinkles.... The script was written by ... Martin Brest, who's also directing.... He called me up one day and said, "Mr. Burns, I want you to wear different glasses in this movie. Can I stop by and have you try on a pair."
>
> "Sure, why not."
>
> Well, he came in on a Thursday with a photographer, a lightning man, three suitcases full of eyeglasses, and a consulting optometrist. They set up the lights, I put on glasses, I took off glasses, and they kept taking pictures. Well, it didn't take long; by the following Wednesday Martin was satisfied. Then he decided that I would need a different hair style. He wanted me to look like somebody else. That seemed strange, if he wanted me to look like somebody else, why didn't he hire somebody else? But I guess that's show business. When he asked me to go to the wig-maker I told him I'd be glad to but he'd have to wait for a few days until my eyes got back in focus.[9]

George Burns was seemingly ever-present in the culture, not to mention ageless. Getting older seemed to energize him, as thought the looming prospect of his own mortality meant that he would have fewer opportunities and less time to produce a solo body of work by which he would be remembered. So the breakneck pace of the movies, television appearances, nightclub shows, private performances, and charity fundraisers weren't enough. George, the child who couldn't read well, the man who had to memorize his scripts, was determined to turn out more books. *The Third Time Around* was published in 1980. *How to Live to Be 100— or More* came out in 1983. *Dr. Burns' Prescription for Happiness* was published in 1984.

The titles are particularly revealing. George Burns had a wider mission than being an entertainer. He sought to provide people a guide to aging. He put out a video in which he illustrated how he exercised at home. To illustrate his own determination to age well, he had Irving Fein book him at the London Palladium for his 100th birthday. (It would be one of the few bookings he had in his life that he could not fulfill.) He began to tell people his one-liner: "I can't die — I'm booked."[10]

That was not just a joke. It was a philosophy of life, and not just his own life. He was convinced that he really *had* found the fountain of youth, and he wanted to share its waters. He tricked age by thinking young, by acting young, by keeping his mind and body active, by looking at life with a twinkle in his eye, by laughing and finding material to laugh about, by setting aside time in which he didn't allow bad news to enter his mind, by a sheer will that he had developed as a child not to let life defeat him. As he wrote:

> I've been young and I've been old, but I never knew when young ended and old began.... Old people are healthier than a lot of young people who died with the same ailment *they* have.... Just because you're old that doesn't mean you're more forgetful. The same people whose names I can't remember now I couldn't remember fifty years ago.... They say you can't teach an old dog new tricks. Who needs new tricks? If you play it right, the old tricks still work.... I enjoy being old. For one thing, I'm still here. I like being older than I was yesterday. And I'm looking forward to being older tomorrow than I am today. When you're young, if you're lucky, you get older. When you're middle-aged, if you're lucky, you'll get to be old. But when you're old ... you're in a holding pattern — that's it. It's sort of a reward for being young all that time."[11]

He summed up his philosophy in another way as well:

> I love show business and I'm lucky to have spent my whole life in it. I think that's really the secret to a long life. I would rather be a failure in something that I love than be a success at something that I hated to do.... You can't help getting older, but you don't have to get old.... Never retire! Retire? I'm doing better now.... I'm making old age fashionable. People can't wait to get old.... There's nothing you can do about dying. Like in vaudeville, if they didn't like your act, they'd cancel you. The manager would knock on your door and give you back your pictures if you were canceled. Well, when the guy knocks on my door, I'm not going to answer! Let them keep the pictures.[12]

George really believed that the mind could control the body, that attitudes could change lives. He had, after all, survived his father's death. He had overcome poverty and the early indifference of audiences and bookers. He had ignored the pleas of some of his family members to find a respectable business. George Burns, though, always had his will and his sense of humor, his determination to do what he wanted to do in life. He always claimed that he would have been happy just to stay in show business, whether or not he had been a success; that the very idea of happiness was grounded in the act of doing what you wanted to do. But he had seen his vaudeville friends, some of whom had been great successes, turn out to be forgotten and poor. That is, George Burns's prescription for happiness works well for the successful.

George Burns continued to travel for the rest of his life. He famously said, "I can't die. I'm booked," and he meant it. He was supposed to play the Palladium Theatre in London on his 100th birthday but, due to health, had to cancel.

Few of his friends who had not succeeded looked as kindly upon life as he did. Still, George would no doubt argue that the prescription fuels happiness, that happiness itself is an elastic term and people define it very differently.

And he wanted to demonstrate what he meant. In 1989, he starred in *The Wit and Wisdom of George Burns*. It is a 45-minute video, and in it George literally takes audiences through his daily exercise routine. It is a bit unnerving to watch him as he bends and stretches. After meeting his house staff, the viewer follows George to his office where he meets with Irving Fein and Jack Langdon. From there it's on to Hillcrest for lunch. As always, George plays some bridge. The video ends with George performing — not in front of a bunch of the nostalgia-filled elderly but, tellingly, in front of a college audience.

The video is revealing, in both a good and a bad way. George talks to Arlette and Daniel D'Hoore (the couple who take care of him) and Red Buttons at Hillcrest, and the viewer (to whom he is illustrating his exercises) in exactly the same way. The best interpretation of this is that George is always on, a performer in public and private, a man with nothing to hide. But there is another, less benign, interpretation. George has performed for so long that any real self has disappeared. There is no Nathan Birnbaum, the civilian. There is only George Burns, the performer. He has volunteered to give up his identity for his success and acclaim. Perhaps he wanted to do so. However, beneath the kind façade and the jokes, it is possible to feel profound sympathy for Nathan Birnbaum who may or may not even realize the price that has been exacted from him to become George Burns. His views on aging are expanded in the video:

> Age is a state of mind, an attitude. I see people that the minute they get to be sixty, they start practicing to be old. They start taking little steps. They drop food on themselves. They take little naps when you're talking to them. By the time they get to be 70, they've made it. They're now a hit. They're now old. Not me ... I like young people. I don't think it's good when older people just hang around each other comparing gravy stains ... unless it's expensive gravy. And I'm not interested in yesterday.... I'm 93 and I love my age.[13]

While he may have given up a lot, it is also true that the prescription to laugh, to exercise, to look forward to each new tomorrow, to eat well, to be simultaneously satisfied and hungry for more from life is an excellent one for those with the temperament to follow it.

His prescription also included an active interest in women. He kept that out of his prescription formally, but it was there by example. He came close to marrying several women in his old age, but each time he stopped himself, or the women helped him stop himself. But George liked to date very young women, at least very young for him. Doing so added to the gossip around him which kept him in the news. Dating much younger women made him still feel attractive, a deep need for him all his life. Or perhaps for George, as for so many people, reason stopped at the edge of desire. Perhaps he took his wish to date younger women as a sign not so much of virility but as a sign that he wasn't yet ready to die.

Surely he would have preferred that Gracie were alive to keep him company in his old age, but without her he had to prove to himself that life, however painful, kept going. He remembered Gracie, and he mourned her deeply for a while. He then realized that mourning didn't become a survivor. And so he began to give advice to others about how he had lived and how they could live.

And George retained his interest in helping others. He was honored on his 85th birthday with a tribute dinner by the Ben-Gurion University in Israel. The university planned to name a medical wing "The George Burns Medical Educational Center." Neil Simon and Marsha Mason chaired the event. It was one more indication that in his later years, however tentatively, George sought to find the Jewish part of himself again. Perhaps it was a tribute to his father and mother or even his ancestors. But it is just as likely that George saw in Israel a land where Jews didn't have to hide their identity, and that must have really appealed to him.

George certainly took his own advice about how to live. He never stopped. He wanted to prove to himself and the world that he was beyond aging. Let everyone else be surprised that he could still think well and could walk across the stage in bold strides. He knew he could do it.

Lucie Arnaz noticed George's unique method of preparing for a performance. A half hour before he was to go on, he was fully dressed and ready. Many performers waited until the last minute to dress. Most singers practiced by singing the songs they would perform. The rehearsal calmed them down. George, though, didn't do that. He had a piano in his dressing room and when Morty Jacobs, his accompanist, arrived, the two didn't sing and play the songs that George would perform on stage. Instead, they tested each other's memory, calling out old songs to see if the other recalled it and, if so, if he could sing or play it. The door to George's room was open so that people backstage could hear the songs. What George was really doing was a memory exercise. He trusted his voice. He wanted to keep his mind active.

On September 18, 1985, when George Burns was 89 years old, a new television series, *George Burns Comedy Week*, was broadcast. George served as the host and narrator for what was essentially an anthology series. George was being promoted as the oldest star ever in a television series. But George really wasn't in any of the episodes of the series, so that there simply wasn't enough of George Burns to satisfy his fans. Comedians and actors who appeared on the series included Candy Clark, Samantha Eggar, Fannie Flagg, Howard Hesseman, Robert Klein, Don Knotts, Roddy McDowall, Martin Mull, Joe Piscopo, Don Rickles, and James Whitmore, There were some cute episodes, especially "Christmas Carol II," which imagined Tiny Tim as an adult, beginning to act more and more like Ebenezer Scrooge. Another episode starring Harvey Korman and Valerie Perrine turned out to be the pilot for a short-lived show titled *Leo & Liz in Beverly Hills*. But generally audiences didn't much like George's new show. It lasted only until December 25, 1985. That failure was to be George's last role in a television series.

George, though, continued to be on television and on stage. One critic summarized George Burns' appeal after a 1988 appearance at Caesar's Tahoe:

> You're ready to laugh ... what you're not ready for is to be touched. In George Burns you have the essence of entertaining, everything rolled into seamless, artless charm, pure humor wedded to pure style. As you watch him, warmed and awed by this foxy grandpa in a natty tuxedo, we want him never to leave — not just the stage, us.[14]

George was 92 at the time of this appearance. He had never devolved. He had done just as he said: he was in his own brilliant holding pattern, the perfect comedian, the walking, talking exemplar of the kindness and humor that humans could produce if they wanted to do so. Americans indeed wanted him never to die, for a piece of themselves would go with him.

For a while it looked as though he might keep that promise. He sang "Take Me Out to the Ball Game" during an All-Star baseball game. He donated his vaudeville trunk to the Smithsonian Institution. Streets were named for him and Gracie.

In 1988, George starred in the movie *18 Again!* (which evokes his popular 1980 country-western single, "I Wish I Was 18 Again") about a grandfather and grandson having an accident that causes them to switch souls. George plays Jack Watson, a wealthy playboy about to turn 81. Charlie Schlatter plays David, his grandson who is at the same time approaching his 18th birthday. After the accident, Jack lives life as his grandson. David, though, ends up in a coma. In his new role, Jack gets to see himself in a new way. He ruefully observes that he was not a good parent to Arnie, his son. He kept Arnie at an emotional distance and ignored good ideas to improve the company the family owned. Jack also forced his grandson to join a fraternity at his old alma mater and learns that David is being bullied there. His fraternity brothers make him write their term papers. He discovers, to his horror, that his young and attractive wife, Madeline, is unfaithful to him. When the family makes the painful decision to disconnect David from the life-support system, Jack intervenes and saves his grandson.

Once again, George's screentime is limited. George was, indeed, beginning to slow down—but only onscreen.

In 1989, he produced his book *George Burns: All My Best Friends*. George and his collaborator, David Fisher, filled in another piece of the Burns prescription for happiness: find and keep great friends. The book is one of George's best. His stories about Frank Fay, Eddie Cantor, George Jessel, and, most of all, Jack Benny, were moving. George, in fact, had worked to convince the United States Post Office to issue a commemorative postage stamp honoring Jack Benny. (Such a stamp was released in 1991.) George also wrote about Benny's wife, Mary. George made it clear in the book that he didn't really like her, but that he tolerated her for the sake of his friendship with Benny. The memoir also made clear that he far preferred Harpo Marx to Groucho.

A story about others is revealing, in part, because the choices of which stories to tell can reveal a lot about the teller. Here, for example, is one story George told about Eddie Cantor:

> Even if you had good ratings, if you did something or said something that upset the sponsor, they canceled you. I'm being serious again—I always like to let you know—because I want to tell you what they did to Eddie Cantor. Whether people liked Cantor or not they had to admire his courage. At the 1939 World's Fair he made a speech criticizing Father Coughlin, a priest who used his own radio show to preach prejudice and hatred. The day after Eddie said out loud what a lot of other people were thinking, his show was canceled. He couldn't get a sponsor. Suddenly Eddie Cantor, one of the most successful radio entertainers, was off the air. Grace [sic] and I had him on our show a few times, Jack had him on, but Eddie was very depressed.
>
> He went off the air for a year. Jack saw how depressed he was, so one night he picked up the phone and called the president of the New York advertising agency that represented his sponsor. The president told him that the business people thought Cantor had become too political, that no one wanted their products associated with controversial things like justice and honesty. Jack finally convinced him to meet with Cantor. Cantor gave his word that he wouldn't talk about politics and a few weeks later he was back on the air."[15]

The reason the story is important is that Burns almost never made any reference to politics. Once again, late in life, he recalls slights against the Jewish people who stood up to prejudice. It is telling, of course, that it was Jack Benny, and not George, who had the courage (and the ratings) to stand up for Cantor. But this was one more of a growing number of signs that George wanted to say he was Jewish.

Friends came to see him across time. One evening he was playing in the Concord, a resort hotel in the Catskills. The booking was for a single night, a typical 55-minute act with George singing, dancing, and telling stories. But this performance was different. At its end, one of the Concord's executives came onstage and told George that a friend of his was in the audience. Billy Lorraine, the partner George broke up with just before he met Gracie, walked slowly onto the stage. The 65 years between meetings disappeared, and the two partners performed together again. This time, though, they weren't "Broadway Thieves" stealing the songs and styles of others. They sang in their voices. Everyone in the crowd was deeply moved. But that was George, always remaining connected to his past, even across a lifetime. Billy Lorraine died two years later.

But George Burns kept living. Cathy Carr returned to town and decided that she was going to stay in his house — not at some hotel — when she was visiting. She was given the back bedroom. It was not the nicest room in the house. George was trying to deliver a message, in the most polite way possible. He invited other women to dinner while she was there. She eventually moved out.

And George wasn't through with performing on television. *George Burns Celebrates Eighty Years in Show Business* appeared as a television special in 1993. The show began along the lines of a roast, with comedians making the standard sex and old-age jokes. It was all not very original, and George even didn't look like he appreciated it. He sang a song and delivered a monologue. But George had been concerned. He had always memorized all his work, and now, for the first time in his life, he was concerned that his memory would fail him, that the timing could not work because the words would not flow. He expressed his fears to a former writer who tried to reassure him that the audience would guide him. But that was wrong, George knew. The audience was always a guide, but not a prompter. The audience told him if he was doing well, not how to do what he did. And his fears turned out to have merit. He performed well, but he knew it was time to quit. He would no longer be the performer.

That, of course, didn't mean that he was done with show business. It meant that he couldn't do his standard act, but it didn't mean he couldn't sit in a chair and answer questions, which is what he began to do.

But the signs were beginning to show. Bit by bit, age began to catch up with the elusive George Burns.

It was, for example, impossible not to notice that he was the only one of his generation left. It was horrible enough when Gracie died and then Jack Benny. But it added to his pain when people like George Jessel, Groucho Marx (for all their rivalry), Danny Kaye, and others died. It was as though George was being abandoned, making it harder and harder for him to remain positive and to focus on the future. George joked that he had outlived his doctors, and that he would be glad not to date younger women but women who were his own age. But, he wryly observed with the lifelong twinkle he had in his eye, there simply were no women his own age whom he could date. And if he outlived his friends and doctors, he also outlived his rivals and critics. It was one way to be a triumphant success. There was no one around who could question the veracity of his tales, still rubbed to a high gloss with a vaudeville shine. Even better, critics no longer criticized George Burns. He was a genuine American icon, a force of nature to be admired, not questioned. After all, how could you criticize God? So his songs were old and forgotten and spoken more than sung. So his voice was not exactly comparable to Enrico Caruso's. So his stories were told, retold, and retold again until audiences could literally fill in the punch lines. George was the being from afar who brought comfort and delight. That is what the critics now saw, even if one or two did notice that the "George Burns" created from those stories didn't always resemble the George Burns who had lived through the reality of his life.

But George's act wasn't universally accepted. As John Lahr wrote in his *New York Times* review of one of George's books, *The Third Time Around*:

> It's impossible to dislike a megalomaniac who confides, "By the time I found out I had no talent I was too big a star" ... George Burns has been a star for so long he doesn't know how to stop being famous.... And to see a man of 82 still selling himself is at once tremendous and terrifying.... This compulsion to curry favor with the public, to keep up the image, dishonors both the integrity of the performer and his accomplishments.... Very little of the man and the real life of show business is conveyed.[16]

Lahr makes an interesting point. George was selling himself to the end. But it wasn't an act. It was a *need*. He needed to surrender his self for an image. He had a profound emotional need to prove he was worthy, to show the world that his parents' son was someone of whom they could be proud. It's true, as Lahr asserts, that such an approach does shield the real person, but it is not true that the approach in any way "dishonors" the performer or the accomplishments. George was being George. He told people that he was going to tell stories. It would have been dishonorable for him to stop being George Burns. Indeed, when in his book *Gracie: A Love Story* he revealed an affair, he took some criticism. The audience spoke. They didn't want to see behind the George Burns curtain. And so he very rarely lifted it again.

George's own family kept getting older as well. Sandra got a divorce from Rod Amateau and married Steve Luckman. George had great-grandchildren. Both Ronnie and Sandra stayed out of the limelight, perhaps seeing the negative effects that the general public never observed.

And so, it was at a moment like this that George had the most to tell Gracie as he visited her to talk about what was happening to him. It is easy to imagine George sitting there at Forest Lawn, spinning his stories, saying he was going to be joining Gracie, sighing and perhaps shedding a tear or two. It must have been there, in Gracie's presence, that he felt in between the land of the living and the land of the departed, as though it were a hallway. He surely had a lot to tell Gracie, but even he didn't know when the end would come.

There are various interpretations of his visits to Gracie. In a straightforward way it was simply an ongoing sign of love and dedication. But because this was George Burns, who always deflected tragedy, who didn't like to deal with pain, there is another way to look at the visits. The director Herbert Ross had noted about Jack Benny that George had "never dealt with Jack's death. He had a very strange view of that, of death."[17]

George's visits to Gracie were, in a way, his psychological efforts to keep her still alive, to refuse at some deep level to admit that she was really gone. Such an attitude went all the way back to his father's death. George developed some way to shield himself from the pain, a shield he desperately needed to continue living. He needed those visits to Gracie. He needed to pretend — not in a delusional way, but in some corner of his mind, some private refuge from reality and the world and other people — that somehow she was still alive.

It was on a Wednesday, on July 13, 1994, that George hit his head after slipping in the bathtub in his house in Las Vegas. He had been sitting on a stool to dry himself with a towel. He either stood and fell or fell over while sitting and hit his head on one of the bathroom fixtures. Daniel D'Hoore was downstairs and, upon hearing the fall, ran upstairs, saw what happened, and immediately called for an ambulance. He also called Ronnie and Sandy.

George was taken to Cedars-Sinai Medical Center in Los Angeles to be observed. He had stitches, and he uncharacteristically rested. He seemed all right, at first, as though this 98-year-old man really was invincible. He only stayed in the hospital until July 22. But his speech seemed affected, and he was re-admitted in less than two months. Fluid had collected around his brain, and it had to be drained. This required that a hole be drilled into George's skull. It was on the operating table, on September 12, that he suffered both a minor stroke and a heart attack.

George hoped his recovery would be sufficient to carry on his appearances. But despite the bookings, his health did not allow him to work. His final film appearance — in a cameo role — was in *Radioland Murders*, which was released on October 21. It must have disappointed him profoundly that he had to cancel a January 1995 appearance in Las Vegas to celebrate his 99th birthday. He still went to Hillcrest. But he was down to three cigars a day and an equal number of heavily-watered down martinis. Life was never going to get back to normal.

On February 25, 1995, George received a Lifetime Achievement Award given to him by the Screen Actors Guild. By August 1995, George still fully intended to fulfill his two-week booking at the London Palladium and his booking at Caesar's Palace. Both of these were to celebrate his 100th birthday which would take place on January 20, 1996. Indeed, so excited were fans by the prospect of seeing George that the five Las Vegas shows were already sold out. But by the end of September, it was obvious to everyone that George could not fulfill those bookings. George, though, would not stop. He continued to go to his office, struggling to maintain an entertainer's life to the end.

As George entered his 100th year in 1996, it became painfully clear that he was fading. He couldn't attend a birthday party in his honor being held in Beverly Hills. He tried going back to Hillcrest, but he couldn't walk and required a wheelchair. He had shrunk so that his five foot body seemed even smaller than it was.

George faced his death calmly. As he had written at the end of his book *All My Best Friends*, "I know that sometime there's going to be a knock on my door, and when I open it somebody'll give me back my pictures. And I'll go. But I'm telling you something right now; when I go, I'm taking my music."[18]

George awoke very early on Saturday, March 9, 1996 and felt sick. His doctor was called. The doctor came over and said no more could be done for George. He was not suffering and not in pain. Ronnie Burns stood over him.

George Burns died at 10 A.M. at the age of 100 years and 49 days.

His funeral was held on March 12 at Forest Lawn, alongside Gracie. He was laid out in a dark blue suit and light blue shirt with a red tie. He had on his toupee, his ring, and a watch that had been a gift from Gracie. Three cigars had been carefully placed in his pocket, along with his keys. His wallet was also there with ten $100 bills, a five-dollar bill and three one-dollar bills. The press (and even his show business friends) were kept from being in attendance.

As he had told Ed Bradley, the marker on the crypt was indeed changed to "Gracie Allen & George Burns — Together Again." In life Gracie always had second billing, but for eternity she would have top billing.

It is a show business cliché to assert that a performer's death marks the end of an era, but in the case of George Burns it was true. Part of that legacy involved the people he worked with on his television show and movies and elsewhere in his life. Here is what happened to a few of the numerous important people who played a role in George Burns's life:

Bea Benaderet later starred in *The Beverly Hillbillies* and *Petticoat Junction.* She provided Betty Rubble's voice in the cartoon series *The Flintstones.* She died of lung cancer in 1968, at the age of 62.

Ronnie Burns died on November 14, 2007, at the age of 72. (He was gracious in helping the author of this book.)

Eddie Cantor died on October 10, 1964, at the age of 72.

Fred Clark became a prominent character actor. He died at the age of 54 in 1968.

Bobby Darin won two Grammy Awards before his untimely death on December 20, 1973, at the age of 37.

John Denver was an extraordinarily successful singer before his untimely death on October 12, 1997, at the age of 53.

Larry Gelbart, one of the most successful comedy writers in television history, died on September 11, 2009, at the age of 81.

Bill Goodwin had a show on NBC and bought the Nooks Hotel in Palm Springs in 1956. He died in 1958 of a heart attack.

Harvey Helm, who had worked for Burns and Allen for two decades, died at the age of 66 in 1965.

George Jessel, widely known as "The Toastmaster General of the United States," died on May 23, 1981, at the age of 83.

Al Jolson, the entertainer whom George Burns considered to be the all-time best, died on October 23, 1950, at the age of 64.

Larry Keating went on to star as the neighbor in *Mr. Ed*. He died at age 64 in 1963.

George Burns not only made people laugh but also taught them how to age gracefully. He made an exercise video, constantly dated, and taught America to embrace life. He died on March 9, 1996, at the age of 100 years and 49 days.

Walter Matthau, the widely acclaimed actor best remembered for his role in
The Odd Couple, died on July 1, 2000, at the age of 79.

Harry Von Zell made various motion pictures and then became a spokesperson
for Home Savings and Loan in Los Angeles. He died in 1981 at the age of
75.

Beyond his audiences and all the people in the entertainment business
who were part of his life, George Burns became a part of the culture. One
restaurant chain that wanted everyone to know they would not serve underage
drinkers, put up signs before George died that read that they even card George
Burns. After his death, the signs were changed to say that they even carded
George.

There was an episode of *The Simpsons* titled "Rosebud" in which George
is portrayed as Montgomery Burns's younger brother. When the older Burns
leaves the family home, their father notes that at least George is still around.
A very young George Burns bursts into song in his unique style. He then reas-
sures the audience that such singing will be funny when he becomes elderly.

On October 10, 2002, the Broadway production *Say Goodnight Gracie*
premiered at the Helen Hayes Theatre. The play was written by Rupert
Holmes, who received a nomination for a Tony Award for Best Play, and was
a one-man effort by Frank Gorshin, a popular actor and impressionist. Gorshin was a dead-ringer for George, assuming the voice and look perfectly.
Didi Conn, who never appeared on stage during the performance, had pre-
recorded Gracie's voice. The show ran for 364 performances, and that was
after 27 previews. Gorshin was nominated in the Outstanding Solo Performance category for the Drama Desk Award. Gorshin's efforts were the third
longest-running solo performance show ever. The play won the 2003–2004
National Broadway Theatre Award for Best Play.

The play opens with an unusual premise: George is between worlds, not
yet able to join Gracie. First he must give a performance for God. In his performance he tells his story, beginning with the early years on the Lower East
Side. Carefully stitching together George's stories, Holmes cleverly captured
George's warmth. As audience after audience decided, Frank Gorshin was
almost eerie in his ability to become George Burns.

The play did include, beyond Gorshin and Conn's voice, music and
images from George's life. It was a loving tribute, and its packed audiences
amply illustrated that George Burns may have died, but his spirit lives on.

It is difficult to sum up George Burns's legacy, his importance to the culture. George Burns the man eventually changed into George Burns the idea. He became the embodiment of all that America stands for. He had been born into incredible poverty, with a father who died when George was young. He had suffered failure after failure. And yet, he became the model of the American success story, and like the best of those success stories he had found true love along the way. That love, that partnership, may have been more perfect in the public mind than in the private lives of the couple, but it was nevertheless very real. George Burns proved that you didn't have to be handsome, a white Anglo-Saxon Protestant, or a great singer to succeed. Perhaps that was part of the reason for his appeal: he represented that part in all of us that believes we can reach the top, that only hard work and pluck are needed to make it in this country. In that sense, George Burns was a great American.

His life had spanned the twentieth century. When he was born there were no airplanes. There was barely a movie industry or a record industry. Radio and television were inventions yet to come.

Another part of the great George Burns legacy is a lesson on how to adapt. Like the country in which he was born, George learned to accept change. He didn't bemoan the death of vaudeville as so many others had. He accepted it and moved on to other, newer forms of entertainment. He didn't even stop when his great love and his best friend died. George had a way of putting one foot in front of the other, of never quitting, of refusing to let reality be a barrier between himself and his dreams.

George Burns also stands for a humor that is now out of style in some quarters. He was slightly risqué in private (and in later public performances), but he never swore and was never explicit. He simply wouldn't have done that. His humor rested on language mix-ups and small matters. He didn't take on the big issues of life, or perhaps he did in small bits at a time.

But George had a humanity that will never be out of style. He became a symbol of kindness. He was a warm and caring God in the movies, and so he seemed in life. His humor reached a part of us that longed for such a caring parent or friend. He was the uncle who always found a way to make us feel better, the other person who really understood us, understood that we were in pain and needed a helping hand. We saw in George Burns the kind of person we could be ourselves if we were gentle and funny and loving.

Beyond seeming to illustrate the reality of love, George was also a model of friendship. He loved his friends, and they loved him. It is no surprise that he had so deep a friendship with Jack Benny. George was the most loyal of friends, and even when he didn't like someone — such as with Frank Fay or

Groucho Marx — he kept the friendship. And when he found a newcomer whose talents he admired, a Bobby Darin or an Ann-Margret, he made sure that they got a chance to succeed. He had learned early on how to be generous from Gracie. He spent a lifetime sharing the spotlight, and he didn't feel diminished to bring on a new talent. This was, to understate the matter, not entirely common in show business.

It is no accident that part of George's appeal was in his very longevity. In his old age, the idea of dating much younger women seemed almost innocent, almost charming. Everyone just knew that he really loved Gracie, that these women were no more than substitutes because the real Gracie could no longer be with him.

He seemed to stretch the possibilities of life beyond the normal restrictions. In doing so, he offered to all of us the tantalizing possibility that we, too, can transcend the limits of our earthly existence, that we are truly a special species meant for greatness on this Earth. George Burns could seemingly live forever.

And if there is justice in the world of entertainment, that is just what will happen to George Burns. The vaudeville routines are gone (except when they were re-created on radio and television), but no one who ever saw George and Gracie perform could forget them.

George Burns will be forever linked with his beloved Gracie Allen, and forever a part of the great legacy of American entertainment.

Chronology

c. June 1855: Eliezer (Lipa) Birnbaum is born. He will be known as Louis in America.

c. November 1857: Hadassah Bluth is born. She will be known as Dora in America.

c. 1874: Lipa and Hadassah marry.

c. 1885: Lipa comes to America from Kolbaschow.

c. 1886: Hadassah comes to America along with Annie, Isidor, Esther, and Sarah Birnbaum.

26 July 1895: Grace Ethel Cecile Rosalie Allen is born in San Francisco to George Allen and Margaret Darragh Allen.

20 January 1896: Naftaly Birnbaum is born at 95 Pitt Street, New York City, son of Lipa and Hadassah Birnbaum. He will be called Nathan and will later unofficially change his name to George Burns.

20 April 1899: Hannah Siegel is born.

22 August 1903: Lipa Birnbaum dies at 259 Rivington Street of heart disease, at the age of 47.

23 August 1903: Lipa Birnbaum is buried in a plot owned by the Bnei Chasim Machne Rubin Kolbaschow Teitelbaum Chevra in Union Field Cemetery

c. 1905: Nathan Birnbaum is part of a group called The Peewee Quartet and quits school around the fourth grade.

1910: Nathan Birnbaum is a dance instructor. He enters small-time vaudeville under various names with a wide variety of acts.

5 September 1917: Nathan Birnbaum marries Hannah Siegel.

1919–1920: Nathan Birnbaum works with Sid Gary.

1921: Nathan Birnbaum and Hannah Siegel Birnbaum divorce.

1921–1922: Nathan Birnbaum works as George Burns and teams with Billy Lorraine in an act called "The Two Broadway Thieves."

22 June 1922: Hannah Siegel remarries. Alexander Kleinman is her second husband.

Late fall 1922: Burns and Lorraine break up in Union City, New Jersey. Burns meets Gracie Allen, who agrees to be his partner in a comedy act.

Late fall 1922: Burns and Allen make their first appearance at the Hill Theater in Newark, New Jersey.

1923–1925: Burns and Allen continue to perform, mostly as a disappointment act. For a while, Burns continues to be the comic member of the team until, over time, he makes Gracie the comic and slowly develops her character.

1925: Burns develops a new act called "Lamb Chops" with the writer Al Boasberg.

7 January 1926: Nathan Birnbaum and Grace C. Allen marry in Cleveland, Ohio.

23 August 1926: Burns and Allen open for the first time at the Palace Theater.

25 August 1927: Dora Birnbaum dies.

25 February–4 October 1929: George and Gracie tour the British Isles with their vaudeville act.

10 June 1929: Burns and Allen appear for the first time on the BBC. They go on to perform for 15 weeks.

October 1929: *Lambchops* (also known as *Burns and Allen in Lambchops*), their first film, is released.

1930: Burns and Allen fail an NBC radio audition.

2 August 1930: *Fit to Be Tied* is released.

10 January 1931: *Pulling a Bone* is released.

7 March 1931: *The Antique Shop* is released.

23 May 1931: *Once Over, Light* is released.

1 August 1931: *100% Service* is released.

3 October 1931: Burns and Allen appear with Eddie Cantor and others at the Palace.

15 November 1931: Gracie makes a solo appearance on Eddie Cantor's radio show.

16 January 1932: *Oh, My Operation* is released.

28 January 1932: Burns and Allen appear on Rudy Vallee's radio show

15 February 1932: Burns and Allen appear on Guy Lombardo's show. They appear the following week and eventually become regulars.

11 March 1932: *The Babbling Book* is released.

14 October 1932: *The Big Broadcast* is released.

25 November 1932: *Your Hat* is released.

4 January 1933: Gracie's supposedly missing brother is first mentioned on their radio show as part of a stunt.

17 March 1933: *Let's Dance* is released.

12 May 1933: *Walking the Baby* is released.

27 May 1933: *International House* is released.

5 July 1933: *College Humor* is released.

October 1933: Burns and Allen's last month in vaudeville.

7 February 1934: *Six of a Kind* is released.

27 April 1934: *We're Not Dressing* is released.

8 June 1934: *Many Happy Returns* is released.

19 September 1934: After Guy Lombardo leaves, the radio show is given a new name, *The Adventures of Gracie.*

September 1934: Burns and Allen adopt a baby girl, Sandra Jean.

3 October 1934: The radio show is broadcast on a coast-to-coast hookup for the first time.

20 April 1935: *Love in Bloom* is released.

September 1935: Burns and Allen adopt a second child, a son, Ronald Jon.

10 September1935: *Here Comes Cookie* is released.

20 September 1935: *The Big Broadcast of 1936* is released.

26 September 1936: *The Burns and Allen Show* begins (other titles are also used)

6 October 1936: *The Big Broadcast of 1937* is released.

December 1936: Burns and Allen move to California.

19 December 1936: *College Holiday* is released.

19 November 1937: *A Damsel in Distress* is released.

29 April 1938: *College Swing* is released.

Fall 1938: Burns and Jack Benny are accused of receiving smuggled jewelry.

31 January 1939: Burns pleads guilty. He is given a fine and a suspended sentence.

3 February 1939: *Honolulu*, the last Burns and Allen motion picture, is released.

7 February 1940: Gracie announces a run for the presidency as part of another publicity stunt.

17 May 1950: Last of the regularly scheduled Burns and Allen radio shows is broadcast.

12 October 1950: The Burns and Allen television show premieres.

18 February 1958: Gracie announces her retirement from show business.

15 September 1958: The final original episode of the television program is broadcast.

22 October 1958: *The George Burns Show* debuts. It only lasts until April 14, 1959.

27 August 1964: Gracie Allen dies.

14 September 1964: *Wendy and Me* debuts on TV. It runs until September 6, 1965.

20 January 1966: Willy Burns, George's brother and assistant, dies.

6 November 1975: *The Sunshine Boys* is released. Burns wins an Academy Award for Best Supporting Actor.

7 October 1977: *Oh, God!* is released.

13 July 1979: *Just You and Me, Kid* is released.

December 1979: *Going in Style* released.

28 February 1981: Hermosa Klein, born Hannah Siegel, dies.

18 September 1985: *George Burns' Comedy Week* debuts. It runs until December 25, 1985.

15 April 1988 *18: Again!* is released.

21 October 1994: *Radioland Murders* is released. This is George Burns's final motion picture.

20 January 1996: An ailing George Burns quietly observes his 100th birthday.

9 March 1996: George Burns dies. Three days later he is entombed alongside Gracie at Forest Lawn Memorial Park.

Chapter Notes

Preface

1. George Burns, *The Most of George Burns* (New York: Galahad, 1991), 498.

Chapter One

1. Burns, *The Most of George Burns*, 120.
2. Ibid.
3. Martin Burden, "Have a cigar, George," *New York Post*, January 17, 1991, 33.
4. *60 Minutes*, CBS, November 6, 1988.
5. Ibid.

Chapter Two

1. Lawrence J. Epstein, *At the Edge of a Dream: Jewish Immigrants on New York's Lower East Side: 1880–1920* (Hoboken, NJ: Jossey-Bass, 2007), 14.
2. Herb Fagen, *George Burns: In His Own Words* (New York: Carrol & Graf, 1996), 20.
3. George Burns (with Cynthia Hobart Lindsey), *I Love Her, That's Why* (New York: Simon & Schuster, 1955), 12.
4. George Burns Interview, American Jewish Committee, 1977.
5. Ibid.
6. Lawrence J. Epstein, *The Haunted Smile: The Story of Jewish Comedians in America* (Cambridge, MA: Perseus, 2001), 272–273.
7. Burns, *The Most of George Burns*, 276.
8. Ibid., 283.
9. Burns, *I Love Her, That's Why*, 15
10. *Variety*, October 6, 1922, 21.
11. Gail Rogers, "They Fell in Love at Fifth Sight," *Movie Mirror*, August 1935, 48.
12. Ibid.

Chapter Three

1. *Variety*, April 12, 1923, 20.
2. *Variety*, June 28, 1923, 24.
3. *Variety*, November 1, 1923, 33.
4. Shirley Staples, *Male-Female Comedy Teams in American Vaudeville, 1865–1932* (Ann Arbor, MI: UMI Research Press, 1984), 208.

5. Lawrence J. Epstein, *Mixed Nuts: America's Love Affair with Comedy Teams from Burns and Allen to Belushi and Ackroyd* (Cambridge, MA: Perseus, 2004), 8.

6. Staples, *Male-Female Comedy Teams in American Vaudeville, 1865–1932*, 209.

7. Burns, *I Love Her, That's Why*, 107.

8. Ibid.

9. Mary Jacobs, "This Is Gracie," *Screen & Radio Weekly*, October 1939, as quoted in Clements and Weber, *George Burns and Gracie Allen: A Bio-Bibliography* (Westport, CT: Greenwood Press, 1996), 14–15.

10. Kate Davy, "An Interview with George Burns," *Educational Theatre Journal* (1975), 349.

11. Burns, *I Love Her, That's Why*, 114.

12. Ibid., 115.

13. Ibid., 115–116.

14. Burns, *Gracie: A Love Story*, 68.

15. Ibid.

16. Ibid., 71.

17. Epstein, *Mixed Nuts*, 2.

18. Burns, *The Most of George Burns*, 57–61.

19. Ibid., 62–63.

20. *Variety*, August 25, 1926, 26.

Chapter Four

1. Burns, *Gracie: A Love Story*, 85.

2. Staples, *Male-Female Comedy Teams in American Vaudeville, 1865–1932*, 213–214.

3. Arthur Frank Wertheim, *Radio Comedy* (New York: Oxford University Press, 1979), 200–201.

4. Burns, *Gracie: A Love Story*, 99.

5. Burns, *I Love Her, That's Why*, 148–149.

6. Burns, *Gracie: A Love Story*, 101.

7. Ibid., 102.

8. Ibid., 104.

9. Burns, *I Love Her, That's Why*, 158

10. Ibid.

11. Burns, *Gracie: A Love Story*, 128.

12. Epstein, *Mixed Nuts*, 90.

13. Transcript, *Hollywood Hotel*, Academy of Motion Picture Arts and Science, Margaret Herrick Library.

14. Ibid.

15. Ibid.

16. *Time*, December 19, 1938, http://www.time.com/time/magazine/article/0,9171,772095,00.html

17. *George Burns and Gracie Allen: Great Moments in Show Business*, Epic FLS 15105 (1966).

18. Steve Allen, *Funny People* (New York: Stein and Day, 1981), 97.

19. Burns, *Gracie: A Love Story*, 166.

20. Ibid.

21. Ibid.

22. Ibid., 167.

23. Burns, *Gracie: A Love Story*, 167–168.

24. Ross Firestone (ed.), *The Big Radio Comedy Program* (Chicago: Contemporary, 1978), 204.

25. Ibid., 206.
26. Epstein, *Mixed Nuts*, 53–54.
27. Ibid., 54.
28. Burns, *Gracie: A Love Story*, 165.
29. Epstein, *Mixed Nuts*, 55–56.
30. Staples, *Male-Female Comedy Teams in American Vaudeville, 1865–1932*, 233–234.
31. American Jewish Committee. Tape transcript. New York Public Library, 41–42.
32. Ibid., 40.
33. Firestone, *The Big Radio Comedy Program*, 279–280.
34. Burns, *Gracie: A Love Story*, 223.
35. Burns, *All My Best Friends*, 180.
36. Epstein, *The Haunted Smile*, 61.
37. Burns, *Gracie: A Love Story*, 226.
38. Ibid.
39. Allen, *Funny People*, 93.

Chapter Five

1. Burns, *I Love Her, That's Why*, 195.
2. Burns, *Gracie: A Love Story*, 244.
3. Cheryl Blythe and Susan Sackett, *Say Goodnight, Gracie! The Story of Burns and Allen* (New York: Dutton, 1986), 28–29.
4. Ibid., 175.
5. Ibid., 39.
6. Ibid., 42.
7. Ibid., 44–45.
8. Patricia Mellencamp, *High Anxiety: Catastrophe, Scandal, Age & Comedy* (Bloomington: Indiana University Press, 1992), 317.
9. Ibid., 318.
10. Ibid.
11. *Say Goodnight, Gracie!*, 55.
12. Ibid., 57
13. Ibid.
14. Ibid., 58–59.
15. Ibid., 64.
16. Ibid., 66.
17. Jordan R. Young, *The Laugh Crafters: Comedy Writing in Radio and TV's Golden Age* (Beverly Hills, CA: Past Times, 1999), 40–41.
18. *Say Goodnight, Gracie!*, 100.
19. Ibid., 120.
20. Martin Gottfried, *George Burns and the Hundred-Year Dash* (New York: Simon & Schuster, 1996), 159–160.
21. Ibid., 167.
22. Ibid.
23. Ibid., 168.
24. Burns, *Gracie: A Love Story*, 274–275.
25. Ibid., 275.
26. Blythe and Sackett, *Say Goodnight, Gracie!*, 184–185.
27. Ibid., 185.
28. Burns, *Gracie: A Love Story*, 277–278.

29. Ibid., 278.
30. Burns, *The Most of George Burns*, 453–454.

Chapter Six

1. Blythe and Sackett, *Say Goodnight, Gracie!*, 190.
2. Burns, *Gracie: A Love Story*, 296.
3. Ann-Margret, *Ann-Margret: My Story*, 72.
4. Ibid., 73.
5. Ibid., 76.
6. Alan Young, *Mister Ed and Me* (New York: St. Martin's, 1995), 10.
7. Ibid., 12.
8. Blythe and Sackett, *Say Goodnight, Gracie!*, 194.
9. http://www.people.com/people/archive/article/0,,20065905,00.html.
10. Melissa Miller, *Close But No Cigar: 30 Wonderful Years with George Burns* (Los Angeles: Newstar, 1998), 15.
11. Ibid., 56–58.
12. Ibid., 75.

Chapter Seven

1. Wikipedia, "Smith and Dale." http://en.wikipedia.org/wiki/Smith_%26_Dale.
2. Gottfried, *George Burns and the Hundred-Year Dash*, 234–235.
3. Ibid., 235.
4. Ibid., 238.
5. Ibid., 252.
6. Ibid., 253.
7. Burns, *The Most of George Burns*, 487–497.
8. Ibid., 466
9. Ibid., 468–469.
10. Gottfried, *George Burns and the Hundred-Year Dash*, 273.
11. Burns, *The Most of George Burns*, 475.
12. Blythe and Sackett, *Say Goodnight, Gracie!*, 199.
13. Gottfried, *George Burns and the Hundred-Year Dash*, 291.
14. Ibid., 278.
15. Burns, *All My Best Friends*, 141–142.
16. *New York Times Book Review*, February 10, 1980, 12.
17. Gottfried, *George Burns and the Hundred-Year Dash*, 311.
18. Burns, *All My Best Friends*, 317.

References

The materials included here represent only a small percentage
of the available literature on Burns and Allen.

Books and Articles

Allen, Gracie. *How to Become President*. New York: Duell, Sloan, and Pearce, 1940.
_____. As told to Jane Kesner Morris. "Inside Me," *Woman's Home Companion Magazine*, March 1953.
Allen, Steve. *Funny People*. New York: Stein and Day, 1981.
Ann-Margret, with Todd Gold. *Ann-Margret: My Story*. New York: Putnam, 1994.
Astaire, Fred. *Steps in Time: An Autobiography*. New York: Cooper Square Press, 2000.
Benny, Jack, and Joan Benny. *Sunday Nights at Seven: The Jack Benny Story*. New York: Warner, 1990.
Benny, Mary (Livingstone), Hilliard Marks, with Marcia Borie. *Jack Benny*. Garden City, NY: Doubleday, 1978.
Berle, Milton. *B.S. I Love You: Sixty Funny Years with the Famous and the Infamous*. New York: McGraw-Hill, 1988.
Blythe, Cheryl, and Susan Sackett. *Say Goodnight, Gracie! The Story of Burns and Allen*. New York: Dutton, 1986.
Brecher, Irving; as told to Hank Rosenfeld. *The Wicked Wit of the West: The Last Great Golden-age Screenwriter Shares the Hilarity and Heartaches of Working with Groucho, Garland, Gleason, Berle, Burns, Benny and Many More*. Teaneck, NJ: BenYehuda Press, 2008.
Burns, George. *Dear George*. New York: Putnam, 1985.
_____. *Dr. Burns' Prescription for Happiness*. New York: Putnam, 1984.
_____. *Gracie: A Love Story*. New York: Putnam, 1988.
_____. *How to Live to Be 100—Or More: The Ultimate Diet, Sex and Exercise Book* (*At my age, sex gets second billing)*. New York: Putnam, 1983.
_____. *Living It Up*. New York: Putnam, 1976.
_____. *100 Years, 100 Stories*. New York: Putnam, 1996.
_____. *The Most of George Burns: Living It Up, The Third Time Around, Dr. Burns' Prescription for Happiness, and Dear George—Four Bestselling Works in One Volume*. New York: Galahad, 1991.
_____. *The Third Time Around*. New York: Putnam, 1980.
_____, with Cynthia Hobart Lindsey. *I Love Her, That's Why*. New York: Simon & Schuster, 1955.
_____, with David Fisher. *All My Best Friends*. New York: Putnam, 1989.
_____, with Hal Goldman. *Wisdom of the 90s*. New York: Putnam, 1991.
Cantillon, J.P., and Sheila Murphy Cantillon, eds. *The First 100 Years*. Beverly Hills, CA: George Waverly, 1996.
Cantor, Eddie. *My Life Is in Your Hands*. New York: Cooper Square, 2000.

Carroll, William. *Gracie Allen for President 1940*. San Marcos, CA: Coda Publications, 2000.

Chandler, Charlotte. *Hello, I Must Be Going: Groucho and His Friends*. Garden City, NY: Doubleday, 1978.

Channing, Carol. *Just Lucky I Guess: A Memoir of Sorts*. New York: Simon & Schuster, 2002.

Clements, Cynthia, and Sandra Weber. *George Burns and Gracie Allen: A Bio-Bibliography*. Westport, CT: Greenwood Press, 1996.

Davy, Kate. "An Interview with George Burns," *Educational Theatre Journal*, Vol. 27, No. 3, Popular Theatre, October 1975.

Dougherty, Barry, ed. *New York Friars Club Book of Roasts: The Wittiest, Most Hilarious, and, Until Now, Most Unprintable Moments from the Friars Club*. New York: M. Evans, 2000.

Douglas, Susan J. *Listening In: Radio and the American Imagination*. New York: Times, 1999.

Dunning, John. *Tune in Yesterday; The Ultimate Encyclopedia of Old-Time Radio, 1925–1976*. Englewood Cliffs, N.J.: Prentice-Hall, 1976.

Edelman Rob, and Audrey Kupferberg. *Matthau: A Life*. Lanham, MD: Taylor Trade, 2002.

Fagen, Herb. *George Burns: In His Own Words*. New York: Carroll and Graf, 1996.

Fantle, David, and Tom Johnson. *Twenty-five years of Celebrity Interviews from Vaudeville to Movies to TV, Reel to Real*. Oregon, WI: Badger, 2004.

Fein, Irving. *Jack Benny: An Intimate Biography*. New York: Putnam, 1976.

Firestone, Ross, ed. *The Big Radio Comedy Program*. Chicago: Contemporary, 1978.

Friars' Club. *The Friars Honor Jack Benny, George Burns*. 1972.

George Burns File. New York Public Library. Billy Rose Collection.

George Burns: The First 100 Years. New York: Biograph Communications, 1996.

Gottfried, Martin. *George Burns and the Hundred-Year Dash*. New York: Simon & Schuster, 1996.

Halper, Donna L. *Invisible Stars: A Social History of Women in American Broadcasting*. Armonk, NY: M. E. Sharpe, 2001

Harmon, Jim. *The Great Radio Comedians*. Garden City, NY: Doubleday, 1970.

Hinmon, Dean. *Conversations with "God."* West Conshohocken, PA: Infinity Publishing, 2008.

Jessel, George. *So Help Me: The Autobiography of George Jessel*. New York: Random House, 1943.

Kibler, M. Alison. *Rank Ladies: Gender and Cultural Hierarchy in American Vaudeville*. Chapel Hill: University of North Carolina Press, 1999.

MacDonald, J. Fred. *Don't Touch That Dial! Radio Programming in American Life, 1920–1960*. Chicago: Nelson-Hall, 1979.

Maltin, Leonard. *The Great American Broadcast: A Celebration of Radio's Golden Age*. New York: Dutton, 1997.

Marc, David. *Comic Visions: Television Comedy and American Culture*. Boston: Unwin Hyman, 1989.

_____. *Demographic Vistas: Television in American Culture*. Philadelphia: University of Pennsylvania Press, 1984.

Mellencamp, Patricia. *High Anxiety: Catastrophe, Scandal, Age & Comedy*. Bloomington: Indiana University Press, 1992.

Meyers, Daniel D. *Confessions of a Hollywood Publicist*. Kansas City, MO: Four-Star Press, 2001.

Miller, Melissa. *Close But No Cigar: 30 Wonderful Years with George Burns*. Los Angeles: NewStar, 1998.

Nulman, Andy. *I Almost Killed George Burns*. Toronto, ON: ECW Press, 2001.

Rubin, Benny. *Come Backstage with Me.* Bowling Green, OH: Bowling Green University Popular Press, 1972.

Schwartz, Ben. "The Gag Man: Being a Discourse on Al Boasberg, Professional Jokesmith, his Manner, and Method," in *The Film Comedy Reader,* ed. Gregg Rickman, NY: Limelight Editions, 2001.

Sotheby's. *The Estate of George Burns.* 1996.

Shields, Brooke. *The Brooke Book.* New York : Pocket Books, 1978.

Slide, Anthony. *The Encyclopedia of Vaudeville.* Westport, CT: Greenwood, 1994.

_____(ed). *Selected Vaudeville Criticism.* Metuchen, NJ: Scarecrow Press, 1988.

_____. *The Vaudevillians: A Dictionary of Vaudeville Performers.* Westport, CT: Arlington House, 1981.

Smith, Bill. *The Vaudevillians.* New York: Macmillan, 1976.

Snyder, Robert W. "The Vaudeville Circuit: A Prehistory of the Mass Audience, in James S. Ettema and D. Charles Whitney, eds. *Audiencemaking: How the Media Create the Audience.* Thousand Oaks, CA: Sage, 1994.

_____. *Voice of the City: Vaudeville and Popular Culture in New York.* Chicago: Ivan R. Dee, 2000.

Staples, Shirley. *Male-Female Comedy Teams in American Vaudeville, 1865–1932.* Ann Arbor, MI: UMI Research Press, 1984.

Starr, Michael Seth. *Bobby Darin: A Life.* Dallas: Taylor, 2004.

Tray S.D. *No Applause—Just Throw Money: The Book That Made Vaudeville Famous.* New York: Faber & Faber, 2005.

Weisblat, Tinky. "Will the Real George and Gracie and Ozzie and Harriet and Desi and Lucy Please Stand Up? The Function of Popular Biography in 1950s Television." Dissertation. University of Texas at Austin, 1991.

Wertheim, Arthur Frank. *Radio Comedy.* New York: Oxford University Press, 1979.

_____. *Vaudeville Wars.* New York: Palgrave Macmillan, 2006.

Wilde, Larry. *The Great Comedians Talk about Comedy.* New York: Citadel, 1968.

_____. *How the Great Comedy Writers Create Laughter.* Chicago: Nelson-Hall, 1976.

Wilk, Max. *Interview with George Burns.* American Jewish Committee. October 21, 1971.

Young, Alan. *Mister Ed and Me.* New York: St. Martin's, 1995.

Young, Jordan R. *The Laugh Crafters: Comedy Writing in Radio and TV's Golden Age.* Beverly Hills, CA: Past Times, 1999.

Audio Recordings

A Conversation with George Burns. UAHC (1984).

The Friars Club Honor George Burns and Gracie Allen, 1951. Laughdome.com.

George Burns on Comedy. Laugh.com (2006).

Video

George Burns: An American Legend. Dan Dalton Productions (1996).

George Burns: A Century of Laughter. GoodTimes Home Video Corp. (1996).

George Burns: His Wit and Wisdom. Vistar International Productions (1989).

George Burns: 100 Years of Comedy. Stone Entertainment (1995).

George Burns and Gracie Allen. PPI Entertainment Group (1990).

Websites

George Burns and Gracie Allen http://georgegracie.wordpress.com/

The George Burns and Gracie Allen Radio Show http://theburnsandallenshow.blog
spot.com/

The George Burns & Gracie Allen Show http://www.timvp.com/burns.html

Interview with George Burns http://rogerebert.suntimes.com/apps/pbcs.dll/article?AID=
/19790603/PEOPLE/906030301/1023

Jerry Haendiges Vintage Radio Logs http://www.otrsite.com/logs/logb1008.htm

Official Website of George Burns http://georgeburns.com/

A Tribute to Gracie Allen http://www.gracieallen.net/

Index

Numbers in *bold italics* indicate pages with photographs.

201

PN
2287
.B87
E78
2011